OFFICIAL LETTER BOOKS

OF

W. C. C. CLAIBORNE

1801-1816

EDITED BY

DUNBAR ROWLAND, B. S., LL. B., LL. D.

Director Mississippi Department of Archives and History, Secretary
Mississippi Historical Society, Member American
Historical Association

VOLUME VI.

JACKSON, MISSISSIPPI

Printed for the State Department of Archives and History

1917

Library of Congress Cataloging in Publication Data

Claiborne, William Charles Cole, 1775-1817.
   Official letter books of W. C. C. Claiborne, 1801-
1816.

   Bibliography: p.
   1. Louisiana--History--Sources. 2. Mississippi--
History--Sources. I. Mississippi (Ter.) Governor,
1801-1804 (Claiborne) II. Orleans (Ter.) Governor,
1804-1812 (Claiborne) III. Louisiana. Governor, 1812-
1816 (Claiborne)
F374.C58 1972   976.3'04   72-980
ISBN 0-404-01600-6

Reprinted from the edition of 1917, Jackson, Miss.
First AMS edition published in 1972
Manufactured in the United States of America

International Standard Book Number:
Complete Set: 0-404-01600-6
Volume VI: 0-404-01606-5

AMS PRESS INC.
NEW YORK, N. Y.   10003

OFFICIAL LETTER BOOKS

OF

W. C. C. CLAIBORNE

1801-1816

VOLUME VI.

AMS PRESS
NEW YORK

LETTER BOOKS OF W. C. C. CLAIBORNE

1811–1816

To Henry Clay

New. Orleans 11th Decbr. 1811

Speaker of the House
of Representatives.

I have the honor to enclose you a Petition addressed to the Congress of the United States, from the Ursuline Nuns of New Orleans, & which I will ask the favor of you, to lay before the House of Representatives.—

The Ursulines of this City are held in high estimation.— Their Deportment is exemplary correct, & their temporal cares being wholly devoted to the education of Female youth they have a just Claim to the Patronage of the Government.—

I am, Sir, &ca &ca
Sigd. W. C. C. Claiborne.

To Robert R. Livingston

New. Orleans 11th December 1811.

New York.

Sir,

I am honored with the receipt of your letter of the 4th Ultimo.— The arrival of the Steam Boat at this port is daily expected;— We have heard of her progress down the river, & this whole society manifests a deep interest for her safety & prosperity.— I am fully persuaded, that experience will evince the practicability of navigating the Mississippi without much risk, & I sincerely hope Sir, that yourself & Mr. Fulton may be rewarded an hundred fold for your trouble, Care & expenditures.— Having very much at heart the welfare of the Western Country & being fully impressed with the advantages of Steam Boats on the Mississippi, you may be assured of the promptitude & pleasure, with which I would promote any measure essential to your security; & to the prevention of intrusion on your rights.— But you, no doubt, are apprised of the Change of Government which this Territory is destined very soon to experience.— The Convention of Orleans (now in Session) have determined it expedient at this time to form a Constitution or State Government & to accede to the Terms required by Congress.— I enclose for your perusal the plan of a Constitution as reported by a Committee, and which after undergoing some immaterial Amendments, will, most probably be adopted.— It is very uncertain, whether *or not* I shall be honored with any agency in managing the Affairs of the State;— We have among us, many aspiring Individuals, & it often happens, that the people look upon an officer *long in service,* as old-fashioned, and lay him by, with as little Ceremony, as they would an old Coat; But in whatever station I am placed;— whether I reside here, as a Public Character, or a private Citizen, you will always find me, favorable to the *Navigation Interests* of yourself & Mr. Fulton, & the more so, since I conceive *it* to be intimately connected with the welfare of the Western Country & indeed the whole United States.—

I am &c &c a

Sigd. W. C. C. Claiborne.

To Major Carmick

New Orleans 11 December 1811

of the Marine Corps.

Dear Sir,

Having been informed that the Secretary of the Navy had instructed you with the selection from among the Creoles of this Territory, of three young Gentlemen, to be Commissioned as Second Lieutenants in the Marine Corps, I take the liberty to mention to you Mr. Theobule Montreuil, as a worthy & promising young Man; He is in the prime of Life, perhaps 22 or 23 years of age, & enjoys excellent health; his person is engaging & his Department very correct;— He is connected with a very respectable & numerous family in this Territory, & of the good example which has always been afforded him, he seems to have profited.— Being sincerely of opinion, that Mr. Montreuil would be a Credit to the service, I should be happy to hear that he was Commissioned.—

I am &ca &ca &ca

Sigd   W. C. C. Claiborne.

To Albert Gallatin

New. Orleans 12th December 1811

Secretary of the Treasury.

Sir,

Your letter of the 6th of September was brought by the last Mail.— Previous to its receipt, I had been furnished by the Commissioners of the Western District, with a Duplicate of their Letter to you, in which they declared an intention of conforming to the instructions of the President.— I of course in Compliance with your wishes, returned under Cover to your address, the letter directed to Messrs Garret & Fitz.—

I enclose you a Copy of the Constitution as reported

by the Committee;— It will no doubt undergo several Amendments— But my opinion is, that the general Provisions will be approved by the Convention.

Observing by the late Land Law, that several appointments were to be made in this Territory, I took the liberty to recommend, Mr. Joseph Saul of New Orleans, as receiver of Public Monies for the Eastern District; Mr. John Thompson for the Western;— Mr. Henry Brÿ for the District North of Red River, & Mr. John Clay as Register for this last District.— I really do not know any Citizens better calculated to fill these offices, & am persuaded, they will discharge the duties thereof with Integrity, Zeal and Industry.—

> I am &ca &ca &ca
> Sigd.   W. C. C. Claiborne.

To James Monroe

New Orleans 12th December 1811

Secy of State.
Sir,

I have the honor to enclose a project of a Constitution or form of Government, which is now before the Convention;— It will probably undergo some Amendments, but its general Principles will I think be adopted.—

> I have the honor to be &ca
> Sigd   W. C. C. Claiborne.

To Paul Hamilton

New. Orleans 12th December 1811

Secy of the Treasury
Dr. Sir,

I had the pleasure by the last Mail to acknowledge the receipt of your kind Letters of the 9th Septbr & 27th. of October.— I now address you, more particularly with a view of enclosing for your perusal a Copy of the form of Government for the New State, reported by a Committee, & to add, as my opinion, that its general provisions will meet the approbation of the Convention.—

We have news here, that the English Government had offered satisfactory reparation for the affair of the Chesapeak, but I am not advised of the particulars.— This act of Justice, would have been better timed had it been rendered a few years ago;— At the *present Crisis* it looks very much like a temporizing measure;— designed to amuse & to divide the American people;— But you who have a view of "the whole ground," will best know, in what light to Consider this averture.—

Present me Respectfully to Mrs. Hamilton & to your amiable family.—

I am, Sir, &ca
Sigd. W. C. C. Claiborne.

New Orleans 13th Decbr. 1811

To the Lady Abbess of the Ursuline Convent New Orleans.

Holy Sister!

I have been honored with the receipt of your letter of the 6th Inst:, enclosing the Petition addressed by your Community, to the Congress of the U: States.— I am sorry your letter did not reach me in time, to forward the Petition by the last *Mail;* But it shall certainly be sent by the ensuing one, nor will I omit to state the just Claims of your Community to the patronage of the Government.—

I offer to you, Holy Sister, the assurances of my great respect & sincere friendship.—

Sigd W. C. C. Claiborne.

To John H. Johnson

New Orleans 13th Decbr 1811
near to St. Francisville.

Dear Sir,

The Convention is stil going on with their Constitution;— But every article undergoes ample discussion & of course little progress is made.— Doctor Watkins gave Notice on yesterday, that he should move an Amendment to the Preamble of the Constitution, which would go to make express provision for the County of Filiciana being at any time hereafter received into this State, with the assent of Congress.— My impression is that the amendment will prevail, & I indulge a strong hope that your Country will yet form a part of the State of Louisiana.—

I have addressed a third Letter to the Post-Master General relative to a Port-office near to St. Francisville, & I persuade myself, that the establishment will very soon be directed.—

I am &ca &ca &ca
Sigd.   W. C. C. Claiborne.

To Capt. Gaines

Fort Stoddart.   New Orleans 13th Decbr. 1811.

Sir,

I have received your letter of the 7th Instant.— The complaints of the people on the Bay & River of Pascagoula in Consequence of the non residence of a Judge in the Parish have been general, & to my own knowledge, they have experienced Inconveniences since none of their late Conveyances, Wills, Mortgages, &c have been made & recorded according to Law, & which together with their recent Marriages, can alone be legalized by an act of the Legislature.—I however am pleased to learn, that by your early removal to the Parish these Inconveniences will in the future be removed;— But I ought not to omit saying to you, that a residence on Dog River will be extremely inconvenient to the great Majority of the Inhabitants of the present Parish of Pascagoula;— The Mass of Population is on the Bay & River of Pascagoula, & the great distance the Citizens will have to travel to transact business will (I am well assured) be made a cause of Remembrance & that I shall be entreated to limit the Parish Eastwardly by the Bayou Batric & to create a New Parish extending from Bayou Batric to the Perdido.— If this arrangement should be adopted the office of Judge of the new Parish, will only be acceptable to you in expectation, that the Town of Mobile may soon fall into the possession of the United States & of course within the new Parish.— But this arrangement will not take place, (whilst Mobile is in the hands of the Spaniards) if the necessity for the same should be superceded by your residence on the Bay or River of Pascagoula, where as I have already observed the Mass of the Inhabitants reside, & where the Lands, particularly those on the River, are so fertile as to have attracted (I am told) the attention of Emigrants.—

I know not what has become of the Laws forwarded; —They were sent by the first Clerk in the office to an officer of the Navy who was good enough to forward them on (as I understand) by a Merchant Vessel to Fort Stoddart.—

The bond which you are (to) enter into, must be signed by yourself & two freeholders residing within the Parish, & the sum may be fixed at five thousand Dollars.—

I learn with sincere regret the Domestic Calamity which has befallen you;— It is not easy to bear as we ought such heavy misfortunes; It would indeed be fortunate if we were enabled to call to our aid, those Considerations which Reason & Religion would suggest, & be entirely reconciled to the will of an Omnipotent being,

to whose Mandates all Creation must yield.— But the
heart heavily afflicted, finds greatest relief in its overflowings;— And time, silence & reflection can alone reconcile us to the loss of an Affectionate Companion.—

I sincerely wish you health & happiness and am

sigd.   W. C. C. Claiborne

New. Orleans 16th Decbr 1811

To the Lady Abbess of the Ursuline Convent.

Holy Sister,

I had the honor to forward your Petition, by the last
Mail to the Speaker of the House of Representatives of
the United States, with a request that he would lay the
same before that honorable Body. —By the same occasion, I transmitted the Certificate which came enclosed
in your letter to me, of the 13th Instant.—

I renew to you Holy Sister, & to your whole Community, the assurances of my great respect & sincere friendship.—

Sigd   W. C. C. Claiborne.

By William Charles Cole Claiborne
Governor of the Territory of Orleans.

A. PROCLAMATION

Whereas by an act of the Legislature of the Territory
of Orleans, passed on the 24th day of April of the present year 1811, the biennial election of Representatives
to the General Assembly is directed to *take place, on the
first Monday in October next, and the two following days;*
I do therefore issue this my Proclamation, hereby re-

quiring that *an election as aforesaid,* be holden in the several Counties of this Territory, and that there shall be returned from the County of Orleans six Representatives to the General Assembly; from German Coast two; Acadia two; Lafourche two; Iberville two; Attakapas two; Opelousas two; Point Coupeé two; Rapide two; Concordia one; Ouachita one; Nachitoches one; and from the County of Feliciana *five Representatives,* of which there shall be returned *three* from the Parishes of East Baton Rouge and Feliciana; One from the Parishes of St. Tammany and St. Helana, and *one* from the Parishes of Biloxy and Pascagoula:—

And I do further direct and require that due notice be given of the times & Places of *election* in the several Counties & Parishes aforesaid, and that *the same be,* under the direction of the Parish Judges and other officers, Conducted in the manner pointed out by "An Act prescribing the formalities to be observed in the election of Representatives of the Territory of Orleans," passed on the 4th of June 1806, and "An Act supplementary" to the act last mentioned, passed on the 14th of April 1809.—

[L. S.] Given under my hand, and the Seal of the Territory, at New Orleans, on the 1st of August 1811, and in the 36th year of the Independence of the United States of America.

Signed William C. C. Claiborne

NOTE.— "No person is eligible or qualified to act as a Representative unless he shall have been a Citizen of the United States three years, and be a resident in the District (or Territory) or unless he shall have resided in the District three years; and in either case shall likewise hold in his own right, in fee simple, two hundred acres of land within the same."

No man is entitled to the right of suffrage, unless he

shall possess "a freehold in fifty acres of land in the District (or Territory) having been a Citizen of one of the States, and being resident in the District, or the like freehold, and two years resident in the District."

By an Act of the Legislature, it is made the duty of the Judges or Commissioners of the election, "to cause the title of property of the voter to be exhibited, or in deficit of such title, to administer to the voter an oath, whereby he shall swear, that he possesses truly and Bona fide at least fifty acres of land in the Territory, for at least three months past."

Signed   William C. C. Claiborne.

To John H. Johnson

New Orleans December 18th. 1811

near St. Francisville.

Dear Sir,

Your letter of the ——— Instant, has been duly received.— The proposed meeting of the people at St. John's Plains, will be an interesting one, & I sincerely hope, that the result may prove favorable to the welfare of the County of Feliciana.— In the contemplated address to Congress, I trust the Citizens, will not loose sight of the good old maxim, "Gentleness in the manner, but substance in the thing."— State your wishes, your rights & your grievances with firmness but with all that respect & Confidence due to a free, wise and virtuous government.— Believe me, the government are most favorably disposed towards your District;— I know that the President has nothing more at heart, than the happiness of the People of West Florida and their permanent Connection with the American family, nor do I doubt but a like sentiment is cherished by a Majority of the Members of the Senate & House of Representatives of the United

States. For myself, you may be assured, of my zealous co-operation in whatever concerns the prosperity of Feliciana, & I pray you to Communicate with me without reserve?— Mr Magruder has reported a Memorial to Congress praying that the Tract of Country lying West of the Perdido & below the line of the Mississippi Territory, may be permanently annexed to the Territory of Orleans. — The Memorial is well written, & will I trust be favorably received by Congress.— It will meet some opposition in the Convention.— But if I am not much mistaken, its ultimate adoption is certain.—

The Convention do not progress rapidly with their Constitution;— But as far as they have gone, the provisions seem to me wise, and well adapted to the local situation of the Country.—

> I wish you health & happiness
> Your friend,
> Sigd. William C. C. Claiborne.

To F. Cuming

New Orleans december 20th 1811

Springfield,
   St. Helena.
Sir,

I received on last evening, your letter of the 13th. Instant, with its enclosure.— The movements of the Chactaws are suspicious, & the precautions which the Citizens of Springfield & its vicinity have taken are certainly advisable.— I am sorry, it is not in my power to send you at this time, the Arms & ammunition you request;— But the Contents of your Letter shall be made the Subject matter of a Communication to General Hampton, the officer Commanding the regular forces in this Quarter, & he will be requested, to establish a Military Post, some where in your visinity.— You will be pleased to give me from time to time, information of the Indian movements, & if your safety shall be seriously menaced, you shall speedily receive all the succour in my power to afford.—

I am, Sir &ca &ca &ca

Sigd   William C. C. Claiborne.

To James Brothers

New Orleans Decber 20th 1811

Feliciana.

Sir,

Your letter of the 20th. November enclosing an account of your expenditures, whilst acting as Quarter Master & Commissary under the authority of the Florida Convention, reached me a few days since.— In reply, I can only observe that the Executive Government of the United States, have been advised of the existence of a Number of unadjusted Claims of a similar description with yours;— But that no instructions upon the Subject have yet been received by me.—

I am, Sir, &c a

Sigd.   William C. C. Claiborne

To Paul Hamilton

New. Orleans 20th December 1811.

Private

Secretary of the Navy.

Dear Sir,

Your letter of the 20th. Ultimo, has just reached me. — I offer you my Congratulations on the recovery of Mrs. Hamilton, & as regards yourself, I trust that unlike our old Frigates "in ordinary," you are now entirely refitted, & will for *many, many years,* be employed in active service.—

I have read again & again the Speech of our Excellent President;— It is worthy of him & of the Administration;— All parties who feel for the honor of the Nation, ought at the present Crisis to unite, nor do I know any *point,* to which our measures should be directed with a view to obtain Justice from Great Britain, but *open, avowed & relentless War,* or a *prompt repeal of the orders in Council.*— In a former letter, I stated the view I had taken of the late tender of reparation for the affair of the Chesapeak, & I regret to find, that it is in unison with yours;— This reparation has indeed very much the appearance of "a Tub thrown to the Whale," & if it should tend to diversion of sentiment & action in the Councils of our Nation, the affair of the Chesapeak, will be more humiliating, than I had heretofore esteemed it.—

I hope in God, the proposition respecting the Floridas may in its whole extent be adopted.— In such event, can I not be honored with some immediate Agency in the transaction? There is no service that could be more agre'able to my feelings.—

The Secretary Mr. Robertson has arrived, & I could proceed even to East Florida, without Inconvenience to the Public Interest in this quarter.—

By the last Mail, I sent you a Copy of the Constitution.— The tenth Section was much opposed by the Members representing the County & City of New Orleans;— They wished a Senatorial representation in proportion to Population;— Two Senators are accorded to the City & County, but this Number is not satisfactory, and a serious Schism has arisen.— But no ill effect will probably ensue.—

Present me affectionately to your Lady & family.

I am, Dear Sir, &ca &ca

Sigd.   William C. C. Claiborne

To Judge Rhea

Private & Confidential?

New Orleans December 20th 1811
St. Francisville.

I have heard with sincere regret that you contemplated resigning the office of Judge of the Parish of Feliciana. Can you not make a further sacrifice, with a view to the Public good, & to the Public Satisfaction? It is a fact Sir, that you unite the good opinion of all parties in your Parish, nor is there an Individual, who confides more than myself in your Integrity, prudence & Judgment.— But if you are determined to retire, will you be good enough to name to me from among the old Citizens of the Parish, some one, two or more persons, who you suppose enjoy the Confidence of the people, & would discharge the duties of Judge correctly & honestly.— Two Gentlemen Mr. Gurley & Mr. Bradford will (I am told) be recommended;— they are both young Men & recently settled among you;— A parish Judge should be well known to the people & among other Qualifications should possess a great share of experience & discretion;— His duties as a police officer, are very important to the farmers, & from among that description of Citizens I should prefer to select your successor, if one can be found willing to act, whose general Information was such, as to enable him to decide correctly between parties litigent.—

What is the general Character & standing of Captain Griffith?— I have always considered him a very honest Man, and a Lover of his Country.— Is he prudent, is he Capable, and has he the Public Confidence? I know these are delicate questions, but as this Letter is intended for your sole perusal, so will your answer, be received in entire Confidence, and you may write without reserve.
— But do not understand that my enquiries are confined

to Captain Griffith! Give me the names of such Citizens, established in the Parish, known for their Integrity, patriotism & prudence whom you may suppose best qualified.— I however, must again express a wish, that with a view to the general good, you will continue to give to your fellow Citizens the Benefit of your faithful Public service.—

I am, Sir, &ca &ca
Signed   William C. C. Claiborne.

To Commodore Shaw
New Orleans 23d December 1811
Naval Commander
   on the New Orleans Station.

Having received information from the Collector of this Port, that the Schooner Republican, Pierre Ferre Master, had just cleared out for Aux Coyes, under circumstances, which furnish strong grounds to suspect that she is intended for privateering, I have to request, that you would cause her to be overhauled at the Balize; and if on examination, there should be found on board any Cannon, Arms or Ammunition to justify the existing suspicions, that you would direct that the Vessel aforesaid be detained, until my further orders respecting her, shall be communicated to you.—

I am, Sir,
Very Respectfully
Your most obt:
Sigd. William C. C. Claiborne.

By William C. C. Claiborne,
Governor of the Territory of Orleans.

To all who shall see these presents, & more particularly, the Sheriff of the Parish of Plaquemine:—

Whereas, it has been represented to me that a Number of the Inhabitants of the Parish of Plaquemine, had been fined by the Parish Judge, in Consequence of their not having conformed to the Regulations prescribed by the Judge & Parish Jury relative to the opening & repairing of Roads, during the year 1811.— by virtue of a Law vesting such Judge & Jury with powers to that effect;— and

Whereas, it is further represented, that the Inhabitants fined as aforesaid, are generally Composed of the poorest Class of Society, who were much injured in their Crops by the overflowing of the Mississippi in the same year 1811— And that the payment of the said fines, would prove not only inconvenient, but *greatly oppressive,*—

Now therefore, be it known, that I William C. C. Claiborne, Governor as aforesaid, do by virtue of the general Powers in me vested to grant pardons, have thought proper, & do by these presents, wholly remit *the fines* which have been imposed as aforesaid, upon such of the Inhabitants of Plaquemine as have neglected to open & repair the Roads during the year 1811.— in Conformity to the Parish Regulations prescribed as aforesaid.—

Given under my hand and the Seal of
the Territory at New Orleans on the 24th day
of December 1811.
Signed   William C. C. Claiborne.

To Major McRae

Commg. the Regular
Troops.

Information having reached me that the Negros in the County of German Coast had again evidenced a disposition to rise in Insurrection, & that this spirit was supposed also to exist among the Negros in this City, I have deemed it essential to take some immediate *measures of precaution;*— Among these companies of Militia, in case of alarm by day or night are ordered to rendez-

vous at (————?————)[1] and there await my orders.—
But as the Militia force would be of little use unless well
armed and supplied with ammunition, I must ask the
favour of you, to send to the Principal, (to remain under the care of the City Guard, & not to be used, unless
in case of necessity) about 150 stand Muskets, and several Boxes of Ball Cartridges. As regards the regular
force under your Command, I am assured, they are at
all times in readiness for service, & if the occasion requires, I shall, with entire Confidence, Calculate on your
prompt co-operation.—

I am, Sir, &c a &c a

Signed   William C. C. Claiborne.

To Col. Adlard Fortier

New Orleans December 24th 1811

German Coast.

My aid de Camp Major Fortier will have forwarded
you a Commission by which you are appointed Colonel
of the fifth Regiment of Militia.— You will be pleased
to report to me as soon as possible, the state of this Regiment furnishings &c; & also, with the names of such officers as have resigned or who by a removal from within
the Limits of their Command have vacated their offices;
also to recommend to me, suitable Characters to fill the
several Vacancies which exist; In the mean time you will
cause patroles service to be regularly performed, & all
the police Regulations especially such as relate to Slaves
to be strictly observed.— In case of Insurrection, or other
cause of Alarm, you will communicate to me the particulars by express and also to the Colonels or officers
Commanding the several Regiments of Militia in the
Counties of Acadia, Iberville, LaFourche, & at Baton
Rouge.—

I am, Sir, &ca

Signed   William C. C. Claiborne.

---

[1] Mss. illegible.

To Col. Manuel Andry

New Orleans 24th December 1811

Dear Sir,

The news which reached me on yesterday, of a spirit
of Insurrection having been manifested among the Negros of German Coast, renders it indispensable to re-
organize without delay the fifth Regiment of Militia,
lately under your Command.   I have considered your
removal from German Coast, in the light of a resignation, and have promoted Major A. Fortier to the office
of Colonel.—

I take this occasion to return you my thanks for your
faithful Public services and to assure you of my respect
and Esteem.—

Signed   William C. C. Claiborne.

To Jamse Mather

New Orleans 24th Decbr 1811

Mayor of New Orleans

Since the information I communicated to you on yesterday, no further intelligence has reached me from
above.— I nevertheless deem it a prudent measure of
precaution, to continue the Militia Patroles, and have accordingly ordered on this service for the ensuing night
two Companies of Militia;— they will rendezvous at the
Principal at 8 oClock P.M. and will continue on duty
until the break of Day on the Morning of the 25th.— I
am assured that under your orders, the Police Regulations, will be strictly enforced, & you may rely with Confidence on my Co-operation;— It is only at a time, when
our Vigilance has abated, that the Public Safety is in
danger.—

I am, Sir, &ca &ca &ca
Signed   William C. C. Claiborne.

To Paul Hamilton

New. Orleans 25th Decbr 1811

Secy of the Navy.

My dear Sir,

My two young friends John Raimond Montegut, & Valcout Doriscourt being solicitous to enter the service of the United States, I beg leave to recommend them to the patronage of the President & to solicit for each, a second Lieutenancy in the Marine Corps, in the event of Vacancies. John Raimond Montegut is about 21 of age, a native of New Orleans, & a promising young Man. His father, Doctor Montegut is a highly distinguished & influential Member of Society, and the son seems to have profited of the good example, which has always been afforded him.— Valcout Doriscourt is also a native of New Orleans, he is nineteen years of age, and a very amiable youth;— his father is a worthy Citizen, & his connections are numerous & respectable.— Feeling convinced that these two young Louisianians, would make deserving officers, I take great interest in the success of their applications,— & in which event, I wish you would give me the pleasure of handing them their Commissions. It would be very pleasing to Mr. Montegut & Mr. Doriscourt and to their parents, (in case of their being commissioned) to be attached to the New Orleans station, & from the Circumstance of their being naturalized to this unhealthy Climate, I presume that such an arrangement would be convenient to the service—

I am, Dear Sir, &ca &ca

Signed   William C. C. Claiborne.

To James Pitot

New Orleans December 26th 1811

President of the
Navigation Company.

I have received your letter of the 19th. Instant. There is no tribunal Competent to the decision of the matter in litigation between the Navigation Company, & the Corporation of New Orleans, but the Supreme Court of the Territory.— The division which has arisen in the opinion of the two attending Judges is cause of regret, and it can alone be remedied by the presence of Judge Mathews. I will take the liberty to enclose to that Judge, the letter you have addressed me, and which will no doubt, serve as an additional inducement, to his attending the Court when in session in this City.

I am, Sir, &ca &ca
Signed   William C. C. Claiborne.

To Paul Hamilton

New Orleans 26 Decber. 1811

Secy of the Navy.

We are again disturbed by *apprehensions* of an insurrection among the Negroes.— I believe them myself to be unfounded; But measures of precaution, are nevertheless expedient and these have been directed.—

The Convention will probably bring their session to a Close in ten or fifteen days, & the Constitution as finally adopted, will not materially vary from the *project* submitted by a Committee & of *which* I have already forwarded you a Copy.—

It is represented that the Garrison of Pensacola is in great distress for supplies;— That there is not a Cent in the Military Chest, no prospect whatever of remittance either from Havana or Vera Cruix, & that an abandonment of Pensacola to its dependencies is contemplated.— That the want of Supplies is seriously felt, I have no doubt; but that an evacuation of the province will (in any short time) be the Consequence, I cannot readily believe.—

I am persuaded the English Government have designs on Cuba & that exertions are now making by its Agents to render the occupancy of Havana by an English force a popular act;— The English will endeavor to obtain in the New World, the influence they have lost in the old. A Monopoly of the Commerce of Spanish America will be their object, & the possession of Cuba an incipient measure.— The best Interest of the United States is opposed to Cuba's falling politically or Commercially into the hands of the English.— Nor would it be difficult to prevent it.— The people of Cuba, are for the most part jealous of the English Government, & by no means partial to the English character. The best inforced Men already speak of Independence, & the expediency & necessity of an intimate Connection with the United States of America,— If it comported with the policy of the Administration, to encourage these sentiments they would very soon be openly avowed.— The men in power at Cuba, and for the most part, believed to be favorable to the English Views;— But the prejudices of the people present a great obstacle.— The friends of Independence, (I learn) are impressed with an opinion, that the internal resources of the Island are not equal to the object, and that without a supply of Arms & Money it could not be accomplished.— The Mines of Mexico in Consequence of the troubles there, have for some time been unproductive, & the remittances of Species from Vera Cruix to Havana, have wholly ceased.— If the friends of Independence could know from what quarter, Arms & Money could be procured, it is thought they would soon take a decided stand and the incorporation of Cuba, with the United

States or its dependence upon the American Government, (as was deemed most advisable) would soon follow.—
Accept the best wishes of Dr Sir, &c, &c
Signed   William C. C. Claiborne.

To Commodore Shaw

New Orleans 28th December 1811

Naval Commander.

It has been represented to me that there were grounds to suspect some Frenchmen now in this City of a design to arm & equip a Vessel "for the purpose of surprising Baracoa in the Island of Cuba, plundering its Inhabitants & laying waste the Town." As such an equipment within the jurisdiction of the United States, would be highly improper, it becomes us to take effectual measures to prevent it.— With this view, I request you to order immediately on the Balize Station an armed Brig, & one or more Gun Boats, with instructions to the Commanding Officer to visit every vessel going to Sea; & detain such as from an unusual Number of Men, Cannon, Arms or Ammunition on board, may justify suspicions that their objects are not wholly commercial.— The Officer detaining a Vessel, will of course report to you the *causes*, & these being communicated to me, I will advise you of such further measures as may be proper to be taken.

I am &ca &ct
Signed   W. C. C. Claiborne

To Genl. Wade Hampton

New Orleans Decber. 30th 1811

of the Army of the
United States.

It has been represented to me, that the parish of St. Helena, within this Territory is visited by an unusual Number of Chactaw Indians, whose insolent conduct, sus-

picious movements & daily depredations have excited
some uneasiness among the Citizens.   The Colonel Commanding the Militia of St. Helena, has in consequence,
solicited a supply of Arms & Ammunition, but which it is
not in my power to furnish, unless they be drawn from
the Stores of the United States.— If therefore the convenience of the service permits, give me leave to suggest
the expediency of your establishing a small Military Post
within the limits of the parish St. Helena, and to request,
that you would direct to be deposited at that post a few
hundred stand of spare Arms & a supply of ammunition,
to be delivered to the Militia of St. Helena in case of necessity, on the receipt of Colonel John Thomas, or the
Officer Commanding said Militia.—

I am &ca &ca
Signed   W. C. C. Claiborne.

To Lieut. Lanceville

New Orleans 31st Decbr. 1811

Fort St. Philip.

Sir,

Desirous of availing the Public of your services as
Adjutant General of the Territory of Orleans, I have the
honor to enclose you a Commission. —In the event of
your acceptance, you will be pleased to repair immediately to this City, and await my orders.— Your friend
Major Marigny has obtained, & will enclose Your leave
of absence from General Hampton, who will I presume
accept your resignation in the Army, so soon as it is
tendered.

I am Sir, &ca &ca
Signed   W. C. C. Claiborne.

To Mr. Dawson[1]

Private.   New Orleans 1st January 1812.

A Member of Congress
Dear Sir,

There will be presented to Congress two Petitions from the people, of that part of West Florida, which now forms apart of the Territory, the one praying, that they may be permanently attached to the Orleans Territory, & the other, entreating the Government to make some provision for the payment of the debts contracted under the authority of the Florida Convention—— Permit me to recommend these petitions to your patronage & support;—— It is of great importance to the permanent welfare of the new State, that its boundaries should be enlarged, & I am certain, that the wishes of the petitioners on this point are in unison with their best Interests. — How far it may be politic in Congress, to legislate Conclusively on this subject, until the right of the United States to the Country in question, shall be acknowledged by the Government of Spain, the other claimant, you, who have a view of the whole ground can best determine:— But I presume a Declaration on the part of Congress, that so soon as the question of title shall be settled in favor of the United States, the District of West Florida, extending from the Mississippi to the Perdido, shall form a part of the State of *Louisiana* (the name of the new State) might not be improper, & I am persuaded such a declaration would be received with great satisfaction by the good people in this section of the Union.—

As regards the payment of the debts contracted by the Florida Convention, I am well aware of the delicacy of the subject;— But really Considerations of Justice, plead powerfully in favour of the petitioners.— of the pro-

---

[1] Beginning of Volume VIII.

ceedings of the Conventionalists the United States have profited;— The Revolution, they effected, was the immediate cause of placing the Country in possession of the United States, & it would seem just, that the expences of that revolution, should be paid by the party benefited. — In this quarter the public voice is greatly in favour of the petitioners, & there is a general Sympathy for such Individuals of the Conventional party, as are likely to be held personally responsible ·for these debts, unless the Government should come to their relief,— I pray you Sir, to give me the earliest information of the order, Congress may take on these petitions, & the the probable result.— The Orleans Convention will adjourn in ten or fifteen days;— The Constitution will be purely republican, & will I hope be approved by Congress during their present session.[1]——

> Accept the best wishes of
> Dr. Sir
> Signed/ W. C. C. Claiborne
> ——— ,, ——— ,, ———

To Albert Gallatin

> New Orleans Jany 2d. 1812.

Secretary of the Treasury.
Sir,

I have the honor to inclose you my contingent account for the 4th quarter of the year 1811. amounting to the sum of $418-29c. together with the necessary vouchers.—

> I am &ca &ca
> signed/ W. C. C. Claiborne
> ——— ,, ——— ,, ———

[1] Journal of the Convention.

To James Monroe

New Orleans Jany 3rd. 1812.

Secy of State

Sir,

I had the honor to receive by the last mail, your communication of the 5th Ultimo, together with a Copy of a letter which Mr. Onis had addressed you, in which it is stated that some Frenchmen designed to arm & equip at New Orleans, a Vessel for the purpose "of surprising the port of Baracoa in the Island of Cuba, plundering its inhabitants, and laying waste the Town." My impression is that Mr. Onis has not been accurately advised.— I have had recourse to the most convenient means of obtaining information, and cannot learn that such a project exists.— I nevertheless have recommended to the Collector of the District the exercise of vigilance in his Department, and instructed the Naval Commander on this station, to cause to be visited at the Balize, every Vessel going to Sea, and to detain such as from an unusual number of Men, Cannon, Arms or Ammunition may justify a suspicion that their objects are not solely commercial.—

I am, Sir &ca &ca

signed/ W. C. C. Claiborne

———— ,, ———— ,, ————

By WILLIAM C. C. CLAIBORNE

Governor of the Territory of Orleans

To all who shall see these presents, and more particularly to the Sheriff of the 1st Superior Court District.— Be it known, that by virtue of the powers in me vested, I do direct and require, that the execution of the sentence of death, which has been announced by the Judge of the Parish New Orleans and a Jury duly impanelled according to Law, against the negro man Henry the slave of

Messrs. Laymere & Groux be further suspended until the
first friday in April next.—

Given at New Orleans on
the 3rd day of January 1812.

signed/ W. C. C. Claiborne

——— „ ——— „ ———

———————

To Paul Hamilton

Private.

New Orleans 3rd Jany 1812.

Secretary of the Treasy.

——— „ ———

My dear Sir,

Since my letter of the ———Ultimo, I have experienced much satisfaction in reading the report submitted to
Congress by the Committee of foreign relations.— It is
indeed an interesting state paper; our wrongs are con-
cisely enumerated, and placed before the nation in a point
of view, that must make a sensible impression on every
Citizen who has a soul to feel, & a spirit to support the
rights of his Country.— If the measures advised by the
Committee are adopted, a *Crisis* (which is certainly desirable) must soon arise:——— An *honorable accommodation,* or a *War,* the Justice & necessity of which, can only
be questioned by those who are prepared for Submission.
— I can see no good grounds to fear the issue of a
War;— If the *enemy* depredated on our Commerce, *his*
would be no less annoyed by American cruisers;— If *he*
menaced our sea-port Towns, *his provinces & those of his
ally* would present to us, fair objects of attack:— to the
North, the Canadàs would no doubt attract attention, &
in this quarter, Coba & the other Spanish possessions
should interest our Government. Their destinies are of
deep concern to the United States, and it is all important

that they should be free'd from the Schackles of European Authority and influence.— I fear, lest I may be thought intrusive by so frequently introducing this subject.— But I shall find in your goodness an apology, when I assure you that it is attributable to the pleasure with which I dwell on topicks, which to my mind, is so intimately connected with the welfare and security of my Country.— Cuba in possession of the British, and Havana would become a great naval station.— From Halifax to Jamaica the chain would be complete.— our whole Coast might be blockaded, and the Trade of the Mississippi entirely destroyed. Cuba in possession of the British, and they would maintain there a disposeable force, always ready to be transported to our shores— our maritime possessions would be seriously menaced, and lower Louisiana in eminent danger.— But reverse the scene, and what are the prospects. Cuba in possession of the United States;— Her ports would swarm with our Merchant Vessels, and her immense resources brought into active use.— In time of War our Cruisers would find an advantageous rendezvous, and their Prizes a Convenient Assylum;— The trade of Jamaica and other Islands would be paralized, and the destinies of New Spain at our disposition.— But above all, the great avenue for the Commerce of the Western States would be secured, and a unity of interests established and perpetuated between the several Members of the America family, that would place our Union beyond the reach of change.—

The *Orleans Convention* is yet in session; a contrariety of opinion existed on many points in the constitution as reported, and the discussions were vastly diffusive;— I believe however that *their* labours are now drawing to a close, & will I trust, eventuate in the formation of a Constitution strictly republican & calculated to promote the present & future prosperity of the State.—

New Orleans 5th Jany 1812

Allan B. Magruder Esqre

Dear Sir,

I thank you, for the pamphlet, which came enclosed
in your note of the 30th Ultimo.—— It relates to a very
interesting subject, and will command an attentive perusal.—— I have heretofore seen some extracts from this
publication;—— But the work itself is now for the first
time before me.—— In the course of the morning, I propose to leave the City, on a visit to my friend Mr. Clay;
——On my return, which will be in 6 or 7 days, I should
be happy to see & to converse with you, relative to the
various Land Titles in this Territory;—— our opinions
respecting them, may not be altogether in unison, but I
do not think any material difference, will be found to
exist.

I am, Sir, &c a &c a
Signed/ W. C. C. Claiborne

—— ,, —— ,, ——

To Col. I. B. Labatut

New Orleans 5th Jany 1812

of the 1st Regt of Militia

—— ,, —— ,, ——

Dear Sir,

I enclose you two Commissions which I will thank you
to cause to be delivered to the Gentlemen for whom they
are intended.—— You will be pleased to annex Captain
Gordon & Lieutenant Kennedy to the Company formerly
commanded by Captain Earle.——

I am, Sir, &c a &c a
signed/ W. C. C. Claiborne

—— ,, —— ,, ——

To Albert Gallatin

New Orleans Jany 5th 1812

Secy of the Treasury
Sir,

I have the honor to enclose you Copies of letters which have passed between Commodore Shaw and myself relative to the restraints proper to be imposed upon the intercourse between pensacola and Mobile, and to request, that you would be so obliging as to point out to me, the line of Conduct, you would wish to be observed.——

I am,

Sir,

With great respect

Your mo: ob: Servt

Signed/   W. C. C. Claiborne

———— „ ———— „ ————

To Commodore Shaw

Naval Commander   New Orleans 5th Jany 1812
———— „ ————

Sir,

Your letter of the 3d Instant is before me. ——as regards Vessels entering the Bay of Mobile from Pensacola or any other foreign Port, with Slaves on board, I feel no hesitation in advising you to sieze all such, and to send them to New Orleans for Trial.—— as respects the transportation of British Goods from Pensacola to Mobile, or vice versa, I shall without delay, solicit the advice of the Honorable the Secretary of the Treasury;—— In the mean time, I do not feel myself at Liberty, to prescribe a Rule for your conduct.——

Perdido is considered by me as the Eastern Limit of the Territory of Orleans;—— But the Spanish authoritys being in possession of the Tract of Country, which includes the Town and Fort of Mobile, & is bounded by Dog River, by that branch of it called Bayou Moulins; by a line direct from thence to the Bayou St. Louis (lately called three mile Creek) by the said Bayou, & by the Mobile River & Bay, I do not know that it would be correct, to prohibit their intercourse with Pensacola;—— But in the event, that any British Goods should be landed West of the Perdido, and from without the limits above described, you should immediately Seize the Vessel and Cargo.

I am, Sir, &c a &c a

Signed/   W. C. C. Claiborne

—— ,, —— ,, ——

To George Poindexter[1]

New Orleans 6th 1812.

A Member of Congress

—— ,, —— ,, ——

Dear Sir,

I have for some time past anticipated the pleasure of a letter from you.—— But I see (through the medium of the papers) that you are busily engaged, and can readily find for you an apology.—— I sincerely wish you success in your application for a State authority;—— Territorial Governments are at best necessary evils;—— they are illy suited to the Genius of the American people and should never exist but over small communities, who are neither able nor desirous to manage their own affairs.— I cannot however wish success to your efforts to take from Orleans, the whole of West Florida.[2]——

---

[1] Delegate from Mississippi Territory.

Had you designed to give us a moiety; for example, had you proposed that the Orleans Territory should extend Eastwardly to Pearl River, & the Tract of Country extending from Pearl River to the Perdido to be attached to the Mississippi Territory, I do not know, that the plan would be very exceptionable;—— But your demand for the whole seems to me somewhat extravigant and if granted by Congress, will in my opinion be highly injurious to the New State of *Louisiana* (the name the Convention has preferred) whose best Interests suggest an extension of its Eastern Boundary.—— I myself, would prefer the Perdido.—— But we would compromise & take as far as Pearl River, and leave to your State the Country on the Tombigbee & Pascagoula & the care of one of the great avenues for the Western Commerce, *the Mouth of the Mobile.*

What is the real situation of our foreign Relations? —— Will the Report of the Committee on that Subject, be supported by Congress? The measure recommended seem to me wise and well calculated to bring on a Crisis, which the honor of the nation demands.—— an immediate Repeal of the orders in Council, or open & direct War.——

The Orleans Convention will close its session in ten of fifteen days.—— The constitution adopted will be purely republican, & will I trust be approved by Congress during their present session.——

I am,
Sir,
Your friend
signed/   W. C. C. Claiborne
—— ,, —— ,, ——

To James Monroe

New Orleans 19th Jany 1812

Secy of State

————— „ —————

Sir,

The Commission by which I was appointed Governor of the Territory of Orleans expired on the 17th Instant. —— A high officer of the Government, in a private letter to me, dated at Washington on the 16th Ultimo, says, "You must have received an Account of your reappointment, which met with no difficulty," and this Sir, is the only information I have on the subject. How far, under these Circumstances I am authorized to exercise Executive authorty, being a matter of some doubt, I have taken the Council of the Territorial Attorney General, who is of opinion, that I cannot with propriety, cease to act as Governor, until officially advised that a successor in office had been commissioned.—— By the ordinance, the Secretary can alone discharge the duties of Governor in case of Vacancy, arising from the death resignation or removal from office, of the latter, or in case of his necessary absence.——— The letter of my friend, above alluded to, altho' not official, leaves no doubt in my mind, but I am still possessed of the confidence of the Government, & if such be the case, no act of the Secretary as Governor (in as much as I am not absent from the Territory) would be valid.—— From these considerations with others not necessary to mention, & the support received from the opinion of the Attorney General, I am induced stil to exercise Executive powers.—— I sincerely hope that in this course, there is nothing improper.—— If the trust I have so long had the honor to hold be continued to me, it will be accepted with gratitude & discharged with as pure motives of honest patriotism as ever warmed the breast of man:—— But if this trust has been committed to other hands, it will indeed be cause of much additional regret, that my ignorance of the fact, should have led to a line of Conduct, so contrary to what my feelings would have dictated.——

I have the honor to be, &c a

Signed/   W. C. C. Claiborne

—— „ —— „ ——

To Genl. Wade Hampton

New Orleans 20th Jany 1812

Baton Rouge

—— „ ——

The enclosed Copy of a memorial, signed by sundry Merchants of Nachitoches, will advise you of an act of atrocious violence, which an Armed Banditti have recently committed within the Tract of Country lying between the Arroya Honda and the Sabine on some unoffending Spaniards, and of the desire of the Memorialists, that measures be taken to put an end to a system of Brigandage, which is calculated to destroy all friendly intercourse, between the Citizens of this Territory and the Inhabitants of the Neighboring Spanish provinces. —— The Parish Judge of Nachitoches gives me to understand, that the efforts of the Civil authority are wholly inadequate to the suppression of this Banditti, & he solicits that the Military support prayed for, may be promptly afforded.—— Orders have heretofore been given to the officer Commanding the Militia of Nachitoches on the requisition of the Parish Judge, to turn out the whole or such part of his force as may be necessary for the preservation of good order;—— Detachments have in consequence of some prior depredations of this Banditti been ordered into service.—— But they are not yet suppressed, and if suffered longer to exist, their num-

bers and outrages will probably greatly increase.—— It
is known to you, that the claim of the United States extends to the Sabine, & that in the act of Congress author-
izing the Inhabitants of Orleans to form a Constitution
or State Government, the Sabine is recognized as the
Western Boundary of the Territory.—— Hence it is Sir,
that whilst as the past, I feel no difficulty as to the question of Jurisdiction, I consider it a duty to take *Measures* to prevent a repetition of such atrocities.—— *These*
heretofore ordered having proved ineffectual, I have to
entreat your Co-operation, and earnestly to request, that
you would establish three temporary Military Posts between the Arroya Honda & the Sabine, on the Road leading to Nacogdoches;—— That you would instruct the
Commandants of these Posts to give protection to Trav-
ellers;—— to aid the Civil authority in arresting *offenders* & to hold *them* in safe keeping, subject to the disposition of the Civil Magistrate.—— A number of armed
men assembled very lately near to Nachitoches, with the
design of attacking the Post of Nacogdoches within the
province of Texas, but owing to the treachery of their
Leader, the project was for the moment abandoned:——
It is however not improbable, but it will again be set on
foot, since many persons believed to be concerned (of
which number the perpetrators of the recent murders
and Robberies may be included) are still hovering on our
Western Frontier, and this circumstance furnishes me
with an additional motive for urging the establishment
in that quarter of several small Military Posts:—— As
to the extent of the force, you certainly Sir, can best determine.—— But I presume two or three Companies
would for the present be sufficient.——

I pray you to have the goodness to dispatch my Express as soon as your convenience will permit, and to inform me how far the State of the service may justify
your conforming to my request.—— Since in the event

of your Compliance, I would wish immediately (for the purpose of preventing misrepresentation & dissatisfaction) to advise the Spanish Authorities of the measures we may take, & of the objects in view.—— The preservation of a good understanding with our Spanish Neighbours, will at all times be desirable.—— But it is particularly so at this eventful Crisis.——

I have the honor to be,

Sir,

With great respect

Your mo. ob. sevt

Signed/   W. C. C. Claiborne

—— ,, —— ,, ——

To Judge Carr

New Orleans Jany 20th 1812

Nachitoches

—— ,, ——

Your letter of the 7th Instant, informing me of a recent Robbery & Murder committed, between the Arroya Honda & the Sabine, by an Armed Banditti was handed me on this Morning, together with a Memorial on the subject signed by several respectable Merchants of Nachitoches.—— Impressed with the importance of speedily suppressing this Banditti, & believing that a Regular force can best effect it I have this moment made and shall forward by express to General Hampton a Communication, of which I enclose a Copy for your perusal.—— In the event of General Hampton Compliance with my requisitions, I shall have only to express the reliance I place in your efforts to bring offenders to Justice, & to request you, to call upon the officer Commanding the Regular Troops for such support as may be necessary to enforce the preservation of good order.—— But should the General not feel himself authorized to conform to my wishes, the subject will then be refered to the President for his decision, & in the mean time, I will give to you & Colo. Shaumburg such further Instructions, as the nature of the case shall require & my powers may justify.—— For the present, I can only repeat to you my wish, that you would continue to exercise jurisdiction as far as the Sabine, & that for the due execution of process, you will if it be necessary call upon Colo. Shaumburg of the Militia for Military support, which in obedience to former Instructions, he will furnish with all the prompitude, which the actual state of his Regiment will permit.——

General Hampton is at Baton Rouge to which place, my Express immediately proceeds—— On his return, I shall be enabled to write you more particularly.——

I am, Sir &c a &c a &c a
Signed/ W. C. C. Claiborne

—— ,, —— ,, ——

To Paul Hamilton

private

New Orleans 23d Jany. 1812

Secy of the Navy

—— ,,

My dear Sir,

I have noted with the greatest satisfaction, the decided vote in favour of the resolutions reported by the Committee of foreign Relations, & the passage of a Bill by the Senate providing for the raising an additional force of twenty five thousand Men.— These proceedings promise well:— It now seems that the nation & Government are united, & that the wrongs offered our Country will be avenged.— Do me the favour to embrace an occasion to assure the President, that my services & my life are at the Command of my Country, & that in the event of War I would with pleasure enter the Army.— As relates to the Grade, I beg leave to repeat to you my willingness to accept of *any* which the Government may be disposed to assign me.— Under an impression however, that my knowledge of the adjacent Spanish provinces might be useful, I would prefer to act in this quarter.— Mexico is again represented to be a State of Revolution, & I have no doubt of the fact;— To this Revolution, it would not be difficult to give such direction as might accord with the views & Interests of the United States. *Five thousand* Regular Troops marched to St. Antoine & fifty thousand stand of Muskets would give Independence to Mexico, & banish forever European Influence;—

A very intelligent friend of mine is now engaged in Committing to paper (but not with a view to publication) his Ideas of the importance of Cuba to the United States, & the advantages which would result from the Independence of Mexico.[1]—— I send for your perusal his first Number, & will take the liberty to transmit the others as soon as they are completed.—

The friendly intercourse between the Citizens of this Territory, and the Inhabitants of the province of Tehus, has recently been disturbed by an armed Banditti, who have taken post between the Arroya Honda & the Sabine, & plundered and murdered several unoffending Spaniards.— I shall take such measures as are in my power to disperse this Banditti;— A good Intelligence with our Spanish Neighbours is at all times desirable— But it is particularly so at this *eventful crisis.*—

The Orleans Convention after much discussion & a Considerable share of Intrique & some warmth & division of sentiment will finish their labours, perhaps in two days, by the adoption of a Constitution, which altho' in some parts may be thought defective, is nevertheless

---

[1] Claiborne was an expansionist; he wanted the United States to take by force of arms, if necessary, the Spanish possessions in North America.

purely republican in principle & tolerably well adapted
to our local situation.—
    Present me affectionately & respectfully to your ami-
able Lady & family.   I am &ca &ca &ca
                        signed/ W. C. C. Claiborne
                        ——— „ ——— „ ———

                    To James Monroe
                            New Orleans Jany 24th 1812
Secy of State
——— „ ———
    I have the honor to enclose you a Copy if a Letter
from the Parish Judge of nachitoches advising me of the
Robbery & Murder, of some unoffending Spaniards, by
an armed Banditti, who had taken post within the limits
of this Territory between the Arroya Honda & the Sabine.— You have also enclosed a Copy of a Memorial
upon the subject addressed to me, by several respectable
Merchants of Nachitoches.   On a former occasion I informed you of the Instructions I had given to the officer
Commanding the Militia of Nachitoches to aid the Civil
authority in the preservation of good order,—— But
prompt Co-operation of General Hampton, & by a Letter
(of which the enclosed marked (A) is a Copy) suggested
the expediency of establishing three small Military post
between the Arroya Honda & the Sabine, on the road
leading to Nacogdoches.——
    A very lucrative Commerce is at present carried on
between Nachitoches & the neighbouring Spanish provinces;— But if the System of Brigandage which has recently been practised, be not speedily checked, all intercourse must be suspended, & instead of that good understanding with our neighbours which at present exists, a
spirit of Ill-will & distrust will be generated, which it
may be difficult to conciliate.——— I am, Sir &ca &ca &ca
                        signed/ W. C. C. Claiborne
                        ——— „ ——— „ ———

General Varnum   New Orleans Jany 26th 1812.
    a Senator in Congress
Dear Sir,

I thank you for your esteemed favour of the 22d Ultimo.—— The course advised by the Committee of foreign relations, seem to me to comport with the honor, the
safety of the United States, nor do I doubt the expediency of raising an additional force.—— It is indeed time
for the Nation & Government to unite in avenging our
wrongs.— of the result I feel no apprehension.—— The
Canada's surely will present no serious obstacles to our
Northern Brethren— and in this quarter the Florida's
will be an easy acquisition.— Cuba, Mexico, and the
Spanish American possessions generally deserve our
particular attention.—— The occasion is favorable to
free them from all European Influence either *Commercial* or *Political,* & to effect *whatever else,* the Interests
of the United States may suggest.

A Constitution for the New State is finally agreed
upon, and will be immediately transmitted to Congress;
—— It is purely republican in principle, & *tolerably* well
adapted to our local situation.— I am Dear, Sir, &ca &ca
&ca

Signed/ W. C. C. Claiborne

—— ,, —— ,, ——

To Robert R. Livingston

                    New Orleans 26th Jany 1812
NEW YORK.

—— ,, ——

The practicability of propelling Boats by Steam
against the Current of the Mississippi has been fully
proven, & I take great pleasure in enclosing for your
perusal an official report made to me as to the progress
thro' the water of the Steam Boat "New Orleans" lately

arrived at this port.[1]—— The great advantages resulting to the public from the Steam Boat navigating on the Western Waters, will soon be sensibly felt, & I doubt not, but that yourself and Mr. Fulton who have adventured so much in the undertaking, will be abundantly remunerated.—— If the force of Steam, could be applied to Sugar Mills, & in a manner simple & not attended with great expence, the invention would greatly conduce to the welfare of this Territory, & to the private Interests of the inventor.—— At present the Cane is ground by Mills worked by Horses—— But I have supposed, it would not be difficult to propell these Mills by Steam, & that no greater quantity of fuel would be requisite, than is now used in boiling the Juice.

The Orleans Convention have finally agreed on a Constitution for the New State.—— It is republican in principle, and tolerably well adapted to our local situation.—

Accept assurances of my great esteem

signed/ W. C. C. Claiborne

—— ,, —— ,, ——

To Commodore Shaw

New Orleans January 27th 1812

Naval Commander)
Sir,

I enclose for your perusal a Letter which has been addressed to me, by the Collector of this District, nor do I doubt, but that you will make such disposition of the Armed Vessels under your orders and give to the several Commanders such Instructions as may be best calculated to detect any violations of our Laws.——

I am, Sir, &ca &ca
Signed W. C. C. Claiborne

—— ,, —— ,, ——

[1] The first steamboat navigating the Mississippi arrived in New Orleans, Jany. 10, 1812.

New Orleans Jany 28th 1812.

Mr. William Conway)
 County of Arcadia)
Sir,

I have the honor to enclose you an Extract from the Journal of the Regents of the University, announcing your appointment as an Administrator of the County School of Arcadia, and to subscribe myself,—

With respect and esteem

Your mo: obt. Servt
Signed/ W. C. C. Claiborne

———— ,, ————

To James Monroe

New. Orleans 31st Jany 1812

Secy of State
Dear Sir,

Permit me to introduce to your acquaintance Messrs. E. Fromentin & Allan B. Magruder Esqrs. who are appointed by the Orleans Convention, Agents to convey to the President of the U. States, the Constitution proposed for the New State, & to represent generally to Congress, the Interests of this section of the Union.—

These Gentlemen deserve & possess a great share of the confidence of their fellow citizens, & can satisfy any of your enquiries as to the aspect of affairs in this Territory.—

The Convention having acceded to all the Conditions prescribed by Congress, & the Constitution being founded on principles purely republican, I persuade myself it will be approved.— The general welfare seems to me to require that the authority of the Territorial Government should speedily cease, & that that of the State should

commence.— an early change being confidently anticipat-
td, & apparently sincerely desired, the respect of the people for the existing Government its Laws & agents dimin-
ishes daily.— A careless indifference also, on the part
of some of the public functionaries is observable, & in
case of vacancies, appointments to office are accepted
with reluctance.— Such are the effects already resulting
from the incertitude of our political destiny, & if this Incertitude should be much prolonged, I really fear Sir,
the public service will be exposed to the most serious inconvenience.— For myself, I intertain no doubt, as to the
expediency (at the present moment) of our admission
into the Union, as a Member State.— The great Majority
of the Inhabitants are unquestionably well affected to
the Government of the U : States, nor could any event
tend more to strengthen their allegiance & affection, than
an early reception into the bosom of the American
family.—

Messrs. Fromentin & Magruder are charged by the
Convention with a Memorial to Congress, which prays
for the annexation of a part of West Florida to the New
State.— How far the posture of our Relations in respect
to that District, with Foreign Nations, will permit the
Government to annex permanently, to a State, such part
of Florida as lies west of the Perdido, is not for me to
determine;— But you will permit me to observe, that the
Interests of the New State strongly advise an enlargement of its Limits, & to add that the annexation solicited
would (in my opinion) not only conduce to the Convenience & prosperity of the people, more immediately
interested, but *to the national good.*[1]— I have the honor
to be, &c a

Signed   W. C. C. Claiborne

———— ,, ————

---

[1] See Annals of Congress.

To Albert Gallatin

New Orleans Feby 1st 1812

Secy of the Treasury)
Dr. Sir

Permit me to introduce to your acquaintance, Mr. Allen B. Magruder who has been named by the Orleans Convention one of their Agents to Convey to the President the Constitution for the New State, and to represent generally to Congress, the Interests of this section of the Union.—

Mr. Magruder deserves & possesses a great share of the Confidence of his fellow Citizens, & can satisfy any of your enquiries relative to the aspect of affairs in this Territory.—

The Convention having acceded to all the Conditions presented by Congress, the Constitution being founded on pure republican principles, I trust & hope it will be approved.— Of the expediency (at the present moment) of our admission into the Union as a Member State, I intertain no doubt the great Majority of the Inhabitants are (I am persuaded) well affected to the Government of the U: States, nor is there any thing, that would have a greater tendency to Confirm them in their affections & allegiance, than an early reception into the bosom of the American family.—

Mr. Magruder is well informed as to the nature of the Land Claims in this Territory, & will state to you some amelioration in the Laws relating to them, which Justice would seem to demand.— I learn that there are many claims, founded on the most unquestionable Titles, which have not been presented to the Commissioners.— various are the causes assigned for the Negligence of the Claimants;— some were advised either by ignorant or base men, not to enter their Claims— others assert, that they were apprehensive, it would be attended with a heavy expense; some again plead ignorance of the Laws, & others state, that their title papers, were thrown carelessly aside, & were not found until the time for receiving Claims had expired.— But whatever may have been the cause of this negligence, it is likely to prove injurious to many honest Citizens unless the Government should again deem it expedient to open an office for the reception of Claims— I am aware that the doing so will be attended with inconvenience.— and perhaps some injury to the public Interest:— But with a view to Justice, the first should at all times yield & I trust such restrictions and regulations may be devised & adopted as may effectually guard against fraud.— I am &c a

signed/   W. C. C. Claiborne

———— „ ———— „ ————

———————

To Paul Hamilton

Private,

New Orleans February 1st 1812.

Secy of the Navy
Dear Sir,

I now enclose you two other numbers upon the subject of Cuba & other possessions of Spain in America, which I am assured you will peruse with great pleasure. My friend Captain Shaler lately arrived hence from Havana is the author;— He is a very intelligent Man— devoted to his Country & his whole mind seems employed on objects connected with her Interests.—

The last letter of yours, which has reached me was under date of the   day of   But I can readily account for your Silence. being well aware, that during the session of Congress your official duties engross much of your time.— I hope however you will be enabled to embrace a few leisure moments to inform me of your health & happiness, and of the measures likely to be resorted to by the Government at this interesting Crisis.—

What a heart rending scene passed at Richmond on the night of the 26th of december.— It has harrowed up my very soul, & made me sad & Melancholy.— I knew many of the unfortunate sufferers, and sincerely do I regret their untimely end.— But our sorrow is unavailing;— The Grave will retain its prey and the mind finds no relief in dwelling upon the subject.— The Schism in Society will indeed be long felt.— But we must endeavour to seek Consolation from the Hope, that the *Scene of Gaiety* which was closed upon our friends, has been exchanged for an eternity of Bliss.—

You will very soon receive at Washington the Constitution proposed for the New State;— One of the Gentlemen named to bear it to the President departs on tomorrow, & the other in a few days.—The electioneering Campaign has commenced & my enemies will labour to rise on my ruin;— Already the press groans with abuse of me and it is attempted to convert into crime, acts the most meritorious.— But strong in conscious rectitude, I place great confidence in the Justice of my country.—

From considerations personal & political I am greatly desirous to visit Washington;— But I cannot at this Crisis (with honor) quit my pose.— I owe much to that portion of my fellow Citizens who have long & so firmly supported my administration, & on the eve of a change of Government, I am unwilling to withdraw from among them;— I have morever, buffeted for more than eight years all the Storms of party— & thus far, maintained my ground against the efforts of Intrigue, & the Shafts of Calumny;— New Clouds are now arising & a Tempest near at hand;— Its rage may drive me into port— But never from my duty.—

signed/   W. C. C. Claiborne

To John Rhea

New Orleans Feby 1st 1812

Dear Sir,

I have nominated & appointed as your Successor in office, Mr. Thomas Butler, on whose application, you will be pleased to deliver the records & papers appertaining to the office of Judge of the Parish of Feliciana.— In appointments to office, it rarely happens, that I am fortunate enough to give universal satisfaction;— But in selecting Mr. Butler, I am persuaded, I have reposed confidence in a Citizen, who will administer the Laws with Justice & in mercy, & whose primary object will be to merit the esteem of the good & virtuous.—

As regards Mr. Bradford & Mr. Gurley, (whom the Inhabitants of Feliciana, have recommended) it is impossible for me, to feel towards either an unfriendly disposition— But when the people of a parish seem divided in their wishes as to the nomination of a parish Judge, I deem it expedient to select some worthy & capable Character, in whose favour, neither party had taken an active Interest.— This policy has been observed on former occasion, & experience has convinced me, that it is correct.—

Accept Sir, the assurces of my Respect & esteem,

Sigd. W. C. C. Claiborne

———,,———,,———

To John Rhea

New Orleans Feby. 1st 1812.

Sir, On accepting (as I now do) your resignation of the office of Judge of the Parish of Feliciana, you will permit me to express my sincere regret, for the cause,

which deprives the public of the Benefit of your services;
to assure you of my confidence & esteem; and to add my
best wishes for the restoration of your health.

Signed/ W. C. C. Claiborne

To Thomas Butler

New Orleans Feby. 1st 1812

St. Francisville   )

―――― ,, ――――

Dr. Sir,

Desirous of availing the public of your services as
Judge of the parish of Feliciana, I have the pleasure to
enclose you a Commission,— and to subscribe myself—

With great esteem

Signed/   W. C. C. Claiborne

―――― ,, ―――― ,, ――――

P. S.   The transmission of the enclosed Commission
has been delayed from a report which had reached me,
that you would not accept;— But your friend Mr. Duncan having informed me to the contrary, I now forward
it, with great satisfaction.   (sigd)   W. C. C. C.

―――― ,, ――――

To Col. Pike

New Orleans Feby 2nd 1812

Baton Rouge)

―――― ,, ――――

Dear Sir,

I have received your private Letter with its enclosures.— The attentions of your Brother Officers will make
a just impression, & must have tended greatly to your
personal gratification.— The time I think the time is near
at hand when your Country will need your best services;
— My opinion is that you have the fairest claim for pro-

motion, & I shall in Consequence take great pleasure in promoting your views in life.— I shall address myself in your favour immediately to the President— It seems to me, to be the best course.—

Excuse that short letter— I am much pressed with business.—

Your sincere friend

(Signed)   W. C. C. Claiborne

———— ,, ———— ,, ————

To Major McRea

New Orleans Feby 4th 1812

New Orleans)

Sir,

I have received your letter of the 28th Ultimo— As regards the publication in the Louisiana Gazette to which you have reference, I have only to remark, that the efforts of Calumny have been so long & so uselessly employed against my reputation, that I can apprehend nothing from the present attempt & that I am too strongly fortified in conscious rectitude, to suffer Inquietude from the detractions of the day.— As respects the *statement* about the arms contained in that publication, I did at first suspect, *it* was made on information furnished by you;— But in as much as you have given me the most satisfactory assurances to the contrary & believing you incapable of misrepresentation of facts, I do not object to repeat in writing what I have already said to you verbally, " that my impression now is that the Statement, was not given by you, or with your knowledge."—

I avail myself of this occasion to request you to transmit me as soon as your convenience will permit, a Statement of the arms drawn from the public Stores in this City, for the use of the Militia, by virtue of requisitions from me, or upon the authority or credit of any other person;— Be pleased also to add, the time of drawing such arms & to whom delivered, & the number which have since been returned.

I am, &ca &ca &ca
Signed/ W. C. C. Claiborne

——— ,, ——— ,, ———

To Benjamin Morgan

New. Orleans Feby 7th 1812

New Orleans   )

Dear Sir,

I this moment received a private & very friendly letter under date of the 2nd Inst: from General Hampton, in which, among other things he says,—

"Lieutenant Colo. Pike, with a Complete Company,"
"in addition to the force of Nachitoches, will depart in"
"a day or two, for that place, with such orders and In-"
"structions as are judged best calculated to effect the"
"main object of your letter of the 20th.— The course"
"adopted by the Government will not be departed"
"from; but it will be taken with dignity & executed in a"
"way that will leave no room to doubt, that the proceed-"
"ing measures are to be alone regarded as mere mat-"
"ters of form & civility."

Believing that this *Information* may in some degree influence your commercial arrangements, I give *it* to you with great pleasure.—— I am &ca

Signed/ W. C. C. Claiborne

——— ,, ——— ,, ———

To Mr. Macon

New Orleans February 7th 1812

a Representative in Congress
Dear Sir,

This letter will be delivered to you by Mr. E. Fromentin who bears to the President, the Constitution proposed for the New State, & who is appointed by the Orleans Convention, one of their agents to represent generally to Congress, the Interests of this section of the Union.—

Mr. E. Fromentin deserves & possesses a great share of the public Confidence;— He is a man of education;— of strict Moral rectitude, & is, I am persuaded, ardently attached to his adopted Country.—

The Convention having acceded to all the Conditions required by Congress, and the Constitution being republican, I sincerely hope it may be approved— a change is confidently calculated upon, and I believe sincerely desired.— A delay will greatly disappoint the expectations of the people, and augment the embarrassments which already attend the administration of the temporary Government.— I have no doubt myself, as to the expediency at the present Moment of admitting this Territory, as a Member State of the Union.— There are among us Individuals, from whose principles political & private, a virtuous Government can look for no support;— The intrigues of these Individuals, will certainly be productive of some temporary Inconvenience;— But the great Majority of the Inhabitants, are well affected to the United States, nor could any thing tend more to confirm them in their allegiance & attachment, than an early reception into the Bosom of the American family.—

I am &c a &c a &c a

signed) W. C. C. Claiborne

To a Lady

New Orleans Feby 9th 1812

Permit me the honor Madam to introduce to you, Mrs. F: of this City, who accompanies her Husband on a visit to the City of Washington— The very amiable disposition of this Lady will soon make you acquainted & her virtues will engage your esteem.—

Mrs. F.— can give you the character of this interesting Society accompanied with such details, as will be most agreeable;— She can also state particularly the alarm which has recently been excited here, by that dread phenominon of Nature, an Earthquake.— On the night of the 16th Instant, a trembling of the Earth interrupted the Gaiety of the Season, & many Ladies retired from a Ball Room seriously affrighted. On the evening of the 7th a like trembling, more than the one preceeding, excited our apprehensions.— I was attending (at that time) a Theatrical Representation, which amused & interested a numerous audience.—

The night was unusually serene, and without, and within all was tranquility.— On a sudden, the vibration of the Chandeliers attracted every Eye:— The whole House undulated:— The Comedians ceased to act;— after a moment of most profound silence, a General expression of fear was heard from the Ladies, & an anxiety for *their safety,* filled me with *Inquietude.— It* however was of short duration, for in about a Minute & ahalf the Earth became composed, and to a kind providence we are stil indebted for life & protection.— I am not however, without serious apprehensions, that elsewhere, the *Shock* has been more terrible, & attended perhaps with consequences, that will be regreted by all, who can feel a sympathy for human woe.— The train of reflection, to which this subject naturally leads, presents anew to my view the heart-rending Scenes which took place at Richmond in Virginia, on the evening of the 26th of December last.

— With what sincerity of Heart, do I lament the calamity
that has befallen my Native State;— How greatly do I
sympathise for the misfortunes of that Society with
which, I had the happiness to pass, many of the days of
my Youth.—— I knew many of the unfortunate victims,.
& shall long affectionately cherish their memories.— But
in reflecting on this afflicting occurrence the mind finds no
relief— Our sorrow is unavailing.— We have, indeed lost.
much, but our friends have made a fortunate Exchange;.
—Thro' a few moments of extreme suffering, they have
passed into an eternity of Bliss.—

I am very solicitous to pay my respects in person, to
my friends at Washington;— The period is perhaps, not
distant, when it may be in my power to do so, & it will
be embraced with great satisfaction.— Be so good as to
bear to Mr. G. my best wishes for a continuance of his
domestic, individual, & public happiness, & permit me
the honor Madam to subscribe myself,—

With the most respectful attachment

Your very ob. Hum. Sert.

Sigd   *W. C. C. Claiborne*

To Judge Claiborne

New Orleans 12th Feby 1812

Rapide

——— „ ———

Sir,

You will be pleased to communicate the enclosed writ
of election to Judges Olliver & Hall, who will unite with
you, in causing its due execution.

As respects the enquiry, you addressed to me, concerning Justices of the Peace, I have to observe, that
such Gentlemen residing within the Parish of Rapide, as
were commissioned Justices for said parish, (and whose
resignations have not been tendered & accepted) are con-

sidered as holding their offices, during the pleasure of the
Governor for the time being.— Justices of the Peace,
for Counties (formerly) under a Territorial Law, and in
conformity to the first Act of Congress for the Government of Orleans, held their commissions for four years.
But the Act of the' Legislature erecting parishes, pre-
scribes no term of office for the Justices of the Peace, nor
does the ordinance by which we are now governed.—

> I am,
>> Sir,
>>> Very Respectfully
>>>> Your mo. ob. sert.
>>> Signed   W. C. C. Claiborne

———— ,, ———— ,, ————

To James Monroe

New Orleans 14th Feby 1812

Secretary of State)
Sir,

I have this day drawn a Bill upon you for three hundred Dollars, payable at ten days sight to Abner L. Duncan or order.—

When at the City of Washington, in the summer of
1810, I informed Mr. Smith, (who was at the time Secretary of State) by letter, of a Suit which Mr. Edward Livingston had instituted against the Marshal of Orleans,
who in obediance to the instructions of the President, had
dispossessed Livingston, of a piece of ground commonly
called the Batture, & I took the liberty to suggest the expediency of employing Council to aid the District Attorney in the defence of the Marshal. Mr. Smith, after
having mentioned the subject to the President, authorized me to engage the services of one or two Lawyers, as
I might judge proper;— The amount of compensation

was not fixed by Mr. Smith, but if my memory serves me right, I mentioned three hundred dollars as a reasonable fee, to which he assented.— I have in consequence engaged in the defense of the Marshal Mr. Abner L. Duncan, & the Bill now drawn upon you, is in full for his compensation, unl&ss the suit should be attended with much more difficulty than is contemplated, & in which case, it is to be left to you Sir, to determine his fee. The District Attorney & Mr. Duncan are of opinion that the suit, will be discontinued, on a plea to the Jurisdiction which has been filed;— But if in this expectation they should be disappointed, & the case be submitted to a Jury, I shall employ also in the defence some one of the French Lawyers unless you should instruct me to the contrary.— The suit instituted against Mr. D'Orginoy the Marshal who dispossessed Livingston was upon argument dismissed by the Court;— The suit now pending is against Mr. Fortier, the successor of Mr: D'Orginoy who in compliance with the advice & instructions of the District Attorney, removed Mr. Livingston who had a second time intruded on the Batture.—

I am &ca &ca

Signed   W. C. C. Claiborne

———— ,, ———— ,, ————

To Commodore Shaw

New. Orleans Feby. 14th 1812

Naval Commander)

Dear Sir,

This letter (with its enclosure) will be delivered to you, by Mr. A. Dufour, a promising youth, who wishes to enter the Navy of the United States, as Midshipman. — The only testimonials in his favour, which I have received are enclosed,— You will observe, that the young man & his Mother were under the impression, that it was in my power to place him in the Navy;— I have corrected this mistake, and refered the applicant to you, with an assurance of your sincere disposition to foster merit, wherever it be found.— Permit me to add Sir, that if the convenience of the service permits, & upon further enquiry, you should think proper to place this youth temporary on board of one of the armed Vessels, I will, whenever you may desire it, unite with you, in recommending him to the Secretary of the Navy, for a Midshipman's warrant.—

> I am &ca &ca
>> Sigd.   W. C. C. Claiborne

—— ,, —— ,, ——

——————

To Judge King
>> New Orleans 15th Feby 1812

Opelousas

—— ,, ——

Sir,

I enclose you a writ of election to supply the vacancy, occasioned by the resignation of Mr Allan B. Magruder.—

The Report of the Administrators of the County School of Opelousas, having been laid before the Regents of the University, & approved, the draft of said administrators on the Treasurer of the Territory, for two thousand dollars will be duly honored.—

> I am, Sir, &c a &c a
>> Signed   W. C. C. Claiborne

—— ,, —— ,, ——

——————

To Judge Carr
>> New Orleans 16 Feby. 1812

Nachitoches

—— ,, ——

Dear Sir,

Previous to the receipt of this letter, Colonel Pike will have reached Nachitoches, for the purpose of taking

command of the Troops at that place.— I recommend the
Colonel to your civilities & confidence;— He is a brave &
discrete soldier, and a Man of Integrity & Talents.— I
do not know the particular orders given to Colo. Pike;—
But General Hampton has informed me, that they would
be such as were best calculated (under existing circumstances) to disperse the Brigands in your vicinity, & to
maintain the public tranquillity.—

We are without any recent intelligence from Washington, three mails having failed in succession; The last
advices furnished strong apprehensions of War with
England;— A Bill had passed the two Houses of Congress for raising fifteen thousand additional Troops, &
a proposition was pending for a Considerable increase of
the Navy.—

The report of the Administrators of the County
School of Nachitoches, has been laid before the Regents
of the University, & is approved;— The Bill therefore
of administrators on the Treasurer of the Territory, for
two thousand dollars, will be duly honored.—

I am, &c a &c a

Sigd.   W. C. C. Claiborne

———— ,, ———— ,, ————

Private

To Paul Hamilton

New Orleans Feby 17th 1812

Secretary of the Navy.

———— ,, ———— ,, ————

Dear Sir,

Three successive Mails having failed, we remain without any recent intelligence from Washington.— Mexico
(from latest accounts) was stil in a State of revolution;—
The patriots continued embodyed, and manifested a determined resolution to put down all European authority.— A reinforcement of three thousand regular Troops
from Cadix, had arrived at Vera Cruix;— But it is be-

lieved, a much greater force will be necessary to keep in check, a spirit of resistance to arbitrary power & oppression, which was so generally diffused.—

I await with great anxiety the determination of the Government, with respect to Mobile, & East Florida,— A longer forbearance will produce no good;— on the contrary I fear it may prove injurious.—England & Spain have already expressed much dissatisfaction, at the partial occupancy of Florida, nor would the taking possession of the whole, highten in the least their resentment.— On the contrary a measure of so decided a Cast, would command their respect, and incline them to be cautious in provoking a people, who evinced no fear of war.

If the proposed additional army should be raised, there will be doubtless many applicants for Commissions;— among the number will be my two Brothers, General Ferdinand L Claiborne, & Doctor Thomas A. Claiborne both of the Mississippi Territory.— They have each been in the regular service, & I have the satisfaction to believe, acquited themselves with honor. My Brother Ferdinand I presume, will aspire to the Command of a Brigade, & the Doctor to some appointment in the line of his profession.— For particular information as to their general course & Conduct in life, I refer you to Mr. Poindexter & Govr. Holmes, (who I understand is now at Washington), and should their report be satisfactory, I take the liberty to recommend them to your patronage.— For myself Sir, I can vouch for their *Integrity,* personal firmness & Love of Country, nor would they be less grateful than myself, for any services you may render them.— I felt some reluctance in introducing this subject;— But upon reflection, that delicacy seemed to me to be false, which would induce an Individaul to withhold from his Brother *a just support.*—

If Captain Johnson formerly of the marines, but now of the United States Infantry, should have arrived at

Washington, I beg you to present him, with my best
wishes; His merits are I understand known to you.—
He is certainly an officer of great promise, & will I hope,
meet with promotion in the additional Army;— He is
prudent, brave, attached to his profession, & devoted to
his Country & Government.— I am, &c a &c a &c a

Signed,   W. C. C. Claiborne

————— ,, ————— ,, —————

To the Lady Abbess of the Ursuline Convent

New Orleans 19 Feby 1812

Holy Sister

I have the honor to announce to you, that the Petition
which your Community addressed to Congress, respecting the Military Hospital was read on the 8th of January
last, in the House of Representatives of the United
States, and referred to a select Committee.— I shall communicate to you the final determination of Congress, so
soon as it is made known to me.—

I tender to you Holy Sister, the assurances of my
great respect and sincere friendship.—

signed   William C. C. Claiborne

————— ,, ————— ,, —————

To John P. Hampton

Territory of Orleans

St. Francisville   County of Arcadia Feby 24th 1812

————— ,, —————

Sir

Desirous of availing the public of your services as
Judge of the Parish of Feliciana, I have the pleasure to
enclose you a Commission, and to subscribe myself,—

With great respect,

Your mo. ob. Servt.

Signed   William C. C. Claiborne

————— ,, ————— ,, —————

To Judge Rhea

County of Arcadia Feby 24, 1812

Dear Sir,

Mr. Butler having declined serving as Judge of your Parish, I have appointed Mr. John P. Hampton of St. Francisville, & his Commission will be forwarded from Lafourche, by the Mail of next week. I have not the pleasure of a personal acquiantance with Mr. Hampton; But Gentlemen in whom I confide, represent him "as a young Man of accomplished education— possessing" "a fund of legal information— of exemplary morals, and "the purest Integrity,"— I have therefore every reason to believe, that in Mr. Hampton, I shall find an officer who will discharge his duties with honor to himself usefulness to the public— I am aware that a report is in circulation at St. Francisville, that your County is to be immediately annexed to the Mississippi Territory.— I have myself Sir, no recent information from the Seat of Government on this subject— But my impression is, that the report will prove incorrect.— I ardently wish, (nor am I without strong hopes) that Feliciana will be annexed to the New State of Louisiana;— But if under existing circumstances, Congress should deem it inexpedient at this time, to make such disposition, I hope the County of Feliciana may be erected into a separate Territory.—

I am thus far on my way to attackapas for the purpose of paying my respects to the venerable Father, of my deceased wife Mr. Duralde, and taking to my arms, my dear little Son. I shall probably return to New Or-

leans, on or before the 15th of March, when, & at all times
I shall be happy to hear from you.—

   I am,
    Dear Sir,
     With great respect & esteem
      Your mo. ob. Ser
      Signed   Will C. C. Claiborne

      ——— ,, ——— ,, ———

      Territory of Orleans

   To James Monroe

    County of Iberville Feby 28th 1812
  Secretary of State

——— ,, ——— ,, ———

Sir,

The Commission, by which I am appointed Governor
of the Territory of Orleans, for three years from the 17th
of January last, did not reach me, until this morning.—

The envelope is post marked Washington December
4th from whence, it appears, that it has experienced unusual detention.— Will you do me the favor to bear to
the President my grateful acknowledgements & to assure·
·him of my best efforts to merit a continuance of his Confidence.

I left New Orleans on the 20th Instant, and calculate
on returning there in twelve or fifteen days, and at an
earlier period, if my presence should become necessary.—

   I am,
    Sir,
     With great respect
      Your mo. ob: Servt.
      Signed   W. C. C. Claiborne

      ——— ,, ——— ,, ———

To the Lady Abbess   )
) New Orleans 24th March 1812
of the Ursuline Convent)
Holy Sister!

I have the honor to enclose you an extract from the proceedings of Congress, of the 11th of January last, by which you will observe the very respectful attention paid to the petition from your Community.—

Accept Holy Sister, the assurances of my great Consideration, and sincere friendship.—

Signed/   W. C. C. Claiborne

―――― ,, ―――― ,, ――――

To His Excellency Joel Barlow

New Orleans March 24th. 1812

Minister Plenipotentiary   )
  from the U. S. of America   )
  to his Majesty the Emperor   )
  of France & King of Italy   )
Dear Sir,

My young friends William McFarland Saul & John Dick Saul (the one 17 & the other 16 years of age) left Liverpool on the 9th of November 1811, in the Brig Dolly, Captain Holden bound for the Havana & New Orleans.— The Brig was taken and burnt at Sea by the French Frigate Madusa & the Passengers carried into Brest.— These two young Gentlemen, were born in Virginia, (of which State their Mother is also a Native) & are the sons of my esteemed friend Mr. Joseph Saul of this City;— They departed hence near four years ago for England with a view to the Completion of their education & were returning home, when they were taken and carried into Brest.— I entreat for these youths your kindest protection;— Their father Mr. Saul (late Cashier of the Branch Bank in this City & now Cashier of the Bank of Orleans)

is an excellent Citizen, & the best of Men;— He has taken
measures to supply his Sons with funds, but in the event,
that these should not speedily reach them, do me the
favour Sir, to advance the necessary Sum, to make them
comfortable on their passage home. This act of kindness, will be gratefully remembered, and your order for
the amount either on Mr. Joseph Saul of New Orleans or
myself, will on sight be paid.—

I pray you Sir, to accept the assurances of my great
respect & sincere esteem!

signed/   William C. C. Claiborne

——— ,, ——— ,, ———

———

To His Excellency Governor Maxent

New Orleans March 25th. 1812

Pensacola

——— ,, ———

Sir,

I have been prevented until this moment from acknowledging the receipt of your Excelly's letter of the
7th of January, in consequence of an absence of several
weeks from this Capital, and a necessary attention to
matters of business, which required immediate dispatch.

There was no mistake as to time, in the Communication I had the honor to address you under date of the
27th of October last, and as regards the delay in its delivery, I have only to observe that it is attributable to
unavoidable causes, which to me have been satisfactorily
explained.—

I shall not enter into a discussion of the right of the
United States, *to the tract of Country, extending from
the Mississippi to the Perdido;* Not Sir, that I feel the
smallest difficulty in Confuting *your assertions,* for you

have not thought proper to introduce *an argument;*—
But because, such discussion is without my province.—
It belongs more immediately to the Secretary of State
for the United States, to whom, if your Excellency is
vested with full powers on the subject, I beg leave to refer
you.— My duties in relation to the Territory in question,
are only executive, and to *their* prompt & faithful discharge, I am always ready to proceed.—

Your ungenerous remarks as to the motives and conduct of the United States, deserve no Comments,— The
Character of *my Government,* is its best shield against
reproach, and I should be wanting in respect for the great
& good Men, who administer it, to attempt a serious refu-
tation of charges so evidently unjust and groundless.—

I renew to your Excellency, the assurances of my
great respect.—

signed/   William C. C. Claiborne

———— ,, ———— ,, ————

New Orleans March 26. 1812

To the Officer   )
  Commanding the U. S. Troops)
     at   )
       Fort Stoddart   )
Sir,

Being desirous, that the enclosed Letter to Governor
Maxent, should reach him in safety and without delay, I
have taken the Liberty to enclose it under cover to your
address, and I must ask of you the favour to forward it,
to the Spanish Commandant at Mobile.—

    I am,
       Sir,
          With great respect Your mo: ob: Sevt
             signed William C. C. Claiborne

To James Madison

Territory of Orleans

The President   County of Attackapas Ist March 1812
of the U. States

Sir,

Having been informed, that an additional Army of twenty five thousand Men, have been voted by Congress, & presuming that some officers attached to Regiments now in Service, may meet with promotion in this raised Corps, I beg the Liberty to recommend to your *further patronage,* Lieutenant Colonel Zebulon Pike;— He is in the vigour of life, about thirty years of age, & possessed of a health robust Constitution;— to an enterprising spirit, he unites great perseverance, & the most cool & deliberate courage;— His leisure moments are wholly employed in the improvement of his mind, & to a fund of very general information, he has added a Knowledge of the French & Spanish languages;— His profession is his favorite study, & in theory & practice, is unquestionably, the best disciplinarian (of his grade) in the Army.— Colonel Pike has for a length of time, been on duty in this Territory, & having observed, that on all occasions his conduct was that of a faithful soldier, & an excellent Citizen, I take sincere pleasure in bearing testimony to his merits.—

With sentiments of the most respectful attachment,—
        I have the honor to be,
                Sir,
                        your mo: ob: Sert.
                        signed   W. C. C. Claiborne
                        ——— ,, ——— ,, ———

George W. Morgan

Sheriff of the 1st Supreme)
    Court District.   )

New Orleans March 31st 1812

Sir,

Mr. Joseph Montigut Junr. having been appointed to succeed you as Treasurer of the Territory of Orleans, you will be pleased to deliver to him the Monies of the Territory, & all the records & papers appertaining to that office.—

I take this occasion, to express my entire approbation of your conduct as Treasurer;— It has evidenced, Integrity, Talent, & attention;— It has placed our Revenue Department in a prosperous State, & gives you additional claims to my Confidence & esteem.

Signed/ W. C. C. Claiborne

——— ,, ——— ,, ———
————————

To James Monroe

New Orleans 31st March 1812

Secretary of State

——— ,, ———

Sir,

I had the pleasure a few days since, to receive your letter of the 15th of Feby. enclosing a Duplicate of my *Commission*.— The Original had previously reached me and of which I did myself the honor to advise you, in a letter bearing date the 28th Ultimo.—

The assurance you are kind enough to give me, of the continued approbation of the President, and of the interest you take in being the organ of such approbation, affords me the sincerest satisfaction.— In the discharge of my various (and not unfrequently) arduous duties, the greatest support I could receive is the Confidence of an administration to which I am devoted, from every consideration of principle & gratitude.— This confidence at all times *so cheering,* is particularly so, at the present crisis, when the Territorial government is drawing to a close, & a few Individuals who wishing to direct the destinies of the New State, seem uncommonly solicitous to impress the Public unfavorably towards me.—

I pray you Sir, to accept the assurances of my great respect & Sincere Esteem.—

signed   W. C. C. Claiborne

———— ,, ———— ,, ————

To Judge Claiborne

New Orleans Apl. 4th 1812

Rapides

———— ,, ————

Sir,

The resignation of Mr. Planché having reached me a few days since, I have issued a writ of election to supply his vacancy & which is herewith enclosed— Such frequent elections, will subject the Citizens to Inconvenience; But it is my duty to take care, that the people shall not go unrepresented. We have no recent information from the Seat of Government, & remain wholy unadvised as to the reception of the proposed Constitution for the New State. — The Territorial Legislature will be in Session on the third Monday of the present Month.—

I am, Sir,

Your &c@ &c@ &c@

signed   W. C. C. Claiborne

———— ,, ———— ,, ————

N. B. A similar Letter was written to Judge King to supply of Mr. Posey of Opelousas.—

To Judge Claiborne

New Orleans 6th April 1812

Rapides

——— ,, ———

Sir,

Mr. Sacket, the Sheriff of Rapides having been represented to me, as a person of Ill-fame & Conduct, without special *Charges* being exhibited I request you, if there be *such* to be pleased to state them, together with the proof, if there be any within your knowledge, or in your power to procure.—

In case you should report to me, any special *charges* against Mr. Sacket, I will thank you to inform him by letter of their nature, & to add, that the Governor has instructed you to say, that such explanations or defence, as he may think proper to offer, will be duly Considered.

I am,

Sir,

Your &c@ &c@

signed/ W. C. C. Claiborne

——— ,, ——— ,, ———

To John Graham

New Orleans 31st March 1812

In the Department of State

——— ,, ——— ,, ———

Dear Sir,

Your letter of the 31st December last, has been delivered to me by the person, to whose care it was committed. To this moment I have received no letter from the Secretary of State, in which his name is mentioned, & I have been some what at a loss, as to the degree of countenance proper to show him.— As however, you inform me, that the Government wished his return *to Mexico to be expedited,* I have not hesitated to recommend him to the friendly attention of Captain William Shaler, who will depart for Nachitoches by the first Boat ascending the River from hence to that post— This Stranger has already given me to understand, that he is wholly destitute of funds; & that some advances from me are calculated on.— I presume, I shall not do wrong in soliciting Captain Shaler to advance such sum as may be necessary to make his voyage to Nachitoches comfortable: Were I not to do so, his return to Mexico, would be greatly retarded, unless he should fall into the hands of some of the Intrigues (foreign or domestic) with which this City abounds.

I am, &c@ &c@ &c@

signed/ W. C. C. Claiborne

———— ,, ———— ,, ————

To Judge Meriam

New Orleans 6th Apl. 1812.

Parish of Iberville

———— ,, ————

Sir,

Your letter of the 5th Ultimo, tendering your resignation, as Judge of the Parish of Iberville has been received.—I shall at any time greatly regret the loss of your faithful services.— But they cannot be dispensed with without injury to the Public Interest, until a successor shall have been appointed.— I pray you therefore for the present to continue in the exercise of your official functions, & to have the goodness to give me the names of one, two or more honest Citizens, who in your opinion would discharge the duties of Judge with Integrity Judgment and discretion.—

I am, &c@ &c@ &c@

Signed   W. C. C. Claiborne

———— ,, ———— ,, ————

To William Eustis

New Orleans Apl. 6th. 1812

Secy at War

——— „ ———

Sir,

Do me the favour to name to the President Mr. Horatio S. Sprigg late of the Navy and at present an Inhabitant of the County of Rapides in this Territory, as a Candidate for the honor of a Captaincy in the additional Army.— I have formed the most favorable opinion of Mr. Sprigg.— He is certainly a young Man of great Integrity & firmness of character, & his conduct in this Territory has been marked with great propriety.— My friends Colo Johnson & Judge Claiborne of Rapide, bear honorable testimony of Mr. Spriggs' merits & their letter to me on the subject of his application, is so honorable to him, that I have taken the liberty to enclose it for your perusal.— Colo. Johnson represented Rapide for several years in the Territorial Legislature, & Mr. Claiborne is the Judge of the parish.— They are excellent Citizens & entitled to high confidence.—

I have the honor to be,

Sir,

With great respect & esteem

signed/ W. C. C. Claiborne

——— „ ——— „ ———

To Col. Josiah S. Johnson

New Orleans 6th. Apl. 1812

Rapide.

——— „ ———

Dear Sir,

Your letter of the 15th Ultimo, was delivered to me on this morning.— I have formed the most favorable opinion of Mr. Sprigg, & with great pleasure, I have this moment, addressed a letter to the Secretary at War, recommending him for a Captaincy in the additional Army.— It is very possible, my letter will not reach the Seat of Government, until all the appointments are made. — Had Mr. Sprigg made an earlier application I feel assured it would have been successful.— I entertain however strong hopes, that he will stil meet the patronage to which I consider him so justly entitled.— We have no late news from the Seat of Government, & remain unadvised of the reception of the Constitution proposed for the New State.— The Territorial Legislature will meet (according to Law) on the 20th of the present Month, & I sincerely hope, the Members will be punctual in their attendance.—

I am,
Dear Sir,
With great esteem
Sigd.   W. C. C. Claiborne

—— ,, —— ,, ——

To William Shaler

New Orleans 7th April 1812.

Dear Sir,

To this moment, I have received no letter from the Secy of State, in which Don Jose Bernado Guiterras, (whom I have already introduced to you) is mentioned. But my friend, Mr. Graham who is attached to the Department of State, having informed me by letter, that the Government, wished the return of that Gentleman to Mexico *"to be expedited,"* I beg leave to repeat to you my desire, that you would give him a passage in the Boat in which you ascend to Nachitoches, & to extend to him, during the voyage, your friendly civilities. Mr. Graham does not request me to advance to Mr. Guiterras any money, & says expressly, that he has no authority from

the Government to make such request;— But wholly
destitute as this Stranger is of friends, his return to
Mexico *cannot be expedited,* without some pecuniary assistance;— I therefore Sir, do not hesitate to ask you to
advance him, such sum, as may be necessary for his
prompt departure from this City & comfortable accommodation on his voyage to Nachitoches & in the settlement of your public accounts, I am of opinion that the
same will be allowed you,— provided it does not exceed
in amount the boundary of a prudent economy.—

Accept assurances of my great respect & sincere esteem.—

Signed/ W. C. C. Claiborne
——— ,, ——— ,, ———

To Judges Claiborne and King

New Orleans 7th April 1812

Since my last letter, information from Washington,
as late as the 7th of March, has reached me, at which time
there were strong reasons to believe, that the Constitution, will be speedily approved.— I have in Consequence
thought it a duty to prorogue the Legislature until Wednesday the 20th of May.— This measure is the more expedient, because by the *Constitution,* the election of Governor & Members of the Assembly for the State, is to
take place, on the third Monday, after information of its
approval by Congress, shall have reached Mr. Poydras
late President of the Convention. In the event therefore
of an early approval, the meeting of the Territorial Legislature, *will at least be useless.* But should the Constitution be rejected, or its Consideration postponed, we
shall certainly be informed thereof, previous to the 20th
of May, when the Sessions of the Legislature will com-

mence & may be continued as long as the public interest shall require.—

I am &c@ &c@ &c@

Signed   William C. C. Claiborne

——— „ ——— „ ———

P. S.   Be so good as to communicate the contents of this letter, to the Gentlemen, returned as Representatives for Rapide, as also a Copy of the Proclamation enclosed.

sigd.   W. C. C. C.

——— „ ——— „ ———

To Judge Johnson

Parish of St. Mary's)   New Orleans 7 April 1812.
Attackapas   )

——— „ ———

Dear Sir,

I have only time to enclose you a Copy of my Proclamation, proroguing the Legislature, until the 20th of May. — This measure is become expedient from the great probability there is, of a *speedily approval* of the Constitution & the unutility in such event, of a Session of the Territorial Legislature.— The information on which I have deemed a prorogation proper, did not reach me until this Morning.—

I am,

Dear Sir,

Your friend

signed/ W. C. C. Claiborne

——— „ ——— „ ———

To Placide Bossier

New Orleans 7th April 1812

Nachitoches

Dear Sir,

Enclosed is a Copy of my Proclamation, proroguing the Legislature, until, the 20th of May.— My information from the City of Washington, is as late as the 7th

Ultimo, at which time, there was every reason to believe, that the Constitution for the New State would be speedily adopted.—

> I am, Dr. Sir, &c@ &c@ &c@
>
> Signed   W. C. C. Claiborne

To Col. Moses Kirkland

> New Orleans 7th April 1812.

St. Francisville
Sir,

On this morning, I received information from the Seat of Government as late as the 7th Ultimo, at which time there were strong reasons to believe, that the Constitution proposed for the New State, would be speedily approved. I have in Consequence thought it a duty to prorogue the Legislature until the 20th of May, & my Proclamation to that effect is herewith enclosed.— This measure is the more expedient since by the *Constitution* the election of Governor and Members of the Assembly for the State, is to take place on the third Monday, after information of *its approval* shall have been received by Mr. Poydras late President of the Convention.— In the event therefore of such early approval, a meeting of the Territorial Legislature *will at least be useless.* But if it so happens, that the Constitution be rejected, or its Consideration postponed, we shall probably be informed thereof, previous to the 20th of May, when the Sessions of the Legislature will commence, & may be continued as long as the Public Interest shall require.—

> I am &c@ &c@ &c@
>
> Signed   W. C. C. Claiborne

——— „ ——— „ ———

N. B. A similar letter was written to the several members of the House of Representatives.—

Private.
To   New Orleans 8th Apl. 1812
   Doct. Sibbley   )
   Judge Carr   )
   Colo Shaumburg)
      &   )
   Judge Claiborne.)
   Do me the favour to receive & to extend to my friend
William Shaler Esqr. your kind attentions.— In the
course of his various & honorable pursuits, he has ac-
quired a great fund of information & is esteemed by all
who know him, as a Citizen of great worth, & a Man of
strict integrity, attached to study & to retirement, Mr.
Shaler, during his stay at Nachitoches, would wish to engage some private lodgings:— Any services you may
render him in this respect, or in any other manner will
confer a favour on
                    Dr. Sr.
                      With great esteem,
                         Signed/ W. C. C. Claiborne
                     ———— „ ———— „ ————

To Col. Joshua Baker

                          New Orleans 8th Apl. 1812

Attackappas
Dear Sir,
   Lest my letter of yesterday may miscarry, I have the
honor to enclose you another Copy of my Proclamation,
proroguing the Legislature.— It is a subject of regret,
that the information which induced the prorogation, had
not been received, at an earlier period;— But I persuade
myself the proclamation may reach you in time to prevent a Journey (at this moment) to New Orleans.— I
need not tell you, that the information alluded to, is "the

great probability'' of a speedy approval by Congress of
the Constitution prepared for the New State.—

I am,

Dr. Sir,

With great esteem

sigd.   W. C. C. Claiborne

———— ,, ———— ,, ————

Colo. Joshua Baker)
Attackapas   )

———————————

To Abner L. Duncan

New Orleans 9th Apl. 1812

Sir,

Enclosed are certain papers addressed to me by the
parish Jury of Plaquemine, & a Copy of a *pardon* granting remission of certain fines, to *which* the Jury in their
address have reference.

It seems, that for a Breach of certain Parish Regulations, made in the year 1810, Judg'ments were rendered
in the year 1811, against certain Individuals, & executions
issued thereon.— The Jury contend that the pardon does
not affect these Judgments;— But the persons more immediately interested, say it does. Will you be pleased
to examine the papers & pardon, & to hear the statement
of the Sheriff, which will I believe be a correct one & give
me an opinion upon the subject.—

I am, Sir, &c@ &c@ &c@

Signed/ W. C. C. Claiborne

———— ,, ———— ,, ————

BY WILLIAM C. C. CLAIBORNE

Governor of the Territory of Orleans

A Proclamation.

WHEREAS considerations of public Interest require that the Legislative Body of this Territory which was to have assembled on the third Monday of this Month (April), should be prorogued for a short time, I have thought fit to issue this my Proclamation proroguing the same to Wednesday the 20th of May Next and it is hereby accordingly prorogued.—

> Given under my hand & the Seal
> of the Territory at New Orleans, on
> the 7th of Apl., 1812 & in the thirty-
> sixth year of American Independence.

[S. S.]

Signed/ W. C. C. Claiborne

—————— ,, —————— ,, ——————

———————————

Colo. Moses Kirkland)   New Orleans Apl. 12th 1812.
Captain L. C. Griffith)
James Turner, Esqr.   )
        &   )
Felix Bernard Esqr.   )

Lest my letter of the 7th Inst: may miscarry, I have the honor to enclose you another Copy of my Proclamation proroguing the Legislature, until the 20th of May, & to subscribe myself.—

> With great respect
> Your mo: ob: Servt.
> Signed   W. C. C. Claiborne

—————— ,, —————— ,, ——————

To Albert Gallatin

New Orleans Apl. 13th. 1812.

Secy. of the Treasury

I have the honor to acknowledge the receipt of your letter of the 4th Ultimo, & to add that a Copy of the same, has been transmitted to Commodore Shaw, as a guide for his conduct towards the Town of Mobile, & the District annexed thereto.—

I am, &c @ &c @ &c @

Signed/   W. C. C. Claiborne

——— ,, ——— ,, ———

To Commodore Shaw

New Orleans Apl. 13th 1812.

New Orleans

——— ,, ———

Sir,

I have the honor to enclose you a Copy of a Letter addressed by me, by the Honble. the Secretary of the Treasury, & to request, that you will give such orders, to the Naval Commander on the Mobile Station relative to the introduction of British Goods into the Town of Mobile & the District annexed thereto, & to exportation therefrom, as may conform to the instructions of the Secretary.— For the extent of the District annexed to Mobile, I beg leave to refer you to my letter of the 5 Jany last.—

I am, &c @ &c @ &c @

Signed/   W. C. C. Claiborne

To Judge Ludeline

New Orleans 13 Apl. 1812

Point Coupeé)

Sir,

Your letter of the 28th inclosing a return of the late election at Point-Coupeé, has been duly received.— The equal vote in the case of Messrs. Croizet & Herriait pre-

sents a novel question.— But I presume, another election
must be resorted to.— You probably have received my
Proclamation proroguing the Legislature to the 20th of
May,— lest however it may miscarry, I herein enclose
another Copy.— My impression is that an early approval
of our Constitution, will wholly supercede the necessity
of a Session of the Territorial Legislature; But if in this,
I should be disappointed, altho' your presence in the
Legislature would afford me pleasure, I should nevertheless, sincerely regret the loss of your faithful services as a Judge, & the more so, since I very much doubt,
whether I could supply your place, with an individual,
who would be alike approved of by myself & the Citizens
of your Parish.—

I am, &c @ &c @ &c @

Signed/ W. C. C. Claiborne

———— ,, ———— ,, ————

To John Graham

New Orleans 13th Apl. 1812.

In the Department of State
Dear Sir,
      Enclosed is a letter, which I have addressed to Captn.
William Shaler, relative to the person, to whom you alluded in your letter of the 31st of December.—
      Mr. Shaler was introduced to me by the former Secre-
tary of State Mr. Smith & I have taken it for granted,
that he is stil in the confidence & service of the Government.— His conduct in this City has been marked with
great circumspection & of his Talents zeal & fidelity, I
have formed the highest opinion. I have suggested to
Capt. Shaler, that on reaching Nachitoches, it would not
be proper to shew any further countenance to this
stranger.— No sooner was the arrival of this Man known
in New Orleans, than several Intriguers (believed to be

acting under foreign influence) made attempts upon
him;— But he prudently evaded all their efforts, & kept
himself whilst here quite retired.—

I am, Sir. &c @ &c @ &c @

Signed,   W. C. C. Claiborne

———— ,, ———— ,, ————

———————

To James Monroe

New Orleans Apl. 13th 1812.

Secy. of State
Sir,
I have the pleasure to inform you, that a Detachment
of Troops, acting under the instructions of General
Hampton have dispersed the Brigands who had taken
post, near the Sabine, & that a free & safe Intercourse
has been reestablished between Nachitoches, & the Spanish province of Tehus.—

It is difficult to say, what is the State of things in
Mexico;— My information from that quarter is always
contradictory.— I however believe it certain, that the
Revolutionists are stil in great force, & have cut off all
Communication between the Interior Provinces & the
City of Mexico & the Sea Board.—

Having understood that the Constitution adopted by
the Orleans Convention was laid before Congress on the
4th Ultimo,— & presuming on its being early approved, I
have deemed it expedient to prorogue the Legislature to
the 20th of May.— In the event of such early approval, a
Session of the Territorial Legislature, would be useless,
& the more so, since under the Constitution all the Territorial *authorities* would in a very short time be superceded by *those* of the State.—

I have the honor to be, Sir, &c @ &c @ &c @

Signed/   W. C. C. Claiborne

———— ,, ———— ,, ————

To Geo. W. Morgan

New Orleans Apl. 13th 1812.

Sheriff of the 1st Supreme)
Court District   )

―――― „ ――――

Dear Sir,
    I have received on this evening, such reports from the
Parish of Plaquemine, as make it necessary, that I should
send *them,* a confidential officer, for the purpose of ascertaining & stating to me, the causes of so much disorder.—
I must in consequence ask the favour of you, to ride tomorrow as far as the residence of Judge Latour where
you will (I presume) be enabled to acquire the information wanted.— That Judge, it is said, has left his residence & the records of the parish are exposed to loss &
spoliation.— But as relates to them & other matters, if
you will call on me in the morning, I will give you special Instructions.— You will no doubt, be enabled to return to New Orleans on Wednesday, & I hope that so
short an absence will not subject you to inconvenience.—
                        I am, Sir,
                        (Signed)   W. C. C. Claiborne.

―――――――――

To Geo. W. Morgan

New Orleans 14th Apl. 1812.

Sheriff &c @ N : O :)
Dear Sir,
    It being represented to me, that Judge Latour of
Plaquemine was at this time absent from his Parish, &
that the records & archives of the Parish remained at
the Judge's place of residence exposed to loss & spoliation, I request you to proceed immediately to the residence of the Judge & if you find that officer absent & no
person, by his authority in possession of the papers of

VI—6

his office, you will be pleased to take with you, a Justice of the Peace, or two respectable Citizens, & in his or their presence, affix Seals on the records & archives of the Parish & deliver them, for safe keeping to some one of the Justices of the Peace of the parish aforesaid.—

I will thank you to inform yourself of the nature of the contest which has arisen between Judge Latour & Mr. Shaw a Justice of the Peace & of the causes of so much division among the Citizens & Civil Magistrates of Plaquemine, & to report the same to you.—

I am, Dear Sir, &c @ &c @ &c @

(Signed)   W. C. C. Claiborne

——— ,, ——— ,, ———

To John H. Johnson

New Orleans 20th Apl. 1812.

Sheriff of the 7th Court &c @
St. Francisville

——— ,, ———

The best answer I can return to your letter of the 14th Inst:, is to enclose to your care, a pardon for Doctor Isaac B. Holmes, & to request you to cause the same to be delivered to the Sheriff of the third Superior Court District.—

The interposition of yourself & several other highly respectable Citizens in favour of Doctor Holmes, assures me, that he is a fit object of mercy & I take much pleasure in restoring him to the bosom of him family.—

I fear the prorogation of the Territorial Legislature will be a source of Inconvenience to the people of Feliciana— But the Interest of the Territory generally renders the measure advisable.— In the event of an early approval of the Constitution, a Session of the Territorial Legislature would not only be useless, but attended with an expence, which the Territory (at the present moment) is illy prepared to incur.—

A Bill approving the Constitution formed by the Orleans Convention has passed the House of Representatives; But I am not advised of the details.— It is understood, that the Country from Pearl River to the Perdido, is to be added to the Mississippi Territory;[1]— But of the disposition to be made of the residue of Florida, I am not informed;— I endulge however the pleasing hope that the parishes of St. Tammany, St. Helena, Baton Rouge & Feliciana will ultimately form a part of the State of Louisiana.—

I am, Sir, &c @ &c @ &c @

Signed)   W. C. C. Claiborne

———— ,, ———— ,, ————

New Orleans 20th Apl. 1812

Messrs. Fedk. A. Sumner)
Danl. Brunson &   )
H. Harrison Esqrs.   )
   St. Francisville   )
Gentlemen,

I have the honor to acknowledge the receipt of your several Letters of the 15th Instant, & to inform you, that I have this moment signed a pardon for Doctor Isaac B. Holmes.— Having understood from the Sheriff of New Orleans, that Doctor Holmes was not in his Custody, I have concluded that he was in confinement at Point Coupeé, & shall in consequence enclose the pardon to Mr. John H. Johnson, with a request, that he will deliver it, to the Sheriff of the third Superior Court District.—

I am,

Gentlemen,

Very Respectfully

Your mo: ob: Servt

signed   W. C. C. Claiborne

---

[1] Annals of Congress.   Holmes Letter Books, Mississippi Archives.

To John Dawson

New Orleans 21st. Apl. 1812.

(Private)

a Member of Congress

——— ,, ———

Dear Sir,

Being well assured of the deep Interest you take in whatever concerns the welfare of this Territory, I beg leave to enclose to your care, a *Petition* to Congress from the Regents of the University of Orleans.— *It* will not reach Washington in time (I presume) to be acted upon at this Session; I will only therefore ask of you the favour to present it to the House, & if the object, should (as I have no doubt) meet your approbation I am persuaded, that at the ensuing session, the Petition will receive your support.—

We are awaiting here, with great anxiety, the Ultimate measures of the Government towards Great Britain;— Our wrongs are sensibly felt by every real American & to avenge them, ought to be, & I believe is the wish of the Nation.— The *"Henry Communications"* are much talked of by the Federal Party in this City;— In point of numbers this party is not formidable,— But in exertion, incessant, & point of Intrigue unrivalled.— It would seem, from the Federal papers, that "the Henry "Communications are recoiling on the Administration." But I really cannot see, with what reason.— The Intrigue on the part of Great Britain was of the Basest cast, & of a nature to excite in every American breast, the warmest feelings of resentment.— The development of this intrigue, was a sacred duty imposed upon the executive, & if in doing so, the expenditure of some fifty or sixty thousand Dollars became necessary, there ought not to have been a moments hesitation. You will observe, I

have only seen the Federal comments;— few of the republican papers reach us, & none regularly.—

Will there be any serious opposition at the ensuing
Presidential Election.— I have thought, & I stil hope,
that Mr. Madison will receive an almost unanimous support from the friends of Republicanism;— His course
merits such support, and a grateful nation will justly appreciate his services.—

I take it for granted, that the State of Louisiana is
e'er this, fully acknowledge by Congress, & the people
here, will very soon be called upon to organize the State
authorities.— It is very uncertain whether or not, I shall
be honored with an employment under the State Government. I owe it to myself & to the Administration who
sent & continued me on this Station, to offer for the Chief
Majestray.— But my success is extremely doubtful.—
I have been long in office, & vested with too much power,
not to have excited the Jealouscy of some, & the ill-will of
many.

> I am, Dr. Sr. &c @ &c @ &c @
> (Signed)   W. C. C. Claiborne
> ———— ,, ———— ,, ————

To Judge Ludeling

> New Orleans 21st Apl. 1812.

Point Coupeé)
Sir,

I have the honor to enclose you an Extract from the
Journal of the University of Orleans, by which you will
observe, that you are appointed an Administrators of the
Public School for Point Coupee to supply the vacancy
occasioned by the resignation of Mr. LeBlanc.—

> I am, Sir, &c @ &c @ &c @
> (Signed)   W. C. C. Claiborne
> ———— ,, ———— ,, ————

Walter Gilbert Esqr.)
)   New Orleans 21st Apl. 1812.
Donaldsonville   )
Sir,

I have the honor to enclose you an Extract from the Journal of the University of Orleans, by which you will observe, that you are appointed an Administrator of the Public School for the County of Arcadia to supply the vacancy which the death of Mr. William Conway has occasioned.—

I am, Sir, &c @
(Signed) W. C. C. Claiborne
——— ,, ———

To Julien Poydras

New. Orleans 22d. April 1812.

Point. Coupeé)
Dear Sir,

There is no doubt, but our Constitution has been approved by Congress, & we may expect information to that effect by the next Mail.— I advise you therefore to descend immediately to New. Orleans, in order, that you may be in a situation to discharge with promptitude the high duties devolving upon you. — Messrs. Blanque, Urquhart & Brown have applied to me for a Copy of the Constitution for the purpose of puting it into the hands of a Printer; I replied that I would permit any Gentleman, whom they may name, to attend at the Bank & take a Copy.— But I will not permit the original to be removed, without you shall request it.— Your friends are all anxious to see you at this place, & the more so, since

their wish is, that the first Elections under the New State, should be holden under your orders & Instructions.—
I sincerely wish you health & happiness.—
                    Your friend
                        (Signed) W. C. C. Claiborne

                ――――― „ ――――― „ ―――――

                    To Judge Ludeling

(Private)   New. Orleans 22nd. April 1812.
Point. Coupeé)
Dear Sir,
    It has been stated to me, by Mr. Francis Duplessis of this place that affairs of Interest in which one of your Brothers-in-law is involved will call him to Point Coupeé & in the event that a law process should become necessary, Mr. Duplessis apprehends that the Parish Court will feel some delicacy in taking Cognizance thereof.— From my knowledge of your Disposition, I am assured you will use such influence as you may possess, to bring about between the parties an amicable adjustment either by themselves or Arbitrators of their choice.— But if this cannot be effected, & a Law process be prefered, surely there can be no obstacle to your acting, in the event, that the parties do not themselves object.— My great solicitude to preserve, that happy tranquility at Point Coupeé which has followed your appointment to office, & to put down all germs of discontent has induced me to name to you this subject.—
    Mr. Lanusse informed me, the other day, that a money matter, in which you & him were involved gave him some uneasiness, & added that he should send an agent to Point Coupeé, with a view of settling it amicably.; I replied to Mr. Lanusse that I was certain, you would read-

ily unite with him in such disposition, it being in unison with the Interests of both parties.—

The House of Representatives of the U: States, have approved the Constitution proposed by the Orleans Convention, nor is there a doubt of its meeting the approval of the other Branches of the Government;— Hence we may soon expect, to assume the high stand of a Sister State of the Union, & that the people will very shortly be called upon to elect a Governor of Louisiana; & Members to the General Assembly.—

The State of our Foreign Relations wears a gloomy aspect, & the general opinion seems to be that War is inevitable.

I am, Dear Sir, &c@ &c@ &c@

(Signed) W. C. C. Claiborne

———— ,, ———— ,, ————

To John H. Johnson

St. Francisville   ) New Orleans 22nd Apl. 1812

Dear Sir,

Since my letter of the 20th I have recd information, that so much of West Florida as lies West of the Pearl River is to be annexed to the State of Louisiana, but upon what Conditions I know not.—

I am sorry my proclamation did not reach St. Francisville in time to have prevented the Representatives from Feliciana descending to New Orleans;— It would have been desirable to have issued that Proclamation at an earlier period, but the information on which it was founded did not reach me, until the morning of the 7th Inst:— I assure you, I ardently wish for the period, which shall close my present powers;— The Territorial *Government,* always difficult to administer, is at the present Crisis peculiarly embarrassing;— Territorial Governments are never popular, & now that the one in operation here is drawing to a close, instead of a *shew of respect*, many of the people treat it with the neglect, which a *fallen man* sometimes meets with in Society.— Indeed, had I not prorogued the Legislature, I am very certain, that it would have been difficult to have obtained the attendance of a quorum of the two houses, & this being done, it is not probable that any business would have been transacted.— The inconvenience experienced in your District, relative to Juries (particularly in Criminal cases) is greatly to be regreted.— I have suggested to one of the Judges — to the Attorney General the expediency of holding a special Court in May next at St. Francisville, for the Trial of offenders, & am not without hopes, that it will be done.— In this way, perhaps, the inconvenience may be remedied.— As to the difficulty existing in Civil causes, it cannot be removed but by Legislative interposition. The interest of Creditors will in the meantime suffer; But the Debtors will gain time and really were I to judge from what I see in the Time Piece, a great many of my fellow Citizens in Feliciana must wish some delay in the recovery of Debts.— Its columns are filled with Sales of property taken in execution, & I presume from the pressure of the times, that this property is often sacrificed.—

I do not know, whether, or not Congress has made any provision for the payment of the Debts contracted by the Florida Convention; I gave to the Petition upon that subject, all the support in my power, & such as the Justice of the demand called for.— It seems that the people in East Florida are in a State of Revolution & that the Flag of the U. States is displayed at Amelia Island & at other places.— The aspect of the relations of the U. States with foreign Nations is indeed gloomy and I be-

lieve the warmest advocates for peace, begin now to
think, that war is inevitable.—
>   I am &c@ &c@ &c@
>   Signed/ W. C. C. Claiborne

———— „ ———— „ ————

To William, Pollard

>   New Orleans 27th. Apl. 1812

Mobile District.
>   *Fort Stoddart*

Sir,
>   Your letter of the 5th Instant, (enclosing One Hun-
dred Dollars in Bank Notes) was delivered to me, by the
Gentleman, to whose care it was committed.— I got the
favour of my friend Mr. Saul late Cashier of the Branch
Bank of this City, to examine the several Notes, who having found one for fifty Dollars a Counterfeit, the same is
herewith returned, together with Mr. Saul's Certificate
that it is a Counterfeit, which will enable you, to recover
the amount from the person from whom you may have
received it,— With the remaining fifty Dollars, I shall
endeavor to purchase a Bill upon some Merchant at Havana, & will enclose the same to the American Agent
there, for the benefit of your unfortunate friend Mr.
Cyrus Sibley.— I sincerely regret the lengthy imprisonment of this innocent young Man, & his unhappy Companions,— And am sorry to add, that my best exertions
to effect their release have hitherto failed of success.—
>   I am &c@ &c@ &c@
>   Signed/ W. C. C. Claiborne

———— „ ———— „ ————

To Albert Gallatin

Private

Secy. of the Treasurer)   New Orleans 3rd. May 1812.

Dear Sir,

During the last week, we had reports of an Embargo, & great exertions were made to hasten the departure of Vessels. Having understood that an Individual in this City, was authorized to purchase *supplies* for the Garrisons of Pensacola & Mobile, I addressed a letter on yesterday to Commodore (Shaw) & requested him to detain all Vessels bound to Mobile or Pensacola & charged with provisions.— But the Mail of this Morning having brought to the Collector official Information of the Embargo, I am relieved of further responsibility.—

We learn that a *Bill* for the admission of Louisiana into the Union, has passed both Houses of Congress, & I persuade myself a *Copy* as approved by the President, will be received by the ensuing Mail. I am greatly solicitous for the close of my present powers. The Territorial Government was always difficult to administer— But at the present Crisis, it is indeed vastly arduous & disagreeable; It is viewed in the light of a Merchant on the eve of Bankruptcy;— distrusted by its former friends— abused by Enemies, and slighted by all.— The office of Chief Magistrate of the New State, is deemed desirable by some of the most influential of the Louisianians. My name also is with the people; But with what probability of success, I know not.— much Wealth, & considerable *Intrigue* are enlisted against me.— My old Batture acquaintance, Livingston after having had, (as is believed) a principal hand *in pointing out the mode of electing a Governor,* has undertaken to direct all the Machinery, which can be brought to bear against me.[1] —

---

[1] The ablest man in the Constitutional Convention, and the most influential member of the Committee on the Constitution.

I observe that some War Taxes are about being imposed.— If an Officer for the Collection of the Quota al-
lotted to this State, has not been selected, permit me to
name Mr. Peter L. B. Duplessis of this City, as deserving
the Confidence of the Government.— I can vouch Sir, for
his *Talents,* his *Zeal, industry & Integrity.* Mr. Duplessis is the Marshall of the District, & his conduct is marked with great propriety.— I am sorry to add that his Per-
quisites as Marshall, are not equal to his support.—

Present me with very sincere regard to Mrs. Gallatin
& believe me to be, Dear Sir, &c@ &c@ &c@

Signed/ W. C. C. Claiborne

——— ,, ——— ,, ———

To Commodore Shaw

New. Orleans 2nd. May 1812.

Naval Commander)
Sir,

Having understood that an Inhabitant of this Territory, was specially authorized to purchase a quantity of
flour for the use of the Garrisons at Pensacola & Mobile,
& observing in a hand Bill just published a letter from a
Member of Congress which announces that a General
Embargo for Ninety days had been laid by the Congress
of the U: States, I request you to give orders for the detention of all Vessels bound to Pensacola or Mobile, &
charged with *provisions of any kind.* The probability
is, that by tomorrow's Mail we shall have official advice
of the Embargo.— In the mean time however, I deem it
right & proper *upon the information before me,* to detain
for the present, all supplies destined for the Garrisons
aforesaid.

I am Sir,

Sigd. W. C. C. Claiborne

——— ,, ——— ,, ———

To James Monroe
New Orleans May 2nd. 1812.

Secy of State)
Sir,

Your letter of the 4th Ult:, was received on this morning. The letter to Colo. McKee, which was enclosed, shall be forwarded to Fort Stoddart, where I presume, it will find him.—

For several days past, we have had here private intelligence of the Embargo, & much exertion has been made, to hasten the departure of Vessels.— Having understood that certain individuals were authorized to forward supplies to the Spanish Garrisons of Mobile & Pensacola, I deem'd it right & proper on yesterday to address to Commodore Shaw a letter of which the enclosed is a Copy.— On this day official information of the Embargo has reached the Collector, but of its *general provisions,* I am not yet advised;— If *these* should not extend to Mobile & Pensacola the letter of Instruction to Commodore Shaw, shall be withdrawn.— We learn, that an act for the admission of Louisiana into the Union has passed both Houses, & I persuade myself, that the next Mail, will bring advice of its approval by the President.—

I have the honor to be,
Sir,
With great respect &c@
signed/ W. C. C. Claiborne

To Commodore Shaw
New. Orleans May 4th. 1812

Naval Commander)
Sir,

The Schooner Louise, Captn. LaCoste bound to Mobile, not falling (in the opinion of the acting Collector) under the restrictions of the Embargo Law, I request you to give orders, to permit her to proceed uninterrupted.

The Embargo Law being now in possession of the Officers of the Revenue, whose duty it immediately is to take care, that its provisions be maintained, I have to request you Sir, (until you may receive special instructions upon the subject from the Secretary of the Navy) to permit all Vessels to proceed upon their voyage, who may have obtained regular Clearance from the Collector of Orleans, & which Clearances shall be subsequent to the third of May 1812.

I am Sir,
Very respectfully
Your mo: ob: Servt.
Signed/ W. C. C. Claiborne

„ „

To John H. Johnson

Private

New Orleans May 4th. 1812.

St. Francisville)
Dear Sir,

We have information of the passage of the Bill, by the two Houses of Congress, for the admission of Louisiana into the Union, & by the ensuing Mail we shall no doubt, receive a Copy of the act as approved by the President.—

Florida as far as Pearl River is annexed to Louisiana; But as to the Conditions I remain uninformed— I learn however with much regret that the House of Representatives had not secured to the people of Florida the right of suffrage at the first elections under the State Authority, & I much fear, that the Senate in this particular has not afforded a remedy.— Our admission into the Union being now certain, I do not calculate on a Session of the

Territorial Legislature;— I am sorry for the inconvenience to which your District will in consequence be subjected,— But the general good of the Territory (& more especially the limited resources of the Treasury) will render a further prorogation or a dissolution of the Territorial Assembly advisable.—

I am, Dr. Sir, &c@
Signed/   W. C. C. Claiborne
_____ " _____ " _____

To William S. Caillevet

Parish of Baton Rouge)

Sir,

From the information before me, it becomes my duty, to revoke the Commission by which you were appointed Sheriff of the Parish of Baton Rouge, & it is hereby revoked.—

Signed/   W. C. C. Claiborne
Govr. of Terry. of Orleans

New Orleans)
May 6th 1812)

To Charles Tessier

New. Orleans May 6th 1812

Baton Rouge   )

Dear Sir,

Your letter of the 1st Instant, has been received.— Mr. Vassant has for some time past, talked of his *resignation.*— But to this moment, it has not been tendered. In the event however, of his retiring from his *present office,* I shall be disposed to favour your application.—

Accept my best wishes.

I am, Dr. Sir, &c@

To Judge Wykoff
New Orleans May 6th 1812.

Baton Rouge   )
Dear Sir,

Your letter of the 30th Ultimo has been received & you have herein enclosed, a letter of dismission to M. Caillevet, which you will cause to be delivered.—

We have certain information, that a Bill for the admission of Louisiana into the Union, has passed the two Houses of Congress, and by the ensuing Mail, we shall no doubt, have a Copy of the Act as approved by the President.—

From what I can learn, there will be much division in the City and County of Orleans as to the person to be named Governor;— If therefore the people of the Interior Counties should generally turn out, & can agree on any one individual, they will decide the Contest.—

I am,
Dear Sir,
With great esteem
Your mo: obt. Servt.
(Signed)   W. C. C. Claiborne

——— ,, ——— ,, ———

CIRCULAR Letter to the several

Members of the Territorial Assembly.

Sir,

A Bill approving the Constitution of Louisiana has passed the two Houses of Congress, and by the ensuing Mail, I expect to receive an Official Copy of the act.—

The certainty of our early admission into the Union, as a Member State, will occasion a further prorogation or perhaps a dissolution of the Territorial Assembly. I fear that this suspension of the Sessions of the Legislature may prove inconvenient to some particular Counties; But the general good of the Territory renders the measure advisable.—

Signed W. C. C. Claiborne

—— ,, —— ,, ——

To Abner L. Duncan

New Orleans 15th May 1812.

Attorney General   )
Sir,

The enclosed proceeding in the case of Negro Ben, a slave, the property of Antoine Mendez, Judge of the Parish of St. Bernard having been officially transmitted to me, I have to request you, to inform me, whether the course pursued, is in conformity to Law.— From the testimony, I have no doubt of the Guilt of the accused, & see no ground on that point for Executive Interference;— But if the procedure has not been in pursuance to Law, it must be corrected.—

I am, Sir,
Very respectfully,
Your humble. Sert.
Signed/ W. C. C. Claiborne.

—— ,, —— ,, ——

To Wm L. Brent

New. Orleans 14th May 1812.

Attackapas   )
Dear Sir,

Your favours of the 8th & 20th Ultimo were duly received.— I regret, that I had not the pleasure of seeing Mr. Randolph to whose care, the first was committed, &

of forming an acquaintance with a Gentleman of whose enterprise & amiability of Character you speak in such favorable terms.—

The depressed state of our Commerce, cannot fail seriously to affect the agriculturists, & I see little prospect of better times.— Indeed the injustice of England is so pertinaciously persisted in, by her rulers that there is no alternative for the United States, but submission & national Degradation, or immediate & determined resistance.— Under such circumstances, no real American, can for a moment hesitate, or withhold from his Country a tender of his life & fortune.— Every advice from Washington justifies the opinion, that the Government has decided on its course! England must respect our rights, or the wrongs offered our Country will be avenged! The recruiting service prospers beyond example, & Troops are marching from every quarter towards the Canada Frontier.— Detachments of Militia are ordered into service, & there exist the strongest indications of a speedy declaration of war.— I entertain no fears as to the issue of this contest.— In point of *enterprise, personal firmness, & perseverance,* the *American* can nowhere find his *superior,* & when the safety of his Country, is put to hazard, there is no undertaking, that valour can atchieve, from which he will shrink.— For myself, then, I calculate to a certainty on an Invasion of Canada, & that on the plains of Abram, England will learn the fact that the attachment of the people of the U: S: to peace, does not proceed from a fear of War.—

We are momently in expectation of receiving official information of our admission into the Union.— On the 6th of April, a Bill approving the Constitution passed both Houses of Congress, & by the ensuing Mail, we shall doubtless receive a Copy with the Presidents approbation.— It is understood that Florida, as far as Pearl River, with the assent of the State Legislature, is to be added to Louisiana.— There are individuals in this City, & some too, who will probably be in the Legislature, who would withhold this assent;— But I trust a great majority will accede to the proposition with promptitude & pleasure.— For myself I shall view such an acquisition of population & Territory as an event greatly interesting to the present & future prosperity of this section of the Union.—

In this City & its vicinity parties are already formed & Intrigue is the order of the day. There are several Candidates for the office of Chief Majistrate.— My name is among the number, but with what prospect of success I know not. If it should fall to my lot, to be honored on the occasion with the public suffrage, I will accept the trust with gratitude, & deserve it if I can.—

The recommendations of Messrs. Brashears & Jackson to which you allude in your letter of the 20th have not reached me.— Should they *be shortly received,* my intention is to Commission each of them.—

I am, Sir, &c@ &c@ &c@
Signed/   W. C. C. Claiborne

———— ,, ———— ,, ————

To Francis Rivas

New Orleans May 16. 1812

Iberville.   )

Sir,

I have received your letter of the 7th Instant.— The Negro to whom you alude, was pardoned on Condition, that he should remain a Prisoner for life in the Joal of New Orleans, & employed at hard labor.— There is no ground therefore for that uneasiness, which the report of his return to your Parish, has given to yourself & family. It is proper for me to add, that the Judge & Jury

before whom, the Negro was tried, recommended him to
Mercy, & expressed a wish, that the sentence of Death
which was announced against him, might be commuted
for the punishment of imprisonment & hard labour.—

I am, Sir, &c@ &c@ &c@

Signed/   W. C. C. Claiborne

——— ,, ——— ,, ———

To Wade Hampton

New. Orleans 18th May 1812

Private

——— ,, ———

NEW. ORLEANS

——— ,, ———

Dear Sir,

Do me the favour to take in charge the enclosed *packet*
which the bearer will deliver to you.— It encloses a Cot-
ton Blanket manufactured by a very amiable Lady of the
county Attackapas within this Territory.— Be so good as
to present this Blanket in my name to Mrs. Madison, accompanied with the assurances of my great respect, and
best wishes for her health and happiness.—

I sincerely wish you an agreeable voyage & much
prosperity in life.—

I am, Sir, &c@ &c@ &c@

(Signed)   W. C. C. Claiborne.

———————

To Woodson Wrenn

New. Orleans 20th May 1812

Collector &c@   )
      Nova Iberia   )

Dear Sir,

The construction which you have given (I understand) to the Law establishing a port of entry at Nova
Iberia, is I am persuaded erroneous.— It surely never

could have been the design of Congress, to subject the
Inhabitants of Attackapas & Opelousas, who descend the
Waters of the Mississippi annually to New Orleans, with
their surplus productions, in Boats navigated by their
own Negroes, or occasionally a few hired Indians, to the
expense attending Licenses for the Coasting Trade, &
to the Marine Hospital Tax.— Vessels proceeding by
Sea, from one District to another, within the U. States,
are the fit objects of these provisions;— but they could
not have been entended to embrace Barges & other small
craft employed in the Inland Navigation.— With equal
Justice might a Tax be levied on Carts & Waggons engaged in Carrying a Crop to market.—

Desiring sincerely, that the people of this Territory,
may have no just cause of Complaint against the Govern-
ment or its officers, and believing that you are in error,
I entreat you to suspend your further operations in this
particular, until the subject can be referred to the Sec-
retary of the Treasury for his advice and Instructions.—
I am,
Dear Sir,
Very Respectfully
Your obedt. Servt.
(Signed)   W. C. C. Claiborne.
——— „ ——— „ ———

TO THE MAYOR, RECORDER AND MEMBERS OF
THE CITY OF NEW ORLEANS.—

Gentlemen;
The undersigned in obedience to a Resolution of the
Council of administration of the Charity Hospital of New
Orleans hastens to lay before you, the wants of that In-
stitution, & to entreat in its behalf your kindest patron-
age.— The undersigned deems it unnecessary to enter

into details— But he begs leave to state,— "that there "are at this time in the Hospital, thirty diseased and dis- "tressed individuals, & that the Number of applicants "for admission is daily increasing;— that the Hospital "is destitute of most of the convenience essential to the "comfort of the Sick; and that its monthly revenue falls "far short of the actual & necessary expenditures."— Under these circumstances, the Council of Administra- tion, instead of experiencing the pleasure resulting from administering relief to suffering humanity, are sensibly affected by an accumulation of human wretchedness, which duty impels them to witness, & to the alleviation of which their means are inadequate.— Hence it is, that the undersigned has been charged to apply to your Hon- orable Body for immediate succour, & which he now so- licits with all the Confidence that a knowledge of your Benevolence of Justice could inspire.—

> I have the honor to be,
> Gentlemen, &c@ &c@ &c@
> (Signed)   W. C. C. Claiborne

————— „ ————— „ —————
—————

To Walter Shaler

> New Orleans May 23d. 1812.

Nachitoches

————— „ —————

Dear Sir,

I am endebted to you, for your very interesting let- ter.— By the present opportunity, I send you all the News-papers, which were brought me by the Mail of this Morning.   I will write you fully by the Western Mail which leaves this on the 25th Instant.—

I wish you health & happiness—and am,

> Your sincere friend
> Signed/   W. C. C. Claiborne

————— „ ————— „ —————

To Col. Thomas Cushing

New Orleans May 24th 1812

Dear Sir,

I beg you to recollect, to mention to the Secretary at War, the wishes of Colo. Wakeville;— If his resignation in the army has not been accepted, it really would be serving a very honorable man to permit his name to remain on the list of officers, *but without pay*.— It would moreover be considered as a particular favour done to me;— For should it so happen that under the new order of things in this Country, I mean, under the State authority, my friend Lanceville should not be continued in his present office of Adjutant General I should be greatly gratified to learn, that it was in his power to resume his former Station in the Army of the United States.— I wish you an agreeable voyage,— and am

(Signed)   W. C. C. Claiborne

———— ,, ———— ,, ————

To James Monroe

New. Orleans May 21st 1812.

Secy of State

———— ,, ————

SIR,

In consequence of the repeated failure of the Mails, we remain without any recent intelligence from the Seat of Government. On the 6th of April, we learn, that a Bill for the admission of this Territory as a Member State of the Union, had passed the two Houses of Congress, & in daily expectation, of receiving a Copy, as approved by the president, I have a second time, prorogued the Territorial Legislature;— Its session would have been expensive & entirely useless;— Indeed such is the anxiety of the people for a change of Government, & so little are they disposed to respect *Authorities whose ex-*

istance will only be momentary, that I doubt, whether if a prorogation had not taken place a quorum could have been formed, & if formed, I am persuaded no business would have been transacted.—

On a former occasion, I advised you of the arrest of certain Individuals, who had committed depredations between Arroya Honda & the Sabine;— I have now to add, that they were indicted before the Superior Court for Robbery, & two of them convicted.—A motion in arrest of Judg'ment was submitted on various grounds;— But the want of Jurisdiction was principally relied on.— The motion however was not sustained, & the offenders have been sentenced to seven years imprisonment at hard labour.— It is known to you Sir, that the tract of Country between the Arroya Honda & the Sabine, is stil claimed by the Spanish Authorities, as a part of the province of Tchus, & I am not without apprehensions, that the incorporation of that Tract with the State of Louisiana will create some dissatisfaction;— I trust however, that the people of Spanish America, will soon take rank among the Nations of the Earth, & establish for themselves a Government with which the United States may negociate on all matters interesting to the New World.—

My letter of the 14th of February last informed you, that in the case of Livingston against Fortier late Marshal of Orleans, a plea to the Jurisdiction of the Court had been filed.— This Plea has since been overruled, & the merits on its merits is set for Trial on tomorrow. I have in consequence, engaged in defence of the Marshal, & in aid of the District Attorney (& Mr. Duncan already employed) Mr. Peter Derbigny a french Lawyer of eminence.—I have promised Mr. Dubigny a fee of three hundred Dollars, & for which amount, I shall draw a Bill upon you,— I am sorry to subject the Government to this additional expense;— But the exertions of Mr. Livingston are unremitting— His Talents considerable,

& an address, (which is of the most engaging cast) is made subservient to his purposes.— To do justice then to the cause of the Marshal which is in fact, that of the Government, requires the exercise of great Judgment, discretion & professional research.— The authority in which I have employed Council in defence of the Marshal, is particularly detailed in my Letter of the 14th of February, & of which, lest the Original may have miscarried, I herewith enclose you a Duplicate.—

I have for some time past, considered a War between the U. States & Great Britain highly probable.— Indeed it seems to me, that unless the orders in Council are speedily revoked, & other wrongs atoned for a longer— forbearance, would compromise the honor, the Independence of our Country.— The causes of dispute are not unknown to the American people for they have been the subject of discussion, not only in the Capitol & the Cabinet, but in every Cottage.— English apalogists may be found on our Sea Board, in the persons of English Agents, factors & old Tories.— But surely there can be no real American who does not feel sensibly the Indignities the injuries offered his Country.— Thro' the medium of the public prints I have received general information as to the preparations for War. But to this moment, I remain unadvised as to the particular means of defence intended for this section of the Union.— General Hampton took his departure on yesterday for the United States, & General Wilkinson's arrival is momently expected, by whom I presume, the measures of offence or defence contemplated in this quarter will be communicated to me.

I have the honor to be,
Sir, &c@ &c@ &c@
(Signed) W. C. C. Claiborne

——— „ ——— „ ———

To Judge Johnson

New Orleans May 26. 1812.

Parish of St. Mary's

Dear Sir,

The last mail brought us information of the approval of the Constitution, & Mr. Poydras is now engaged in preparing his proclamation, & will I understand issue the same on Tuesday next.   The election is to take place the 4th Monday after the date of the Proclamation, & which will be the 29th of June.—

It gives me pleasure to learn, that you are talked of as Representative for the Parish of St. Mary, & sincerely hope, that you may meet a very general support.— My venerable friend Mr. Duralde & Major Ollivier, are I learn, spoken of for the Senate.— Of the Major I have formed the most favorable opinion & have great confidence in his firmness & virtue;— I should be sorry therefore to see him & Mr. Duralde brought in contact.— Their political views, I am told are *in unison,* & it seems to me, that yourself & other of their mutual political friends, might induce one or the other to diction [decline].—

It has been represented to me, that pains had been taken to injure me in Attackapas & that among other things, it had been asserted, that I had in the most positive & solemn manner promised the appointment of Sheriff to a Creole Gentleman, & the very next day nominated G. W. Morgan— This report is untrue; It arose from a friend of mine with whom, I was conversing, relative to the appointment of a Sheriff, misunderstanding me;— I was passing a just eulogium upon one of the Candidates, & my friend received the impression, that it was my intention to appoint this candidate & he stated such his impression to several Citizens.— The fact is, I had no such design.— Apprehending the death of Mr. Cenas for some time previous to its taken place, I had determined on Mr. Morgan as his successor, & so informed some of my friends.— I could have no object in promising the appointment to another, & in truth I never did;— The report originated in error & was first given Currency without any design to injure me;— It is now propogated by Malice, & used for electioneering purposes.—

I owe it to myself Sir, & to you, who I consider as my friend to inform you of another means, my enemies take to injure me.— Soon after receiving possession of Louisiana, & early in January 1804, I wrote an Official Letter to the Government, in which I took a general view of the state of the District;— Spoke with great freedom of the abuses of the Spanish Government, & some of its agents— And took occasion, to say something of the general character of the Louisianians;— I have not this letter by me, but its contents are sufficiently fresh in my memory to say to you, that there was not a sentiment, which evidenced the smallest ill-will towards the people of the Country;— This letter was communicated in Confidence, by the President to Congress, & a few days afterwards, there appeared in one of the federal Gazettes, a publication purporting to be the substance of my letter, in which I am represented as speaking in Terms the most contemptible & the most ill-natured of the Louisianians. — This misrepresentation, has been published & re-published in this City (I believe) fifty times, & is again relied on by my enemies to injure me.   I have said, & I repeat it, that this publication did not contain the substance of my letter;— My language is perverted & my feelings towards the people of this Country greatly misrepresented. — In a private letter also, from Mr. Jefferson, dated in July 1804 & which I have shown to several of my friends in speaking of this publication he declares it to be a false statement, & says that some' one or more persons must have clubbed memories & malice to make out the forgery.—

> I am, &c@ &c@ &c@
> (Signed)   W. C. C. Claiborne

———— ,, ———— ,, ————

To the Officer)   N. Orleans May 27th 1812.
   Commanding at)
     Fort St. Phillip)
  —— ,, ——)

Sir,

    It being represented to me, that a mulatto man, a slave of Major Lanusse of this City, who fled from the service of his master, had taken refuge on board of a French Privateer, now lying opposite Fort St. Phillip, I have to request of you the goodness to accompany the *Bearer,* on board of said Vessel, & if he should find the said Slave, that you order the Captain of the Privateer immediately to deliver him up.— In case of a refusal, you will be pleased to detain the Privateer, until you shall hear further from me on the subject.

> I am,
> Sir,
> Very respectfully
> Your obedt. Servt.
> Signd.   W. C. C. Claiborne

———— ,, ———— ,, ————

To the Lady Abbess
      New. Orleans May 29th 1812
of the Ursuline Convent

———— ,, ———— ,, ————

Holy Sister

    I have the honor to enclose you, a Copy of an Act of Congress ''to authorize the Secretary at War to ex- ''change Lands, with the Ursuline Nuns in the City of ''New. Orleans.''

The provisions of this Law, will I trust, meet the wishes of your Community, & prove beneficial to the very useful Institution under your direction.— I avail myself also, of the present occasion to transmit to you Madame a letter to "The Ursuline Nuns of New Orleans," from the honorable Mr. Duncan a Member of Congress, & to whose patronage, I had particularly recommended your Petition to the Government.

Do me the favour Madame to thank La Mere Gensour (?) for the portrait, of the Holy Father, the Pope Pius 7th. His sacred character, his misfortunes, & his fortitude & resignation must command for him the respect & the sympathy of the Christian world.— My dear little Son will be much pleased with the presents of La Mere Gensoul, & in his name & behalf I return thanks.—

I highly approve Madam of the cautious circumspections with which you acted in relation to Miss Sarah Ann Godberry; You have an important charge, & cannot be too careful of the female youth committed to your care; But in this particular case, I hope & believe that the course pursued, is correct since previous to my second letter to you on yesterday, I received in writing a declaration from three Gentlemen, that to their knowledge, it was the wish of M. Godberry that his Daughter Miss Sarah Ann, should accompany Madam Godberry to the United States.— I renew to you, Holy Sister, the Homage of my great respect, & sincere friendship.—

Signed/ W. C. C. Claiborne

————— ,, ————— ,, —————

To Commodore Shaw

New Orleans 5th. June 1812

Naval Commander
　　at
NEW ORLEANS

———— ,, ————

Sir,

Your letter of yesterday, (in which was enclosed for my perusal one to you, from Lieutenant Carter) has been received.— If the Spanish Agents should think proper to withdraw the whole or any part of the Troops, now at the Fort of Mobile, they ought *not to be opposed;* the contrary such facilities as they may need, & we could conveniently render, should be afforded them.— But no Vessel from Pensacola or elsewhere with foreign Troops on board, should be permitted to pass up the Mobile Bay, & I request you Sir, to give special order to that effect.—

I have information (which may I think be relied on) that a reinforcement from Havana was daily expected at Pensacola, & the probability is, that the *relief* which the Commandant at Mobile spoke of, would turn out to be an additional force.—

I am, Sir, &c@ &c@ &c@
Signed/   W. C. C. Claiborne

———— ,, ———— ,, ————

To Mr. Trudeau

New Orleans 6th. June 1812.

Recorder &c@)
Sir,

I ask the favour of you to lay before the Honorable the City Council the enclosed report of a Committee appointed by the Board of Administration, to enquire into the wants & actual State of the Charity Hospital.— This report, will bring to the view of the City Council, the forlorn situation of this Charitable Institution, & they will see, that without some speedy & effectual succour it cannot long remain an Assylum— for the unfortunate. Indeed without assistance from some quarter the Board of Administration, see no alternative but wholly to abandon the Institution.— We know not where to apply for that assistance, with more propriety, than to the City Council. Charged as it is with the general Interest of the Citizens, that of the poor & distressed has primary claim, to attention, & will I am assured receive the most prompt & indulgent Consideration.

With sentiments of the greatest respect
I have the honor to be,
Signed *W. C. C. Claiborne*

Received New. Orleans 18th June 1812 of Governor Claiborne Fifty Dollars in Bank Notes to be delivered to Lila Sibley at the Havana
$50.   Signed/   Stephen Kingston

—— „ ——

I declare that the above receipt to be a true Copy from the Original.—

Claude Dejan, Pri Secy

To Commodore Shaw

N. Orleans 15 June 1812

Naval Commander)

Sir,

The Bearer Mr. Stephen Kingston having been appointed by the President of the United States, American Consul at the Port of Havanah, & it being important to the Public Interest, that he should speedily reach his place of destination, I request you (if the State of the

Service permits) to give orders to the Officer commanding the Brig Viper, to receive Mr. Kingston on board, &
to proceed to the Havannah with all convenient dispatch.— It will be an accommodation to Mr. Kingston,
If you could conveniently give him a Conveyance to the
Balize, where the Viper I hear is now stationed.—

I am &c@ &c@
Signed/   <i>W. C. C. Claiborne</i></div>

HIS EXCELLENCY, THE CAPTAIN GENERAL
of the Island of Cuba.—

Sir,

Give me leave to congratulate your Excellency on
your safe arrival in the Island of Cuba, & to offer you
my best wishes for the happiness & prosperity of your
Excellency's administration.— In the course of the Terrible War which has so long desolated Europe, it has
heretofore been the favored lot of the U: States, to remain in Peace;— I fear however, the time is not distant
when the injustice of one, or perhaps both of the Great
Belligerents will force my Country from that neutral
position, which she is so desirous to maintain; But in
any event I trust that between the U. States & Spain,
there will exist those friendly relations, which the Interest of the two Nations so strongly advise.—

I avail myself of this occasion to introduce to your
Excellency a subject on which I had the honor to address
your predecessor, the Marquis of Somernelas, & which
motives of humanity urge me to renew.— Among the
prisoners of State at Havannah, are ten native Americans, who whilst acting under the authority of the Florida Convention, were taken in armes, in the year 1810,
near the Fort of Mobile, & sent to Cuba.— Their friends
& relatives who reside at this time, within the Territory

committed to my care have never ceased to make to me
their entreaties & to implore on their behalf my intercession.— Yielding to the humane feelings which such
entreaties so naturally inspired, & encouraged by the
known benevolence of your Excellency's character, I
take the liberty to recommend *these unhappy men,* to
your clemency, nor can I withhold the expression of a
fond hope, that after an imprisonment of such long duration, their release may not be found opposed to the Policy & Justice of your Excellency's Government.—

I tender to your Excellency, the assurances of my
high & respectful Consideration.—

Signed/ W. C. C. Claiborne

———— ,, ———— ,, ————

To Diego Murphy

New Orleans June 18th. 1812

Sir,

I have received your letter of the 16th. Instant.— The
Capture of the Brig from Vera Cruix, & the misfortunes
of her Captain & Crew are to me sources of sincere regret.— The *request* you make of me, to facilitate the return of these *unfortunate strangers* to their Country I
take pleasure in complying with, & I have the honor to
inform you, that the Officer Commanding the armed Brig
Siren, now lying in this port, has orders to receive & to
convey them to the port of Vera Cruix.— The Siren will
be in readiness for Sea on tomorrow & will depart as
soon thereafter as may suit your convenience.— I take
this occasion to assure you Sir, that the Naval force on
this Station is instructed, to give protection, to all Vessels coming within our Waters, & confiding as I do, in
the Zeal & activity of the several Naval Commanders, I
persuade myself that the French Cruisers hovering on

this Coast, will not escape their vigilance should they attempt to commit any outrages within the Jurisdiction of the United States.—

I tender you the assurances of my respect & esteem

Signed)   W. C. C. Claiborne

——— ,, ——— ,, ———

To the Capt. Genl. of Cuba

New. Orleans June 18th. 1812

Sir,

I have the honor to enclose for your Excellency's perusal, a Copy of a letter addressed to me, by the Spanish Commercial Agent at this place Don Diego Murphy, as also of my answer thereto.— The event which has given rise to this Correspondence is by me sincerely regreted, & I persuade myself that *one* of a like nature will not again occur.— The unfortunate subjects of Spain, whose return to Vera Cruix, Mr. Murphy has solicited me to facilitate, will embark in two or three days on board of an armed Vessel of the U: States, & will I hope, reach in safety their place of destination.—

I renew to your Excellency the assurances of my high & respectful consideration.—

Signed/   W. C. C. Claiborne

——— ,, ——— ,, ———

To His Excellency The Governor of Vera Cruix.

Sir,

The Commercial Agent of Spain at this Port Don Diego Murphy having solicited me, to furnish a Conveyance to Vera Cruix, for some Spanish subjects, who having been plundered at Sea by a French privateer, had

arrived at New. Orleans, in great distress, the Naval
Commander on this Station Commodore Shaw has dispatched on this service the United States armed Brig
"The Siren" Commanded by Captain Carrol, whom I
beg leave to recommend to your Excellency's Civilities.
I renew to your Excellency the assurances of my
great respect & Consideration.—

Signed/   W. C. C. Claiborne

———— „ ———— „ ————

New. Orleans   )
June 24 June 1812)

———————————

To Capt. Carroll

Commanding the)   New. Orleans June 25th. 1812
    Brig Siren   )

Dear Sir,

My young friend Mr. Bosch, to whom you have been
pleased to give a passage, visits Vera Cruix solely with
a view of paying his respects in person to some of his
relations who reside at that Place. Mr. Bosch is a native of Louisiana, & being a Citizen of the U: States has
received my passport;— It may happen however that the
authoritics of Vcra Cruix, may be opposed to his entering the City— I will therefore, thank you to mention to
the Governor, the object of Mr. Bosch in visiting Vera
Cruix, & if you find that his landing is in the least disagreeable, I advise & request that he may remain on
board of the Siren.— I should be sorry, that this young
man should experience any difficulty, or that his visit to
Vera Cruix, should excite the smallest suspicion.—

I sincerely wish you a pleasant voyage, & the enjoyment of health & happiness.—

Signed/   Wm. C. C. Claiborne

———— „ ———— „ ————

To Stephen Kingston

New Orleans June 25th. 1812

Fort Plaquemine.   )

Dear Sir,

I sincerely regret the disappointment which you have experienced.— The puting to Sea of the Viper, was an event which it seems the Commodore had not anticipated.— But he says her cruise will not be long,— & perhaps it may be best that you await her return to the Balize.— In the mean time, I presume you may pass your time agreeably at the Fort & in the Country around, & more particularly if you should ascend the River as far as a Captain Johnson's.— As regards the "Siren", I stand committed; Mr. Murphy has been assured that she should proceed directly to Vera Cruix & land there, certain Spanish subjects. But were it not so, all my Controul over the Navy, is now at an end;— I have been *officially advised,* that on the 30th. of April last, the day on which the Territory, by an Act of Congress, became a State, I ceased to be an officer of the U: States, & of course, I do not consider myself, as having any further Controul over the Navy.—

I have nothing new or important from Washington. — It is still reported that War is probable; But I begin to think that it will end in a War of Words.—

The electoral struggle is in full vigour; the virulence of faction increases, & new Calumnies are issued every hour.— For myself, I feel much indifference as to the event— My mind is in that State which the Scripture represents to be desirable.— "Happy is the man who "expects nothing, for if he gets nothing he will not be "disappointed."—

Commodore Shaw is of opinion that the Viper will certainly return to the Balize in eight or ten days.— The disappointment is disagreeable, But it probably may eventuate well.— Had you reached Havanna pending the

Embargo, you might not perhaps have been received.—
If I have formed a correct opinion of your mind the
great ills of life would give you no serious concern & the
"miseries of human life," as Mr. Cunning calls them,
do not I am sure excite a moment's inquietude.—

> Accept my best wishes
> Signed/   W. C. C. Claiborne

To James Monroe
near New Orleans June 27th. 1812

Secretary of State
Sir,

As *the Tract* of Country which lies between the Mississippi & Pearl Rivers is not yet *included within the
State of Louisiana,* nor annexed to the Mississippi Territory, *it* has been considered as forming at the moment
the Territory of Orleans.— If this opinion should be
deemed correct, I beg the favour of you to announce to
the President my resignation as Governor of Orleans
from & after the date of this letter.—

I take this occasion to express my most grateful
thanks for the high Trust so long confided to me; — A
Trust I the more estimate, as coming from two successive administrations which with principles purely American, have done as much, as *in these times,* could possibly
have been done, for the honor, the safety & happiness of
United America.—

With every sentiment of esteem & respect,—

> I have the honor to be, &c@
> Signed   W. C. C. Claiborne

To Albert Gallatin

                    near New Orleans 27th June 1812
Secy. of the Treasurer
Sir,
   I have had the honor to receive your letter of the 25th
Ultimo, & shall in obedience to your directions, close my
accounts against the U : States, for contingent expences,
with the 30th. of April 1812. As that tract of Country,
which lies between the Mississippi & the Pearl River, is
not yet included within the State of Louisiana nor annexed to the Mississippi Territory, it has been considered as forming at this moment the Orleans Territory.
I do not know that this opinion is correct, but as doubts
may arise upon the subject, I have this day, forwarded
my resignation as Governor of Orleans to the Honble.
the Secretary of State for the U : States.—
                    I am, &c@ &c@ &c@
                    Sig. W. C. C. Claiborne
                ———— ,, ———— ,, ————

To James Monroe

Private   New Orleans 27 June 1812
Secy of State
Dear Sir,
   Mr. Magruder delivered to me your very friendly
letter, & to which I shall reply more fully in a few days.
— This state is for the moment, in great agitation, & the
approaching election for Governor engrosses every mind.
The people appear much divided, & it is very uncertain,
which of the Candidates will succeed.— On the 29. Inst;
the trial of strength will commence;— In this City, the
vote will be nearly equal;— But it is believed by my
friends, that in the Interior Counties I shall be honored
with a Majority.— The opposition to me, is very violent,

& I am undergoing all the Calumny which Malice can invent.— Among my opponents Mr. Ed. Livingston & Mr. Thos. Robertson are particularly conspicuous;— But whatever may be my Lot, I am happy in the belief, that neither of these Gentlemen will receive in this quarter, proof of Public Confidence.[1]—

Enclosed is my resignation as Governor of Orleans which has become necessary, in order to remove all doubts as to my elligibility to the office of Governor of Louisiana.— I have a sincere friendship for Mr. Dawson, & highly appreciate his long & faithful pubilc services.— I am persuaded, that in this state his prospects *would be favorable;*— But at this moment I cannot express myself *as freely* upon the subject, as I could wish. — The election being over I will write to Mr. Dawson fully & frankly.— In the mean time he must not venture on a voyage hither during the summer Months.— In the fall he may come on with safety to his health, & then at all times, he will find me disposed to advance his Interest in Life.—

I am, &c@ &c@ &c@
Signed/   W. C. C. Claiborne

——— ,, ——— ,, ———

To Thos. B. Robertson

New Orleans July 4th 1812

NEW ORLEANS

——— ,, ———

Sir,

On the 27th. Ultimo, in a letter to the Secretary of State, I announced to him my resignation of the Office of Governor of the Orleans Territory.— It would seem by Mr. Gallatin's letter of the 25th. of May (a Copy of

---

[1] The newspapers of the day reflect the public excitement.

which I requested Mr. Vassant to hand you) that in his opinion no such Territory existed;— But as the Tract of Country which lies between the Mississippi & Pearl Rivers, is not yet included within the State of Louisiana, nor annexed to the Mississippi Territory, an opinion has prevailed that this Tract formed for the present the Orleans Territory.— I will not undertake to say, that this opinion is correct.— But as the ordinance has provided, in the event of the resignation of the Governor, that his powers shall devolve upon the Secretary, I have deemed it my duty to address you this letter.—

I am &c@ &c@ &c@

Signed W. C. C. Claiborne

To Mr. Dawson

New. Orleans July 4th. 1812

A Member of Congress

Dear Sir,

I have only time, to acknowledge myself indebted to you, for several interesting letters, & to add, that I will answer *them fully in a few days.*— I am persuaded that a removal to this State, would be favorable to your Interests;— But you must not venture on a voyage hither, during the Summer Months;— In the fall season you may come on, without endangering your health.— The election for Governor took place on the 29th. Ultimo:— I have a Majority in every District, from which returns have been received & the General opinion seems to be that I shall obtain thro'out the State, a vote of two to one, over the other Candidates;— How far the Legislature will be disposed to sanction the choice of the people, I cannot possitively say;— But at this time, the prospects of complete success are very favorable.— Accept my best wishes & believe me to be,

With great respect

Your sincere friend

Sigd. W. C. C. Claiborne

—— ,, —— ,, ——

To Albert Gallatin
Private
New Orleans 6th July 1812

Secy of the Treasurer
Dear Sir,

Returns of the late election for Governor, have been received from Orleans, German Coast, Accadia, Iberville, Point-Coupeé, & Concordia.— In each of these Counties, I have obtained a decided Majority, & the general opinion, seems to be, that I shall receive thro'out the State, a vote of at least two to one over the other Candidates.— How far, the Legislature may be disposed to confirm the choice of the people, I will not undertake to say; But at this moment, the prospect of my election, is very flattering.

Permit me to recommend Mr. John Clay of this Territory as a fit person, to be appointed Register of the Land-Office for one of the Districts in West Florida; His Talents are equal to the duties of the Office, & I am persuaded his Integrity may be relied on.

Present me with great respect & regard to Mrs. Gallatin

I am,

Dear Sir,

Your friend

Sigd. W. C. C. Claiborne

—— ,, —— ,, ——

To James Monroe

New Orleans 6th July 1812.

Secy of State

———— ,, ————

Sir,

General Wilkinson is in the River & his arrival in the City momently expected. We learn by the Mail of yesterday, that a Declaration of War, against Great Britain, had passed the House of Representatives on the 4th Ultimo, & information as to the decision of the Senate, is awaited with the greatest solicitude.— From Vera Cruix we have such accounts of the Successes of the Revolutionists as to leave no doubt as to their ultimate Triumph;— Mr. Shaler now at Nachitoches informs me that he had advised you of a design of sundry Citizens of the United States, to rendezvous at some point West of the Sabine, & there to take up arms in favour of the Revolutionists; It is believed, this design is not yet abandoned, but that its execution will be delayed until the question of Peace or War is finally settled by Congress.— A Gentleman on this morning put into my hands the enclosed Copy of an Article of Association, which was secretly circulating in the County of Rapides for signatures;— But at the same time, assured me, that no movement would be made, until further intelligence was recd from Washington.— The advice which on a late occasion I gave to the Civil Authority at Nachitoches, to bring the Law to bear against any person or persons engaged in setting on foot within the Jurisdiction of the U: States a Military expedition or enterprise against the Dominions of a foreign Prince or State, at Peace with the U: States, & my instructions to the Officer Commanding the Militia to give all necessary aid to the Civil Magistrate, supercede *for*

.the *present,* the necessity of further interference on my
part.[1]—   I have the honor to be, Sir, &c@ &c@ &c@
Signed/   W. C. C. Claiborne

To Judge Carr

New Orleans July 8th. 1812

Nachitoches

———— ,, ————

Sir,
     I have issued an order to Colonel Shaumberg to fur-
nish a Militia escort to Don Apolinas Mazmila as far as
the Sabine, & in the absence of the Colonel, it will devolve upon the officer next in Command, to carry the or-
.der into effect.—
     At the late election in New Orleans, & the adjacent
Counties for a Governor of Louisiana, I have been honored with a decided Majority over the Other Candidates;
From the Western Counties no returns have yet been received.—
     The President of the United States has recommended
a Declaration of War against Great Britain;— The
proposition was acceded to by the House of Representatives on the 4th Ulto. & we are awaiting with great solicitude the decision of the Senate.— Where it is understood, there is great diversity of opinion.—
                    I am, Sir, &c@ &c@ &c@
                    signed/   W. C. C. Claiborne

To Don Diego Murphy

New Orleans June 27th 1812

Commercial Agent for   )
      Spain at N. Orleans)

Sir,
     The outrage committed by a French Cruiser on a
Spanish Schooner that had anchored at the Balize, of

———————————

[1] Another evidence of Spanish friction.

which you inform me, is sincere regret, & the Naval Commander on this Station, will take the measures which so flagrant a violation of the Jurisdiction of the United States, has rendered necessary.—

As relates to the Pilot at the Balize who is charged with acting & abetting in this outrage I shall cause an enquiry to be made into his conduct, & if proved culpable, he will receive a strong proof of my displeasure.—

I am,

Sir,

Very respectfully

Your obdt. Servt.

Sigd   W. C. C. Claiborne.

——— ,, ——— ,, ———

To Commodore Shaw

New Orleans July 9th 1812

Naval Commander

——— ,, ———

Sir,

I hasten to inform you, that by an express, this morning arrived from the City of Washington, I have been officially advised that War was declared on the 18th day of June last, by the Government of the U: States of America against the United Kingdoms of Great Britain & Ireland & the dependencies thereof. — You will of course loose no time in communicating this important intelligence to the several Officers (subject to your orders) on distant Stations, & I am particularly desirous that your dispatches for the Balize may reach there in time, to prevent the departure of the Siren for Vera Cruix;— But if she should previously have sailed, permit me to suggest to you the expediency of forwarding advice of the War, *by a Pilot Boat,* to the Commander of the Siren, accompanied with such further orders, as in your judgment, the Crisis may demand.—

I am, Sir,

Very respectfully

Your obdt. Servt.

Sigd   W. C. C. Claiborne.

————— „ ————— „ —————

To Paul Hamilton

New. Orleans July 9th. 1812.

Secy of the Navy

Sir,

I this day received by express from Washington, official information of the declaration of War on the part of the U: States against the U: Kingdoms of Great Britain & Ireland & the Dependencies thereof.— If there was ever a just & necessary War, that which our Country has waged, is the *one;* It was the only measure that could preserve the Independence of the Nation;— That could make our Government respectable at home or abroad, & I trust in God, we shall be enabled to make its miseries recoil *most heavily* upon the enemy.

I inform you with regret, that the Brigs Siren & Viper are at Sea, & may probably fall in with British Cruisers, without a previous knowledge of existing hostilities.— About the middle of the past month, a Mr. Stephen Kingston lately appointed by the President, Consul at Havanna, arrived at New Orleans, & having satisfied me (from a view of his instructions) that the Government was solicitous for his speedy arrival at his port of destination, Commodore Shaw at my request gave him passage in the Brig Viper.— This Vessel was on the Balize Station, & being ordered to cruise in the Gulph Southardly, I did suppose a run to Havannah (so near her cruising ground) would subject the service to no inconvenience.— The Siren has been ordered to Vera Cruix, with some spanish passengers. Two French cruisers or pirates (believed to have been fitted out at New. Orleans) captured & plundered on our Coast a Spanish Brig bound from Vera Cruix to New Orleans, in search of provisions for an almost starving people; The Captain, passengers & Crew, were put on shore, & reached New Orleans poor & miserable;— The Spanish Consul (Mr. Murphy) solicited me to facilitate the return of these unfortunate strangers (particularly the passengers) to their homes & families, & at my request, Commodore Shaw ordered the Commander of the Siren to receive (Mr. Murphy furnishing the necessary stores) & to land them at Vera Cruix.— The Siren had been ordered to cruise to the Westward as far as the Latitude of the Sabine, & to proceed on to Vera Cruix, would not probably have taken her more than thirty-six hours from her Cruising Station.— I had availed myself also of Mr. Kingston's visit to the Havannah, to renew my efforts, with the Captain General of Cuba, to obtain the release from confinement, of ten native Americans, who (whilst acting under the authority of the Florida Convention) were in the fall of 1810, taken in arms near Mobile; & being desirous, that my interference in behalf of these unfortunate men, should be accompanied, with some proof of a disposition on my part, not to be wanting in a return of good offices, I the more readily accorded the request of Mr. Murphy.— I hope the fortunes of War will so far favour the Siren & Viper as to enable them to return safely into port, but in the event of their capture, my regret will be much increased, if the smallest censure should attach to Commodore Shaw— perhaps I was wrong in having ordered those Vessels to a Spanish port, at so perilous a Crisis;— But I remained for some time without official information, as to the course of our Government, & private accounts altho' contradictory, were

such, as to leave on my mind, an impression, that a declaration of War, would not have been proclaimed at so early a period.—
I have the honor to be, &c@ &c@ &c@
Signed/ W. C. C. Claiborne
————— „ ————— „ —————

To James Monroe

New Orleans July 9th 1812.

Secy of State
————— „ —————

Sir,
Your letter of the 19th Ultimo, enclosing a Declaration of War on the part of the United States against the United Kingdoms of Great Britain & Ireland & the dependencies thereof, was delivered to me on this morning.— Of the justice of the necessity of this appeal to arms in support of our Country's rights, every faithful Citizen must be convinced & I am persuaded, that the President, (supported as he will be by a brave people) will be enabled to draw the Contest to a speedy and honorable conclusion.— General Wilkinson who has been several days in the River, is expected here, in the course of the day;— I shall see him immediately on his arrival, & will cordially, Zealously & actively unite with him, in all his measures of defence & offence.—

We have election returns from every County in the State except three;— The majority is so decided in my favour, as to leave little doubt, but that the Legislature which is to assemble on the 27th Instant will confirm the choice of the people.[1]— I am at this moment, acting as

---

[1] The failure of the opposition to Claiborne shows that he overestimated its strength.

Governor of Louisiana, under the Constitution of the State.—

                I have the honor to be, Sir, &c@ &c@
                        Signed/ W. C. C. Claiborne

————— ,, ————— ,, —————

———————————

TO THE Master WARDEN

                        & Wardens of the port of
                        New Orleans

Gentlemen,

Antonio, one of the branch pilots at the Balize, is charged with being in correspondence with certain French cruisers which hover on our Coast, & that on a late occasion, he, or some person in his employ, was aiding & abetting a privateer, in cutting out a Spanish Schooner, which was at anchor within the Mississippi.— I request you Gentlemen to make enquiry into Antonio's conduct in this particular, & to transmit me the result.— It has been suggested, that the Captain of the Brig Sally Ann late from New York, & the Gentlemen who came passengers in said Vessel can give satisfactory information upon this subject.—

                        I am,
                        Gentlemen
                            Very respectfully
                                Your obedt. Sert.
                        Sigd   W. C. C. Claiborne.

————— ,, ————— ,, —————

New Orleans)
9th July 1812)

To Paul Hamilton

New. Orleans July 20th 1812 ,

Secy of the Navy

Since my last letter, I have had no intelligence from the Viper or Siren; As relates, to the latter Vessel, I omitted in my last to inform you, that immediately on the receipt of the Declaration of War, Commodore Shaw dispatched a *Messenger* to the Balize, with a view of preventing her departure ;— But previous to his arrival, she had gone to Sea.—I advised the Commodore, to dispatch a Pilot Boat after her with information of the War, & orders to return to port with all possible dispatch, which I believe he has done.—

There are several privateers, fitting out at this port, & the Citizens concerned are very anxious that Commissions for Letters of Marque & reprisal, should be sent out.—

The General Assembly of the State, will be in session in 9 days.— it is understood, that at the late election for Governor, I obtained a great Majority of the vote of the people, & the general opinion seems to be, that the popular sentiment in my behalf will be sanctioned by the Legislature.—

I am &c@ &c@ &c@
signed/   W. C. C. Claiborne

——— ,, ——— ,, ———

To William Eustis

New. Orleans July 20th 1812

Sec. at War

Dear Sir,

My esteemed friend, the father of Soniat Dufassat Junr. whom the President was pleased to appoint an Ensign in the third Regiment came to me the other day, &

VI—9

handed me the letter of appointed (herein enclosed) which had been addressed to his Son, & requested me to return it to you, accompanied with his best thanks, & to beg that his Son may be considered as resigned.— Some months after young Dufassat's application for a Commission he went to France on private business, & the Interests of his family (in relation to an Estate there) requiring his absence from the U: States for several years, the father has thought it his duty, in behalf of his Son, to tender his resignation. I have a young Creole friend of this City, Mr. Charles Dutillet, who is extremely desirous to enter the Army, & I beg leave to recommend him for Mr. Dufassat's Vacancy.— Young Dutillet is a native of New Orleans 18 years of age, a very *promising Boy;* & the Son of Colonel Dutillet, who filled for some time with great credit the office of Adjutant General of the Orleans Territory.   In expectation, that the President may be pleased to confer the Commission of Ensign on young Dutillet, I have advised him to join the army immediately as a Cadet, & shall beg the favour of General Wilkinson to receive him in that Capacity.—

The taking immediate possession of Pensacola & Mobile is essential to the safety of this section of the Union, & I persuade myself it may comport with the views of the Government, to give orders to that effect.—

It is understood, that at the late election for a Governor of Louisiana, I received a great Majority of the vote of the people & the general opinion seems to be, that the popular sentiment in my behalf, will be confirmed by the Legislature, which will be in session on the 27th Instant.

I am &c@ &c@ &c@
Signed/   W. C. C. Claiborne
———— ,, ———— ,, ————

To Albert Gallatin

(Private)

New. Orleans July 20th 1812.

Secy of the Treasury
Dear Sir,

I am earnestly requested to mention to you, Mr. Audley L. Osborn as a Candidate for the appointment of Register in one of the Land Districts, established in West Florida. Mr. Osborn is at present Judge of the Parish of St. Helena; in the County of Feliciana; He possesses great integrity of Character, & believed to be a very good lawyer.— I beg leave also, to renew my application in behalf of Mr. John Clay;— If there should be a vacancy in the office of Register for the Eastern District of Orleans, I really think Sir, Mr. Clay may be safely trusted with that appointment;— He is a man of business, & by no means deficient in Talents;— In managing his own affairs he has been heretofore unfortunate, perhaps imprudent;— But as to his Integrity, his Creditors have given him an honorable testimonial & of which I recollect on a former occasion to have transmitted you a Copy.—

Our old acquaintance Mr. Poydras is elected a Senator of the State for the County of Point Coupeé;— This Legislature will be in session in 9 days, & the general opinion seems to be that my nomination by the people as Governor, will be confirmed.—

Considerable quantities of flour are passing daily from hence to Pensacola & Mobile;— I consider the taking immediate possession of these places as essential to the safety of this section of the Union, & I learn with regret, that General Wilkinson has no orders to that effect.—

I am &c@ &c@ &c@
Signed/ W. C. C. Claiborne
——— ,, ——— ,, ———

To James Monroe

Private

—— ,, ——

New Orleans July 20th. 1812

Secy of State

Your dispatch of the 19th Ulto furnished the latest intelligence which I have received from Washington.— General Wilkinson is here, & making the necessary dispositions of the Troops under his orders.— For the present, I cannot afford him all that Co-operation, which I desire;— I am at this time Governor of the State *in expectancy only;* It is understood that I have a great Majority of the vote of the people, & the general opinion seems to be, that the Legislature (which will be in session in 9 days) will sanction the popular sentiment in my behalf; But until my nomination is confirmed, I feel a delicacy in taking any measures, with a view to permanency, & indeed my present powers (as Governor pro: Tem: under the Constitution) do not permit it.— A New Spanish Governor has arrived at Pensacola accompanied by 150 Troops Men of Colour & Blacks & Mobile stil remains in the quiet possession of the Spanish Authorities.— I consider the taking immediate possession of Pensacola & Mobile absolutely essential to the safety of this section of the Union, & I learn with great regret, that Genl. Wilkinson has no orders to that effect.— Considerable supplies of flour & salted provisions have been exported from hence to Pensacola & Mobile, & since the Declaration of War, the Shipments to these places augment daily.— We have much contradictory information, relative to the State of things in Mexico.— It was a few days since, reported, that the patriot Chief Rayon was killed, & that his second in Command Morales had been defeated.— But this is now contradicted, & the patriots are represented to be in peaceable possession of the

whole Country, except Vera Cruix, the City of Mexico,
& very few interior *provences,* to which it seems the Revolutionists, have not yet turned their attention.— A very
respectable Citizen of this State, who was formerly in
the Spanish service, put into my hands the other day
some reflections he had committed to writing relative to
the State of things in Mexico; A perusal may not be unin-
teresting & therefore I take the liberty of enclosing you a
Copy.

I have the honor to be,
Dear Sir,
With respect & esteem
Your mo: obedt. Serv.
Signed/   W. C. C. Claiborne
———— „ ———— „ ————

New Orleans July 24th. 1812

HIS EXCELLENCY   )
  GOVERNOR ZUNIGA)
    PENSACOLA   )
Sir,
    I am honored with the receipt of your letter, under
date of the 12th. Inst: & shall without delay transmit
the same, to the President of the U: States.— As regards
to the stile & aspect of your Excellency's Letter, I shall
make no comments.— But I cannot refrain from observing that your reproaches against my Government are
unmerited, & that your menaces will divert no American
officer, from the course of conduct, which his duty en-
joins.—
    The tract of Country, extending from the Mississippi
to the Perdido forms a part of the Territory, ceded by
France to the U. States under the name of Louisiana &
possession of the whole tract, with the exception of a

small District "which encludes the Town & Fort of Mo-
"bile, & is bounded by Dog River.— & that branch of it
"which is called Bayou Moulins; By a line direct from
"thence to the Bayou St. Louis (lately called three mile
"Creek) & the said Bayou & the Mobile River," has been
taken by the U: States, & their Jurisdiction & authority
over same asserted.— I have only to add that such possession will be supported & the necessary means employed to repel aggression.—

I tender to your Excellency the assurances of my
great respect & high Consideration.—

Signed/   W. C. C. Claiborne

——— ,, ——— ,, ———

To James Wilkinson

New Orleans 24th July 1812.

Commg. the U. S. Troops
   on the Mississippi & Mobile

I have the honor to enclose for your perusal a Letter
from the Spanish Governor of Pensacola, as well as of
my answer.— You will observe the terms of reproach
which this foreign Agent uses towards this Government
& the language of Menace which he has thought proper
to address to me; You will also observe General, the assurance I have given him, that the possession which has
been taken of West Florida will be maintained, & the
necessary means employed to repel aggressions.— It
only remains for me to express a wish that our opinions
on this subject may be in unison, & that you will give
the orders proper for the occasion.—

I am, &c@ &c@ &c@
(Signed)   W. C. C. Claiborne

——— ,, ——— ,, ———

To Gov. David Holmes

Private

——— „ ———

New Orleans July 27th. 1812

NATCHEZ

——— „ ———

I am not without apprehensions that the menacing stile of the Spaniards letter has been dictated by the English, & if so, it is not improbable, but our possessions on the Mobile, may be exposed to insult.— Under this impression, permit me to suggest for your Excellency's Consideration, the expediency of sending a Confidential officer to Mobile, with authority to array the Militia, & to repel aggression. So soon as the State authorities here shall be organized which will be in a few days, you may rely with Confidence on their zealous support, & you may be assured also of General Wilkinson's prompt Co-operation.— The General Assembly of Louisiana will form a quorum on this day, & will on tomorrow proceed to the election of a Governor;— an opinion exists that my nomination by the people, will be confirmed perhaps unanimously.—

I am, &c@ &c@ &c@
Signed/ W. C. C. Claiborne

——— „ ——— „ ———

To Gov. Holmes

New. Orleans July 27th. 1812

NATCHEZ

——— „ ———

I have the honor to enclose you a Copy of a Letter, which has been addressed to me by the Governor of Pensacola together with my answer thereto.— The letter of the Governor, evidently denotes a hostile disposition, & I trust your Excellency will agree with me in opinion, that no time ought to be lost, in making the necessary preparations to maintain our possessions on the Mobile & to repel aggression.—

It may be proper to inform you, that in the course of my late administration as Governor of Orleans, I instructed the several Civil Officers in Commission for the County of Feliciana, to exercise authority over the whole tract of Country, extending from the Mississippi to the Perdido, excepting indeed a small District, which encluded the Town & Fort of Mobile, & is bounded by Dog River, by that branch of it which is called Bayou Boulins; by a line direct from thence, to the Bayou St. Louis (lately called three mile Creek) & the said Bayou & the Mobile River: Neither Dolphin Island nor fish River, (the points alluded to by the Spanish Governor) fall within the above defined limits, & of course, were the District stil subject to my Government, I could not & would not, (unless ordered by the President), do an act, which might be construed as a relinquishment of the Jurisdiction of the U: S: over the same.— As regards Dolphin Island, I gave no particular order to take possession of it; But I stated to Commodore Shaw generally that Dolphin Island, & all other Islands bordering on our Coast & lying West of the Perdido & East of the Sabine, were considered as being within the Jurisdiction of the U: S:, & I requested that our cruising Vessels would anchor near to said Islands, & that Crews would land thereon, whenever their convenience made the same desirable. I presume that the Crew of some of our Gun Boats, have landed at Dolphin Island & hoisted the American flag; But I remain uninformed of the particulars.—

I take this occasion to enclose your Excellency a list of the Civil Officers which were appointed by me for the parishes of Biloxy & Pascagoula, & which parishes are

now annexed, by an Act of Congress to the Territory
under your Government:[1]—
      I have the honor to be, &c@ &c@ &c@
                        Signed/ W. C. C. Claiborne
                        ────── „ ────── „ ──────

GENTLEMEN of the SENATE

Desirous of availing the public of the services of Lewis Barthelemy Macarty, of New Orleans, I do hereby nominate him Secretary for the State of Louisiana.—
                        Signed/ W. C. C. Claiborne
                        ────── „ ────── „ ──────
New. Orleans   )
July 30th. 1812)

GENTLEMEN of the SENATE, and HOUSE of REP-

RESENTATIVES.

I have the honor to lay before you, a paper purporting to be a Copy of an Act of Congress, entitled "An Act
"granting to the Governor of the State of Louisiana for
"the time being, & his successors in office, a lot of ground,
"& the buildings thereon." I have received no official
Copy of the above Act; But the paper enclosed, having
having been transmitted to me, by a Member of Congress,
I have no doubt, but it is a true Copy from the Original.
— Whatever may be the construction Gentlemen, which
you shall give to this Act, I trust, in the event, the Senate
& House of Representatives of the State should deem

───────────────────────────────

[1] For full account of the Gulf Coast acquisition see Encyclopedia of
Mississippi History, p. 816.

proper to occupy the Government House, that some suitable building for the residence of the Governor with convenient apartments, for the office of the Secretary, may
be provided at the expence of the State.—

Signed/ W. C. C. Claiborne

—— ,, —— ,, ——

To James Madison

New Orleans August 2. 1812

President of the U: S:
Washington City
Dear Sir,

I have the honor to inform you, that on the 30th Ulto.,
I entered upon the duties of my office as Governor of
Louisiana to which I have been called by a vote of the
people of the State & of the general Assembly.—

Yielding to the feelings of a grateful heart, I eagerly
seize this occasion to return you my sincere thanks for
the high Confidence you were pleased to repose in me,
during the late Territorial Government, & to assure you,
that in the course of my services as Governor of Louisiana there is nothing, I more desire, than to promote the
views of your wise & virtuous administration, & to give
you individually proofs of my most faithful & respectful
attachment.—

(Signed)   W. C. C. Claiborne

—— ,, —— ,, ——

To Simon Favre

New. Orleans 4th Augst. 1812

Pearl River

—— ,, ——

Sir,

Having received information that the Chactaws of the
lower Towns had committed depredations in the settlement on Pearl, Leaf & Checkasaw-hey Rivers, & had discovered a hostile disposition towards the U: S: I have

directed to them "a talk" herein enclosed, & which I commit to your care.— I request you therefore, to proceed without delay to the nation & after assembling the Chiefs & Head Men to deliver & explain to them my address;— and to which you will add such observations of your own, as you may think best calculated to incline them to Peace & friendship.— Should you meet with Mr. Silas Dinsmour the agent of the U: S: for the Chactaws, or with Mr. Pitchylynn,[1] or any other person in the nation in the employ of the U: S:, you will explain to them the object of your visit, & request their Co-operation.—

During your stay in the nation, you will make enquiries & transmit me on your return, information on the following points.— 1st Whether the Creeks & Chactaws have been furnished with Military supplies at Pensacola & Mobile— & if so, by whom— to what amount & with what views.

2n. The number of warriors in the Chactaw nation & what portion of them are supposed to be under English or Spanish influence.

3 The names of the Town, where the Spaniards & English have the most partisans & the Character of the Principal Chiefs of these towns.—

4 Whether the Prophet, had sent talks among the Chactaws, & whether his Brother Ticumsey had visited them.—

You will be pleased to keep an account of your expenses, which together with such reasonable Compensation for your services, as the Legislature of Louisiana shall think proper to prescribe, shall be allowed you.—

I am, Sir, &c@ &c@ &c@

(Signed)   W. C. C. Claiborne

——— ,, ——— ,, ———

---

[1] Encyclopedia of Mississippi History, Vol. II, p. 431.

General Jas. Wilkinson   New Orleans Augst. 5th 1812
    Commg. the U. S. Troops.
Sir,
    About seven leagues north of the Fort St. John, & immediately back of the plantation of M. Bernard Bernowdy on the German Coast, there are the remains of a small Fort on the Lake Pontchartrain at a place called Tiganyou. At that spot, the Chactaw Indians are in the habit of crossing the lake, & in former times, they took that route in all their hostile visits to the settlements on the Mississippi. The French afterwards had a few Men stationed at Tiganyou, & recent information of the unfriendly disposition of the Chactaws, induces me to suggest for your Consideration, the expediency of sending *there,* a subaltern & fifteen or twenty men. It would I am sure give much satisfaction to the inhabitants on German Coast, several of whom have expressed to me, their great desire to see that position occupied.— If events should require your whole force to be concentrated, I will relieve the Command you may send to Tiganyou, by a Detachment of Militia, so soon as the Legislature shall pass a Militia Law, which is now under discussion.—
            I am, Sir, &c@ &c@ &c@
                (Signed)   W. C. C. Claiborne
        ——— ,, ——— ,, ———

FELLOW CITIZENS of the SENATE and HOUSE of

REPRESENTATIVES.

    I am very grateful to the people of Louisiana for the distinguished proof of confidence, they have been pleased to afford me, nor am I insensible Gentlemen of the honor confered, by your sanction of the popular sentiment in my behalf.— Diffident of my talents, & deeply impressed with the magnitude of the trust committed to me, I should despair of a successful result, were it not for the benefit of your enlightened councils.— Man is rarely enabled to conduct his own concerns in a manner pleasing to himself, & how much more difficult is it to manage satisfactorily the affairs of a Government. As far as regards my agency, I cannot promise myself the happiness of pursuing a Course which shall command General approbation. To conciliate public sentiment, & to satisfy the wishes of all, require a perfection in wisdom & virtue, to which I lay no claim. It will, I fear, be often my misfortune to mistake the public interest; but I shall never do so intentionally.— There notwithstanding will be individuals, who endeavor to *magnify my errors into crimes*. But the repose of an approving conscience is not easily disturbed, & as in times past, so in times to come, I shall view with calmness, the turbulence of political contention, & meet with composure the clamour & bitterness of opposition. With these feelings Gentlemen, & a *firm reliance on the justice of my Country*, I have entered on the duties of my office, *without the smallest aprehension*, other than what arises from an extreme solicitude for the general welfare.—

Having witnessed the moment when the authority of the United States was first extended over this important, interesting & delightful district; having assisted for near nine years, in its progress from Colonial dependence to state soveignty, & so frequently experienced the kind indulgence of its generous Inhabitants.— there are no motives which can influence an ingenuous mind;— no considerations of honor & gratitude but combine to render the prosperity of Louisiana, an object of my fondest affections.— Receive then Gentlemen, my warmest congratulations on the happy event, which has made her a Member of the great American confederacy, & secured for ourselves & posterity, the blessings of liberty, Laws

& safety, Always a friend to Representative Government,' believing it to be the one best calculated to advance the happiness of society, I anticipate the most favorable results from your present deliberations.— Your devotion to the public good & your wisdom to discern it, will ensure the earliest attention to the various & fit subjects of Legislation. The consideration of the Act of Congress, which provides for an enlargement "of the limits of the State," has justly been esteemed as of primary importance. By that act a considerable tract of Country rich in natural resources and highly improved by the hand of industry is, with the assent of the Legislature, to be added to Louisiana. This accession of *population, of wealth and of strength,* was earnestly desired by the Convention of Orleans, & the general government in according it, has given a further proof of regard for the welfare of this section of the Union, which you Gentlemen, will I am assured highly appreciate.—

The constitution of the State, points to several objects of high concern; which claim your most deliberate reflection. On a wise & just arrangement of the judicial department, depends the best interests of the community.— The great outlines are prescribed; but the details are left for Legislative provision.— The Judicial power "is to be vested in a supreme Court with appelate jurisdiction only, & in such inferior courts as the Legislature may think proper to establish." Your first care should be to facilitate the approach to the tribunal of last resort, & render it accessible to the most indigent Citizen; An accumulation of legal forms & ceremonies should be studiously avoided;— they augment expences & become oppressive; they obstruct the streams of Justice, & eventually divert their course. In organizing inferior courts, your own knowledge of the local situation of the several counties, & of the habits & sentiments of your Constituents, will be your safest guides;— we have seen the operation of the Parish Court system, & experience has made us sensible of its defects.— *These* should be remedied. But let us not proceed with an impetuous hand, or we may mistake innovation for reform, & instead of amendment present only a change. The duties of the Attorney General and "the number & duties also of District Attorneys" are to be determined by Law. These will necessarily depend upon & be adapted to your judicial arrangements. But I am persuaded Gentlemen, you will in no instance, depart from that wise policy which forbids an unnecessary increase of offices.

At this eventful crisis, it is highly essential, that this State, should be fully represented in the Senate & House of Representatives of the U: States, & that timely provision be made for the exercise of its important suffrage, at the approaching election of a President & Vice President. To this end you will take the necessary measures, nor do I doubt, but they will be such as the purest principles of Patriotism shall advise.

To carry into effect the articles of the Constitution, which secures to the Citizens of New Orleans, the right of appointing the officers necessary for the administration of police pursuant to the mode of election to be prescribed by the Legislature," your Co-operation is necessary & ought to be speedily rendered. The *interest* of this great & growing City, is intimately connected with *that* of the State, & *cannot be too affectionately cherished.*

The regents of the University of Orleans will lay before you Gentlemen, an interesting view of the College of New. Orleans, & of the several County Schools under their superintendence.— You will notice with great satisfaction the progress of science, nor do I doubt your readiness to contribute by such means as may be in your power, to its further advancement. Education gives to the mind all the perfection of which it is susceptible, and prepares our youth for the high destinies which await them. On the rising generation rest the happiness of parents, & the best hopes of the State. Let our children be reared in the paths of knowledge, of virtue & patriotism, and whilst they will maintain the rights, the honor the glory of our Country, their general deportment will be such as to occasion the grey hairs of those who watched them in their infancy, to go down without regret to the grave.—

GENTLEMEN of the HOUSE of REPRESENTA-TIVES.

The proper accounting officers will present you a Statement of the receipts & expenditures for the past year. The liberal donations of the last Territorial Legislature to literary instructions; the remuneration accorded to sufferers during the late insurrection, & the heavy expences incurred by the Convention of Orleans, made serious impressions on the public Treasury. There nevertheless remains a fund equal to present exigencies, & I indulge a fond hope that the Charges incident to a State Government, may all be met without resorting to further taxes. But to this end, it is indispensible that punctuality in the collection of the revenue be enforced, & the most prudent economy in its expenditure observed. We are all Gentlemen sensible of the pressure of the times, & must unite in the most economical course.— The hand of industry no longer meets a liberal reward; most of the productions of the soil are perishing in our possession, & the payment of the existing imposts is becoming seriously inconvenient to many of our fellow-Citizens.

GENTLEMEN of the SENATE and of the HOUSE of REPRESENTATIVES.

There is yet another subject, to which, I am urged by the strongest considerations of duty to invite your attention.— The Militia, says the Constitution, is to be organized in such manner, as may hereafter be deemed most expedient by the Legislature.— It is with regret I have to observe, that this force does not exhibit that arrangement, order & discipline which can alone render it respectable. The causes may in part be found in this existing Laws, which I pray you to revise & to render more efficient. The contrariety of language spoken by the Citizens of Louisiana; the dispersed situation of settlements & the inconvenience which attends the frequent assemblage of corps for exercise & inspection, present serious *obstacles;* but *these* should serve only as incitements to further exertion, until every improvement is given to our militia system, which existing circumstances will admit.— At all times, such would be our duty. But at this perilous crisis, the safety of our Country imperiously demands it; The U: States are engaged in a War, to the calamities of which, this section of the Union is greatly exposed. We know not the moment when the enemy may menace the sanctuary of our dwellings & convert to his use, the fruits of our industry. A sense of common danger, should unite every heart, & strengthen every arm. If ever War was justifiable the one, which our Country has declared, is that war.— If ever a people had cause to repose with confidence on their Government, we are that people. From the days of the great Washington to the present period, the desire of our rulers has been to preserve peace with all nations, & to keep aloof from those destructive conflicts which are filling the world with widows & with orphans. With this view the most pacific policy has been pursued; omitting nothing which justice required, & doing nothing which neutrality forbid. Remote from the Scene of Carnage, & indulging in no sympathy for the belligerents, but such as invited acts of kindness to all,'' we had a right to expect exemption from aggression. But in this degenerate era,

VI—10

innocence itself cannot arrest the hand of violence.
When the Government of Great Britain first aspired to
the base pre-eminence of becoming the highwayman of
the Ocean, our illustrious statesmen opposed the ab-
surdity; the wickedness of her pretensions, & made repeated appeals to her justice.— But they appealed in
vain. When our unprotected commerce became a prey
to rapacity, & our Countrymen navigating the high Seas
were impressed into her ignominious service, & made to
fight the battles of their oppressors, we again prefered
remonstrance to resistance.— But this moderation has
been received as timidity, & in proportion to our forbearance has our wrong multiplted. Our Laws are derided,
& our rights outraged. The harbours of the U : States
have been blockaded & their own waters coloured with
American blood. Seeking redress by negociation, the
sword still rested in the Scabbard & we called it peace.—
But such a peace presented no claims to an American
heart, it was accompanied with dishonor, & leading fast
to the ruin of our Country. The day however of retribu-
tion has at length arrived.— The Government which to
a long list of injuries, has added an attempt to dismem-
ber the happy union, which made these States free & independent. The Government whose Agents are busily
employed in exciting the ruthless Savage to murden our
women & Children has much to answer for.— The collected wisdom of the American nation has declared the
remedy, & a great, brave & determined people will apply
it.— A War exists between the United Kingdom of Great
Britain & Ireland & their Dependencies & the U : States
of America. War is not the greatest of evils; a base
submission to aggression would have been a greater
curse— it would have entailed dishonor, cowardice, vas-
salage upon ourselves & posterity. The independence of
America was the fruit of eight years of toil & of danger,
& to maintain this inestimable ''heritage'' the sword is

again unsheathed. The wrongs of England have been long & seriously felt;— they are visible in the decline of our Sea port towns; in the ruin of commerce & the languor of agriculture. The recourse to arms may increase the pressure; but let it be recollected, that whatever sacrifice we make, is offered on the altar of our Country; a consideration which will reconcile a faithful people to every privation. The President of the United States calculates on every aid, which it is in the power of Louisiana to give, "as well to mitigate the evil of War to our "own Citizens, as to make it effectual against the enemy." In so reasonable a request, let not our Chief be disappointed. For years he has laboured to avert the storm, & now that it rages in all its fury, let us endeavor to carry him & our Country safely thro' it. Union is in itself a host. It is numbers, strength, and security.— Let every man put himself in Armour.— Age itself, should be prepared to advance against an evading foe: our young men should hasten "to the tented field," & tendering their services to the Government, be in readiness to march at a moments warning, to the point of attack.— In such a contest, the issue cannot be doubtful. In such a cause every American should make bare his bosom. "Where justice is the standard, Heaven is the warrior's shield."

Signed/   W. C. C. Claiborne

New Orleans   )   ⸺ ,, ⸺ ,, ⸺
July 30th 1812)

To James Monroe

New. Orleans July 26th 1812

Secy of State

⸺ ,, ⸺

Sir,

I have the honor to enclose you Copy of a letter, which the Spanish Governor at Pensacola, has addressed to me, together with my answer, & also a Copy of a letter from

me to Genl. Wilkinson.— The whole of this Correspondence, shall be transmitted to Governor Holmes, of the
Mississippi Territory with whom the authorities of
Louisiana, (so soon as they can be organized) will cordially unite in repelling aggression.

I am, Sir, &c@

Signed/   W. C. C. Claiborne

―――― „ ―――― „ ――――

GENTLEMEN of the SENATE!

I have received a Copy of your resolution of the 6th
Inst:, by which you "advise the Governor to nominate
Mr. Thomas B. "Robertson, as a Candidate to fill the
office of Secretary of State."

The ninth section of the third article of the Constitution speaking of the powers of the Governor, says.—
*"He shall nomi*nate & appoint, with the advice & con-
"sent of the Senate, Judges, Sheriffs, & all other officers
"whose offices are established by this Constitution, &
"whose appointments are not herein otherwise provided
"for."

After giving to this section all the Consideration
which its importance merited, my mind became perfectly
convinced, that the power to nominate was vested *exclusively* in the Governor, & that the Constitution had
called upon him *imperatively to* exercise it.— I did in
Consequence on the 30th Ulto. nominate Lewis Bartholemew Macarty of New Orleans, as a fit person to fill the
office of Secretary of State.   The right to *approve,* or
disapprove of that nomination, is, by the Constitution
given to the Senate.   Whenever therefore Gentlemen,
you shall notify me of your disapproval, I will nominate
another Citizen possessed of my confidence, & whom I believe also to be deserving of yours.— In the mean time, I
cannot & will not act upon any nomination made me by

the *Senate,* because by doing so, I should depart from my Construction of the Letter & spirit of the Constitution and abandon a Trust committed to me by the People of Louisiana.—

Signed/ W. C. C. Claiborne

New Orleans)
August 7th. 1812)

To Judge Carr

New Orleans August 7th 1812

Nachitoches

——— „ ———

Sir,

I cannot without considerable inconvenience to the public Interest, accept for the present, your resignation, as Judge of the Parish of Nachitoches, & I request you to continue in the functions of that office, until you shall be advised of the appointment of a Successor.—

Having understood that a project to invade the Spanish Province of Tehns, was stil in agitation by a number of individuals at or near Nachitoches, I must solicit your attention, to my letter of instruction under date of the 30th of July 1811, & must again request your vigilance in the maintainance of Law & good order.

An Act of the Congress of the U: States declares "That if any person shall, within the Territory or Juris-"diction of the U: States, begin or set on foot, or pro-"vide, or prepare the means for any Military expedition "or enterprise, to be carried on from thence against the "Territory or Dominion of any foreign Prince or State, "with whom the U: States are at peace, every such per-"son so offending shall upon conviction, be adjudged "guilty of a high misdemeanor, & shall suffer fine & im-"prisonment at the descretion of the Court, in which the

"Conviction shall be had, so as that such fine shall not
"exceed three thousand Dollars, nor the Term of im-
"prisonment be more than three years."—

I am, &c@ &c@ &c@

Signed/   W. C. C. Claiborne

———— „ ———— „ ————

A Message from the Governor to the Legislature.

GENTLEMEN of the SENATE, and of the HOUSE of
    REPRESENTATIVES!

Being informed that a Bill apportioning the representation, to the Parishes of Filiciana, Baton Rouge, St.
Helena & St. Tammany was at this time under Consideration,— I deem it proper to lay before you, a census of
the inhabitants of *Feliciana & Baton Rouge* taken in the
year 1811, by the proper officers.— No official returns
have been received by me from St. Helena & St. Tammany; But from the inofficial reports of parish officers, &
other Citizens entitled to Confidence, there were in *St.
Helena,* in the year 1811, about two thousand and two
hundred Souls, of which three hundred were Slaves; and
in *St. Tammany* from seventeen to eighteen hundred free
people, and three hundred Slaves.— I have understood,
that in the course of the present year 1812, there has
been a Considerable emigration to the *four Parishes
above mentioned,* particularly to St. Tammany;— But I
have no Documents, on which I could form an accurate
estimate of the Number of these emigrants.—

Signed/   W. C. C. Claiborne

———— „ ———— „ ————

New. Orleans   )
Augst. 8th. 1812)

His Excellency   New Orleans Augst. 9th 1812.
    Governor Holmes
        M: Territory
Sir,
    Since my last letter, I have heard nothing further of
the hostile Movements of the Chactaws.— You have enclosed, a petition addressed to me by the Inhabitants on
Pearl River, & a letter from the Judge of the parish of
Biloxy,— Considering that the Inhabitants of the parishes of St. Helena & St. Tammany within this State,
were equally exposed with those of Biloxy & Pascagoula
within your Territory to Indian Depredations, I thought
it my duty, to take some immediate means to ascertain
the Disposition of the Chactaws, & if possible to incline
them to peace.   With this view, I have sent Simon Favre
a Man entitled to Confidence & possessing great influence with the Chactaws into the Nation, with a Talk to
the Chiefs of which a Copy is enclosed.— The report of
Mr. Favre shall be forwarded to you, & on this & all other
occasions I shall be happy to unite with you in every
measure essential to the safety & defence of our Country.—
            I am Sir, &c@
                Signed/ W. C. C. Claiburne
            ———— ,, ———— ,, ————

            To James Wilkinson
            New. Orleans August 9th. 1812.
Commg the U: S: Troops
    I enclose you a letter from a Citizen of Nachitoches,
which after reading,.I will thank you to return to me, It
announces, that a Military expedition was preparing at
or near Nachitoches against the Spanish province of
Tehus;— I have written to the Judge of the parish of

Nachitoches, requiring his vigilance in the Maintainance of Law & good order, & informing him of the provisions of the Statute, which forbids the preparing or seting on foot within the Jurisdiction of the U: States, a Military expedition against the Dominions of a State at Peace with the U: States.— I request you General, to give on this occasion the necessary orders to the officer Commanding at Fort Claiborne, & that you require him to give immediate & effectual assistance to the Civil Authority.—

I am, Sir, &c@ &c@ &c@
Signed/ W. C. C. Claiborne

—— ,, —— ,, ——

To Diego Murphy

New. Orleans 10th. Augst. 1812

New Orleans

—— ,, ——

Sir,
Your letter of the 7th. Ins: has been received.— As long since as the 30th of July of the past year, I gave the necessary Orders to the proper officers at Nachitoches to observe all due vigilance in maintaining our Laws, & to prevent any Military expedition or enterprise, against the Dominions of a Prince or State with whom the U: States are at peace from being began or set on foot within the Territory or Jurisdiction of the United States. These orders have recently been renewed, & I persuade myself, will have the desired effect.—

I salute you, Sir, with friendship & respect
(Signed)   W. C. C. Claiborne

—— ,, —— ,, ——

A TALK from

WILLIAM C. C. CLAIBORNE, Governor of the
State of Louisiana & Commander in Chief
of the Militia thereof, to the Chief Head
Men & Warriors of the Chactaw Nation.

Brothers

I salute you in friendship, & beg you to open your
Ears, that you may hear my words,— Many of you remember me, when I was a Chief at Natchez, & know that
I never deceived you. My friendly disposition towards
you remains unaltered, & since I have been a Chief at
New Orleans, I have always been just to the red men.—
Brothers! When I have a journey to make, I take the
nearest path, turning neither to the right nor to the left,
but keeping straight on;— So it is when I send out a talk
— my manner is to speak plain, & to ease my heart at
once, of what I have to say.—
Brothers! The English who live beyond the big Water have done the Americans much harm;— they have
robbed us of our property— compelled many of our people to serve on board of their Ships of War, & spilt
American blood.— The President of the U: States, & his
head Men have determined upon satisfaction; the Tomahawk is raised & our hearts are cross.— This a quarrel
Brothers between white people, & does not concern the
red Men; We know well the English, & have no fear of
them.— More than thirty years ago they made War
against the U: States. We were then a young people, &
the enemy thought to crush us;— But they found Men &
Warriors to combat them, & returning to their Ships,
they left our Country to ourselves, & made peace upon
our own terms.
Brothers! We have now grown up to manhood, & can
the better fight our own battles.— I say again this quar-

rel does not concern the red Men.— Let them therefore remain quiet & join neither side. Your squaws & little Children will rest undisturbed in their Cabbins Your old Men will discourse & smoke without fear, under the shade of the Trees, & your Warriors may hunt & dance & be merry until they have an enemy of their own to strike.

Brothers! During the last War between the Americans & the English, the cherokees, & the Creeks & the Northern Indians joined with our Enemies.— And what followed?— The Indian Country was often visited by the big knife Men; Towns were burnt & fields of Corn destroyed; the women & little Children had to sleep in the mountains & many a brave warrior was laid low.— And what Brothers was the recompense for all these sufferings? Some trifling presents! A few shirt Blankets— some kegs of Rum & two or three dozen Medals made of bad Mettle.

Brothers! I have heard some bad news from Pascagoula & Pearl Rivers.— It is said the Chactaws have committed many robberies & that blood has been spilt. What does this mean? Do the English want the poor Indians to fight their battles & are you such fools as to sell your lives for a few goods? Has the proffet sent bad talks among you? or has his Brother Ticumsey made you believe that the Northern Indians are strong enough to drive the Americans into the Sea?

Brothers! The proffet says that he is the Son of the great Spirit, & can prevent powder from burning, & deprive a Ball from a riffle of its force. Some of the followers of this pretended "Son of the great Spirit" believed him & made an attack some moons past on the American Army. But as formerly the powder hurt & the Balls penetrated, the Indians were defeated.— Many were killed & the proffet turned out to a liar.— Ticumsey is a Warrior; But he is a *Mad Man* & knows not what he says, or what he does. Beware of him, or he will bring you into trouble.—

Brothers! Your father the President of the U: S: loves his red Children & wishes him to live in peace,— He loves also his white Children, & will suffer no Nation to strike them with impunity. He possesses the power to punish his enemies, & the will to do it.— The Chactaws are a small people, & when compared to the Americans are but a handful.— You may make War; But you will soon sue for peace.

Brothers! I am told that a Council fire is now burning & that white Beads & Wampum are passing between you & the Creeks.— Let this talk be read at the Council, & tell the Creeks to hold it fast. Say to them in my name, to keep their bad Men at home or evil will fall upon their nation.—

Brothers! I am told you go often to Pensacola & Mobile. Listen not to any bad talks you may hear there; But sell your skins & return in peace to your Cabbins or to your hunting ground. The Spanish Chiefs if they are your friends will give you the same advice; But there are wicked people every where, & if you find such at Pensacola or Mobile, turn your backs upon them— But Brothers I must conclude— Many words are soon forgotten— Take Simon Favre by the hand, & whatever he tells you in my name, believe him, for he is a good Man, & will neither betray me, nor deceive you.

I have nothing more to say Brothers— but to express a wish, that the Tomahawk between the Americans & the Chactaws may long remain buried.[1]—

                              Signed/ W. C. C. Claiborne
New Orleans Augt. 1812.

---

[1] The Creeks were unable to induce the Choctaws to join them in their attack on the people of Mississippi Territory.

To John Dawson

New Orleans Augst. 10th. 1812

Virginia

Dear Sir,

Attribute not my long silence to a want of friendship;
— But to the Political Storm to which I have been exposed, & the disposition, I felt, to await addressing you
until I had made a safe harbour.— During the late contest for Governor, my enemies were unusually active,
& had recourse to every means, to injure my private
& public character;— Among my opponents Edward Livingston of New York, & Wm. Robertson (the Secretary
were the most malignant! But after all, I have the pleasure to announce to you, that the people of the State, have
honored me, with a most flattering proof of their confidence.— In the vote of the people, I obtained a majority
in each & every County in the State;— the aggregate
Number of votes in my favour was 2757.— Mr. Velleré
947, & for M. Destrehan 168— On the 28th Ulto. the Legislature proceeded to elect by ballot one of the two highest Candidates in the vote of the people, when there ap-
pared to be 33 votes in my favour, & 6 for Mr. Velleré.—
I entered upon my administration on the 30th. Ulto. &
enclosed is a Copy of my address on the occasion.— I
have before me an arduous Task, & already my difficulties have commenced.— In New Orleans my enemies are
numerous, & they have already succeeded in creating a
serious Schism between the Senate & myself.— The power of nominating to office under the Constitution, is
claimed by the Senate & will be insisted on by me.— How
the difference will finally be settled, I cannot tell. The
Senate are at this time equally divided; Seven decidedly
with me, & Seven opposed;— the first are to a man my

friends, & the latter, with the exception of perhaps, two,
are my political enemies, & I believe personal.[1]

No appointments in the Judiciary have yet been made,
& are not likely to take place for some time. Most willingly would I place you on the Bench of the Supreme
Court of this State.— But in my present difficulties with
the Senate it is extremely doubtful, whether or not it will
be in my power to serve you.— Your absence would prevent a Confirmation of your appointment were you nominated— & the great doubt as to the disposition of the
Senate towards *either* of us, make it impossible for me to
invite your removal here, with any certainty of the patronage of the Senate.— Your old friend Poydras is President of the Senate, & is most favorably disposed towards
you;— But his influence & mine united, can only divide
the Senate. Cannot the General Government give you
some desirable employment in this quarter? I will pay
attention to passing events, & should I see any way of
serving you at Washington, I will eagerly seize the occasion. After some short residence among us, I am certain it would be in the power of your friends, to advance
your Interest under the State Authority.— I pray you to
write me from time to time, & keep me advised of the
successes of our little Navy & of the Northern Army. I
am grieved at the course Massachusetts has taken; the
address of the Representatives of that State to the people, is vastly humiliating & will be read with sorrow & by
every lover of his Country.— I wish to God Congress
had ordered taking possession of the Floridas; Was the
War prosecuted with vigour, promptitude & decision, it
would soon become popular!—

Genl. Wilkinson is here, but can take no effectual
means for the protection of this Section of the Union,
until he is authorized to take Mobile & Pensacola! **If**

---

[1] This attempt to embarrass Claiborne was of course prompted by
old political enemies.

the English should have any designs in Louisiana, they will certainly possess themselves of these places, & I think, we should anticipate them.—

I will do myself the pleasure to write you again in a few days.—

I wish you health, happiness & prosperity

And am,

Dr. Sr. With great respect,

signed/ W. C. C. Claiborne

——— ,, ——— ,, ———

To James Monroe

New Orleans Augst. 10th. 1812

Scy of State.

Dr. Sr.

Do me the favour to forward the enclosed letter to our friend Mr. Dawson; It acquaints him of my sincere desire, to advance his interests, & of the pleasure I would feel in placing him in the Judiciary of this State;— But such is my present difficulty with the Senate of this State, that I cannot promise my friend, the support he so justly merits.

I succeeded to the Government of the State by an overwhelming majority of the vote of the people, & in the Legislature by a vote of 33 to 6:— But notwithstanding Sir, it will be with extreme difficulty, that I shall be enabled to get along with the Government. New Orleans is the seat of Government;— My enemies here are very numerous & after resorting to every expedient which malice could invent, to defeat my election they seem determined to throw every embarrassment not only in my way, but in the way of the public Interest & safety. The Intriguers have already succeeded in creating a serious Schism between the Senate & the Executive.— The power of nominating to office, under the Constitution is claimed by the Senate, & insisted on by me. The enclosed Copy of my last message will inform you, in what state the business now rests. I learn today, that the Senate are equally divided 7 in favor of the Executive nomination & 7 against.— The former are my warm supporters;— The latter my political opponents, & (with the exception of two) my personal enemies. I believe no appointments in the Judiciary of the State will take place for some months;— In the mean time, I will endeavor to impress my friends favorably towards Mr. Dawson, & with this view, I shall use your letter as also one which Mr. Jefferson has written to me.— With the people of Louisiana I stand well, & in the House of Representatives I have many friends. But the unprincipled intriguers of New Orleans with Livingston at their head will prevent me, from effecting many objects, which accord with the best Interests of the State.

I am grieved at the course Massachusetts has taken, nor can any lover of his Country, read the address of the Representatives of that State to their Constituents without terror & humiliation.—

Gen. Wilkinson is here but can take no effectual means for the safety of this Section of the Union, until he is authorized to take Pensacola & Mobile.—

It is understood that the patriots in Mexico are stil successful— But I have received recently, no information that can be relied on. It is believed that a Number of Americans design to rendezvous at some point West of the Sabine, & to join the revolutionary standard. General Adair is mentioned as the leader of the party, & it is positively stated to me, that the project will soon be attempted. I await with anxiety some orders of the Government upon this subject.— in the mean time, I have thought it a duty, to renew my instructions to the Civil Officers at Natchitoches to be vigilant in preserving order,

& preventing a violation of the Law, which forbids the setting on foot within the jurisdiction of the U: S:, a Military expedition against the Dominions of a foreign state at peace with the U: States.—

East of the Sabine & within the limits of this State, there is a small settlement, called the post of Bayou Pierre, where during the Territorial Government, I never exercised jurisdiction,— It is within what has heretofore been called the neutral ground, that is to say, between the Harroya Honda & the Sabine;— there is at present at that post a Civil Majestrate acting under a Spanish Commission.— I must necessarily extend to that settlement the authority of the State of Louisiana & I am not without apprehensions, that it will be illy received by our Spanish neighbours.—

> I am, Dr. Sir &c@ &c@ &c@
> > Signed/ W. C. C. Claiborne

————— ,, ————— ,, —————

—————————

To Judge Carr

New. Orleans August 12th. 1812.

Nachitoches

————— ,, —————

Sir;

Having received information that in this City, & elsewhere in this State, certain individuals were engaged in raising Troops for the avowed purpose of invading the Dominions of Spain, a State in amity with the U: States, it becomes my duty to issue a Proclamation, of which you have enclosed several Copies.— I persuade myself, that so soon as the Contents of this Proclamation shall be known, the parties engaged in this unlawful project will abandon the same;— But if it is persisted in, I confidently expect you will act with promptitude & decision, & that you will cause to be arrested, & bound to their good behaviour all persons concerned, or that you will send them

in to New Orleans for trial before the District Court.—
Genl. Wilkinson has given the most positive instructions
to the officer Commanding at Fort Claiborne, to afford
on this occasion, to the Civil Authority all necessary
aid.— I am &c@ &c@

(Signed)   W. C. C. Claiborne

——— ,, ——— ,, ———

GENTLEMEN OF THE SENATE, & OF THE HOUSE OF REPRE-
SENTATIVES!

Involved as we are in War, with one of the most
powerful Nations of Europe:— menaced with Indian
hostilities, & exposed from within to Casualties of serious
import, I feel it a duty to urge the Legislature, to take
with promptitude, *such measures,* as the safety of the
State shall advise.— Among these, the immediate passage of a Law; which shall point out the mode of appointing Militia Officers, is highly essential.— Many vacancies
exist, & there is no where a power to supply them.— The
Consequence is, that the Militia already disorganized,
is becoming more so every day.— It would indeed be desirable that a Militia System more efficient, than the one
left us by the Territorial Government should be adopted;
But to mature such, would require much reflection, & be
attended with greater delay, than the present perilous
Crisis permits.— I entreat you therefore Gentlemen to
remedy some of the most prominent defects of the existing Laws, & to put it in the power of the Executive, to
array in defence of the State our whole force, or such
part thereof, as the occasion may demand.—

On turning my attention to the interior situation of
the State, I perceive with regret, that within the parishes
of Feliciana Baton Rouge, St. Helena & St. Tammany
(which have recently been annexed to Louisiana) the

Civil Authority has become so weakened & relaxed, that the laws have lost much of their influence, & in the parish of St. Tammany particularly are scarcely felt.— I advise therefore Gentlemen, that such provisions as you shall think proper to prescribe for these parishes, may be passed with all convenient dispatch.—

In organizing the Judicial Department, I recommend an early decision, as to the expediency of continuing the Parish Courts, which is the more necessary, since vacancies have arisen in the parishes of Iberville, & Avoyelle, which the public Interests require to be speedily filled.— To the due preservation of the Law & of good order it is requisite, that an additional Number of Justices of the Peace, be named in several of the parishes:— But it devolves upon the Legislature, to declare in what manner they shall be appointed.—

Signed/ W. C. C. Claiborne

—— ,, —— ,, ——

New. Orleans   )
Augst. 14. 1812)

To James Wilkinson

New. Orleans 14th Augst. 1812

Dr. Sir

An excellent Company of Volunteer Militia, lately formed, & consisting of about fifty Citizens of good Character & standing are in complete uniform & wanting only arms, to be in readiness for service.— can you loan me fifty stands of muskets? I will give you my special receipt, & will pledge myself, to have them returned in the same good order in which they are received, whenever you or the Officer Commanding the District shall require.— This Company of Volunteer Militia, will be on duty on Thursday next, & wish to obtain arms in time, to have them previously put in Complete order!

I am, Dr. Sir,

Your obedt. Servt.

(Signed)   W. C. C. Claiborne

——— „ ——— „ ———

GENTLEMEN OF THE SENATE, AND OF THE HOUSE OF REPRESENTATIVES!

I have the honor to lay before you, a report of the Regents of the University of Orleans, accompanied with a general plan of the College in New Orleans, and several Copies of the Rules & Regulations prescribed for that Seminary.

(Signed)   W. C. C. Claiborne

——— „ ——— „ ———

New. Orleans   )
Augst. 14th 1812)

To Judge Carr

New. Orleans 14th Augst. 1812

Nachitoches

——— „ ———

Since my letter of the 12th. I have understood, that many persons from different parts of this State, & from the Mississippi. Territory, were on their way to Nachitoches, with a view of joining in the expedition against the Spanish Dominions:— They are said to consist principally of Native Americans, & those I hope, will on seeing my proclamation, desist from their project.— But if otherwise, I have only to repeat my request, that you would act with energy, & cause the Laws to be respected.— You may call (with confidence) upon the of-

ficer Commanding at Fort Claiborne for all necessary
aid; he has been instructed to afford it.—

                         I am, Sir,
                              Very Respectfully
                         signed/   W. C. C. Claiborne

                    ————— ,, ————— ,, —————

                         To Judge Steele

                    New Orleans 17th Augst. 1812

    Baton Rouge)
Dear Sir,
    Shortly after issuing the enclosed proclamation, a
Man of the name of William Francis came to me & said,
he had intended to proceed to Nachitoches in a barge,
with a number of passengers, whom he believed designed
to join the *Mexican expedition,* & understanding the Government approved the *same,* he had not supposed any
blame would attach to him.— But finding from the Proclamation, that the expedition was unauthorized, he
should no longed favour it, or any person concerned; &
on proof of his sincerity, he delivered me four stand of
U: S: Arms, which were found in possession of some of
the persons, who had engaged their passage.— The next
day Francis again came to me, & said that having taken
in freight for Natchitoches, his private Interest required
he should proceed thither;— But as it was probable, suspicion would at this time attach to all Boats proceeding
to that quarter, he solicited for his security a passport,
which I furnished him, under a belief that he was sincere
in his professions of respect for the Laws. I have this
moment been informed, that the whole of this conduct
was a finesse & that Francis left this place two days
since with all the persons who had originally engaged to
accompany him.— I have therefore to request, that you
would take means to see Francis, as soon as he should
reach Baton Rouge & demand of him his passport, & on

receiving it, that you should say to him, that he had deceived me, & that I had requested you to obtain the passport & to transmit it to me.— I have further to request, that you would cause the Francis's Barge, the Passengers & Crew to be examined, & if there be reasonable ground to suspect, that the object of the voyage to Natchitoches is in any manner to co-operate in the expedition against the Spanish Dominions, that you will bond Francis & the passengers to their good behaviour, or have recourse to such other precedure, in conformity to the Laws, as may in your Judgment be deemed correct. I am, Sir,

Signed/   W. C. C. Claiborne

————— ,, ————— ,, —————

New. Orleans 18th August 1812.

My dear Sir,

I have received your friendly letter, & am very thankful for the Interest you take in my welfare.— I owe the people of Louisiana many obligations for the high honor confered on me, & the first object of my heart shall be to advance their prosperity;— But the difficulties in my way are considerable & not easily surmounted; already my enemies have succeeded in dividing the Senate & Executive; The former claims under the Constitution, the power of nominating to Office, & pretend that the duty of the Executive is to Commission, such persons as the Senate shall select. This doctrine being opposed in my judgment to the Spirit or letter of the Constitution, I cannot & will not submit to it. The Consequence is, that no appointments have been made, nor will any take place, until the Delegation from Florida, shall decide the contest.—

In volunteering your services, we have another proof that the Spirit of Seventy Six is not yet extinguished;— the Example is inestimable, & will produce the happiest effect; the Commissions for the Company shall be forwarded as soon as the Legislature, shall pass a Militia Law, now under Consideration; But, for the present I can do nothing (officially) in forwarding the patriotic exertions of yourself & Captn. Bellenger, in as much, as I have no authority to issue a single Commission— but I hope the Legislature will in a few days relieve me from this embarrassment. I rejoice at the prospect of your becoming a permanent Citizen of Louisiana;— be assured of my friendship, & of my sincere disposition to serve you. You ought to occupy in the Militia of the State that high rank to which your long & faithful service entitle you, & the first opportunity shall be embraced by me to confer it;— Under the Civil Government, whenever it is in my power to serve you, I shall give a proof of my confidence, in your virtue & patriotism. I am one of those, who feel grateful to the Soldiers of the Revolution.— I consider them as the fathers of my Country, & having great claims on the public patronage.

In the affair of McFarland, the conduct of Judge Wykoff & the Citizens, & of Captn. Ballenger meet my entire approbation. I am sorry that the arrest of the Offenders, was attended with so much bloodshed,— But their resistance made it indispensable, & the example may, & I hope will, have a good effect.—

Give my best wishes to Captn. Ballenger & say to him, that I shall answer his communications by the ensuing Mail.—

I am, &c@ &c@ &c@
(Signed)   W. C. C. Claiborne

——— ,, ——— ,, ———

To James Wilkinson
New. Orleans 21st Augst. 1812

Sir,

Your letter of the 14th Instant, was received on the day of its date; I am awaiting with great anxiety, the passage of a Militia Law, now before the Legislature, which I hope, will be so framed, as to enable me, to act with decision & promptitude on the subject of your Communication; In the mean time, I can only repeat to you the pleasure I shall take in zealously co-operating in all measures, essential to the safety of this Section of the Union.—

> I am,
> Sir,
> Your obdt. Servt.
> (Signed)   W. C. C. Claiborne
> —— ,, —— ,, ——

GENTLEMEN OF THE SENATE & OF THE HOUSE OF REPRESENTATIVES!

I have the honor to lay before you a letter, which General Wilkinson has addressed to me, by virtue of instructions from the President of the United States.

It being important that I should act on this occasion with promptitude, I beg leave to repeat my solicitude for the early passage of such regulations respecting the Militia, as you may deem expedient.—

> Signed/   W. C. C. Claiborne
> —— ,, —— ,, ——

New Orleans   )
Augst. 22nd 1812)

GENTLEMEN OF THE SENATE & HOUSE OF REPRESENTATIVES!

Between the Red River & the Sabine & within the chartered limits of Louisiana, there is a settlement commonly called the post of Bayou Pierre, to which the authority of this State, has not yet been extended.— This Settlement (which is believed to consist of fifty families) is too remote from Natchitoches, to annex it conveniently to that parish;— I submit therefore the expediency of creating by Law, another parish, which shall include the post of Bayou Pierre & of making provision for the appointment within the same of a parish Judge, Justices of the peace, & such other Civil Officers as may be necessary to the preservation of good order, & the due execution of the Laws.—

(Signed)   W. C. C. Claiborne

New. Orleans   )
Augst. 25. 1812   )

A Circular Letter from the Governor.

To   New. Orleans Augst. 25. 1812.

Judge Steele,   )
Judge Hampton)
Judge Osborn   )
      &   )
Judge Warner   )

I have the honor to enclose you a Writ of election, & to request that it may be duly executed.— I also enclose for your instruction a Copy of the Constitution, & several Copies of the Act of the Legislature apportioning the representation of that part of Florida annexed to the State of Louisiana & for other purposes. The Laws refered to, in the Act aforesaid, as governing elections within the former limits of the State of Louisiana, are two Acts of the Territorial Government, the one entitled "An Act prescribing the formalities to be observed in the "election of Representatives of the Territory of Orleans" passed on the 4th of June 1806, and the other An Act supplementary to the Act last mentioned, passed on the 14th of April 1807.

I am, &c@ &c@ &c@
(Signed)   W. C. C. Claiborne

GENTLEMEN OF THE SENATE & OF THE HOUSE OF REPRE-
    SENTATIVES!

The collection of the Taxes by the several parish
Judges, has at all times been considered by them as a
very unpleasant duty.— It has already occasioned several resignations, & in some instances prevented Citizens, in whom the public placed high Confidence, from accepting the office of Judge.— I much fear a continuance
of this regulation may induce the Judges to retire & that
at the present period, when the durability of the Parish
Court system is so very uncertain, I shall experience difficulty in filling satisfactorily, the vacancies which exist
or such as may arise.— With a view therefore to prevent embarrassments, & the better to secure a punctual
collection of the revenues, I suggest for consideration,
the expediency of providing by Law, for the division of
the State into *five or more Collection Districts,* & for the
appointment within each of a Collecting Officer, or that
some other means be resorted to, calculated to ensure *a
faithful accountability,* & upon terms the least expensive.

                    (Signed)   W. C. C. Claiborne
New. Orleans 28th Augst. 1812

To Col. Tousard

                    New Orleans Augst. 31st 1812.

French Consul   )
    New Orleans)
Sir,

I have the honor to acknowledge the receipt of your
letter under date of the 29th Inst: making a tender of
your own *Services* in defence of this State & those also of
the Subjects of France who have found an assylum in
Louisiana, & requesting permission to organize a separate Corps under your Command.

I justly appreciate the generous motives by which you are actuated; but previous to returning a positive answer to your request, I must ask the favour of you to make me acquainted with number & names of the Gentlemen who propose to form this Military association.—

        I am, Sir, &c@ &c@ &c@

           (Signed)   W. C. C. Claiborne

———— ,, ———— ,, ————

GENTLEMEN OF THE SENATE & HOUSE OF REPRESENTATIVES*!*

In several of the parishes, an augmentation of Justices of the Peace, is essential to the Convenience of the Citizens, & to the maintenance of good order.— I therefore recommend, that previous to the adjournment of the Legislature, the mode of appointing these Officers be permanently fixed, or that the Executive be vested with Authority to appoint & Commission during the recess of the Legislature such number of Justices of the Peace, as may be found necessary to the due execution of the Laws.

           (Signed)   W. C. C. Claiborne

———— ,, ———— ,, ————

New Orleans)
1 Sept: 1812)

A Message from the Governor, returning a Bill with his objections.

GENTLEMEN OF THE HOUSE OF REPRESENTATIVES!

I have considered, the Bill, entitled, "An Act supple-"mentary to An Act to regulate the Conditions & forms "of the emanicpation of Slaves"— & I now return it to the House, in which it originated with the following objection!

It puts to hazard the character, the peace of mind & even the Lives of unoffending Citizens, by subjecting them to be denounced by Slaves, to whom the Bills holds out such inducement, the promise of freedom as to expose innocence itself to accusation.— In some instances the Provisions of this Bill may tend to bring Offenders to punishment; But as I fear they might also operate to the injury & oppression of good Men, I should regret to see them introduced into our Code of Laws.—

(Signed)   W. C. C. Claiborne

—— ,, —— ,, ——

New. Orleans
Sept: 2d 1812

———

GENTLEMEN OF THE SENATE AND OF THE HOUSE OF REPRESENTATIVES!

Having under stood that a Memorial from the administrators of the Charity Hospital of New. Orleans, was now under consideration, I have thought it a duty to lay before you, two original Letters which have been addressed to me, shewing the deplorable State, to which that Institution is reduced for the want of funds.—

(Signed)   W. C. C. Claiborne

—— ,, —— ,, ——

New. Orleans   )
September 4th 1812.)

A Message from the Governor, making several nominations.—

GENTLEMEN OF THE SENATE!

Several parish Judges having resigned, & the Public interest requiring that their successors should be speedily appointed, I have the honor to submit to the Senate for their advice and *Consent,* the following Nominations to wit:

John Dutton of Point-Coupeé to be Judge of the Parish of Iberville in the place of Nathan Merian resigned.

Kenneth McCrummins of Avoyelles to be Judge of that parish in the place of Thomas F. Olliver, resigned.—

Ranson Easton of Attackapas to be Judge of the Parish of St. Martin in the place of Seth: Lewis resigned—And Edward Lauve of Natchitoches to be Judge in the place of John C. Carr, who has tendered his resignation.

I take this occasion also to renew to the Senate the nomination of Lewis Bartholemew Macarty of New Orleans as a fit person to fill the office of Secretary of State. —In conducting the business of the Executive Department the aid of that officer is essential & the public service will be promoted by such an appointment.— It is very questionable whether the Secretary of the late Territory of Orleans, is at this time authorized to act as Secretary of the State of Louisiana. The powers given to that officer in the Schedule to the Constitution were evidently designed to be only temporary. The 19th Article of the 3 Section of the Constitution says, "A Sec-"retary of State shall be appointed & Commissioned "during that term for which the Governor shall have "been elected, if he shall so long behave himself well."—In order to meet this Constitutional provision, immediately after being sworn into office, I had the honor to nominate to the Senate, a Secretary of State. It would seem also, from the Resolution entered into by the Senate on the 6th of August last, that on their part, they were alike impressed with the necessity of appointing & Commissioning a Secretary of State, for and during the time mentioned in the Section of the Constitution above refered to.

Signed/ W. C. C. Claiborne

——— ,, ——— ,, ———

A Message from the Governor, returning a Bill with his objections.

GENTLEMEN OF THE SENATE!

I have considered the Bill, entitled "an Act for regu-"lating the Election of Representatives for this State "to the Congress of the U: States," and I now return it to the House, in which it originated, in order that the first Section may be so modified as to meet what I presume to have been the object of the Legislature, an early election.—

The Bill (which was presented to me on yesterday the 3rd of September) directs an election to be holden on the fourth Monday in September next,— and of course if approved in its present shape, the Election would be postponed to a very distant day.—

As the first Section of this Bill must necessarily be reconsidered, it seems to me desirable to render the same more explicit.— Two elections are contemplated to be holden in the same days;— The one for a Representative to the present Congress, whose term of service will expire on the 3rd of March next, & the other for a Representative to the next succeeding Congress, whose term of service will expire on the 3rd of March 1815.— If the Judges of the elections were directed to furnish on the occasion two separate Boxes, & to make the result of the examination of each Box the subject of a distinct & separate return, it would prevent confusion & Irregularity.

As regards the proper period for holding these elections, I shall not oppose the *will* of the Senate & House of Representatives; But I am of opinion, that information of the same, cannot be generally communicated throout the State, in less time, than six weeks.—

(Signed)   W. C. C. Claiborne

————— „ ————— „ —————

New. Orleans   )
Septber 4th 1812   )

———————————

A Message from the Governor, returning a Bill with his objections.

GENTLEMEN OF THE HOUSE OF REPRESENTATIVES!

I have considered the Bill entitled "An Act supple-"mentary to an Act for Regulating & governing the Mi-"litia of the Territory of Orleans" and as I cannot approve the same, I now return it to the House in which it originated.—

I object to the passage of this Bill because it would tend to throw the whole Militia into a State of Confusion & Chaos;— which would at any time, be cause of regret, but at a moment like the present, of War & peril, might prove hazardous to the public safety.— Because some of the provisions of the Bill are contradictory, & others cannot be executed.— And because, there are officers created by the Bill, on whom high duties devolve, & for whose nomination & appointment no provision is made. There are several Regulations proposed that would greatly contribute to the good of the Service:— Among others those contained in the 3rd 14th 16th 17th 18th &

20th Sections would be particularly useful & which I regret it is not in my power to separate from the Sections
which appear to me exceptionable.

(Signed)   W. C. C. Claiborne

„   „

New. Orleans   )
Septber 5th. 1812   )

A Message from the Governor, returning a Bill with his
objections.

GENTLEMEN OF THE HOUSE OF REPRESENTATIVES!

I have considered, the Bill entitled "An Act supple-
"mentary to an Act to regulate the Conditions & forms
"of the emancipation of Slaves"— And I now return it
to the House, in which is originated with the following
objection!

It puts to hazard the character, the peace of mind &
even the lives of unoffending Citizens, by subjecting them
to be denounced by Slaves, to whom, the Bill holds out
such inducement, the promise of freedom, as to expose
innocence itself to accusations.—

The provisions of the *Bill* may in some instances tend
to bring the Guilty to punishment; But as they may & I
fear would also operate to the oppression of good Men, I
should regret to see them introduced into our Code of
Laws.—

(Signed)   W. C. C. Claiborne

„   „

New. Orleans
Septber 6th 1812

A Message from the Governor, returning a Resolution, with his objections.

GENTLEMEN OF THE HOUSE OF REPRESENTATIVES.

I have considered the resolution, declaring "that the Judges of the Superior Court are by the Schedule of the Constitution authorized to proceed in the duties of their offices, & that provision should be made accordingly," and I object to its passage, upon the ground, that it is rendered useless, in Consequence of a Law approved on yesterday, which fixes the Salary of the Judges of the Superior Court.— The Resolution, is therefore returned to the House in which it originated.

                    (Signed)   W. C. C. Claiborne
New. Orleans   )   ——— „ ——— „ ———
September 7th 1812.)
                    ——————————

By WILLIAM C. C. CLAIBORNE
Governor of the State of Louisiana.

Be it known, that if on the fourth Monday of the present month, September, there should not be a Judge of the Parish of St. Martin in the County of Attackapas duly qualified according to Law, to preside at, & conduct the election for Representative to Congress, directed by Law to be holden on that day & the two following days within the Parish aforesaid, then & in that case, I do by these presents nominate & appoint Seth Lewis a Commissioner *ad hoc* to preside at the said election, & to conduct the same according to Law.—

Given under my hand & private Seal,
there being no Seal for the State yet
provided, at New Orleans on the 7th. of September
1812, & in the 37th year of the Independence
of the United States.—

                    signed   W. C. C. Claiborne
                    ——— „ ——— „ ———

A Writ of Election.

WILLIAM C. C. CLAIBORNE
Governor of the State of Louisiana.

To Carlier D'Outremer, Judge of the Parish of Ascension, & A: D: Tureaud Judge of the Parish of St. James, within the County of Arcadia,—

WHEREAS I have received the resignation of Joseph Landry, who had been elected a Senator to the general Assembly of this State, for the County of Acadia, it becomes my duty to issue this my Proclamation hereby requiring & directing that an election be holden, at the usual places of holding elections in the County aforesaid, on the fourth Monday of the present Month (September) & the two following days, to supply the vacancy occasioned by the resignation of the said Joseph Landry, & that the election be conducted according to Law.—

Given under my hand & private
Seal, there being no Seal for the
State yet provided, at New Orleans,
on the 11th day of September in
the year One Thousand Eight hundred & twelve
Signed/ W. C. C. Claiborne

————— ,, ————— ,, —————

A Writ of Election.

WILLIAM C. C. CLAIBORNE
Governor of the State of Louisiana.

To Charles Latour Judge of the Parish of Plaquemine, & A. Mendez Judge of the Parish of St Bernard.—

WHEREAS Godfrey Ollivier, who had been elected a Representative to the general assembly of this State, from the first Senatorial District has resigned his Seat &

the same is now vacant.— I have thought proper to issue this my Proclamation, hereby requiring and directing an election to be holden at the usual places of holding elections in the District aforesaid, on the fourth Monday of this present Month (September) & the two following days, to supply the vacancy occasioned by the resignation of the said Godfrey Ollivier, & that the said election be conducted according to law.

> Given under my hand & Private
> Seal, there being no Seal for the
> State yet provided, at New Orleans,
> on the 11th day of September 1812.
>
> (Signed)   W. C. C. Claiborne

———— ,, ———— ,, ————

To the Banks

New. Orleans 11th Sept. 1812.

Sir,

I have the pleasure to enclose you a Commission by which you are appointed Judge of the Parish of *Avoyelles;* Previous to entering upon your duties, it is necessary to take an Oath to support the Constitution of the U: States & an Oath of office, which any Justice of the Peace in the State, is authorized to administer.— It is also requisite that you enter into a Bond, with two Securities, in the Sum of five thousand Dollars, for the faithful performance of your duties; The form of the Bond will be given you on application to your predecessor in office, & as to your Securities, any Citizens of the State, of fair reputation & possessed of real property, will be accepted.—

> I am,
> Sir,
> Very Respectfully
> Your most obdt. Sert.
> (Signed)   W. C. C. Claiborne

———— ,, ———— ,, ————

To the President   )
  & Directors of the Bank   )
  of Orleans, The Louisiana)
  Bank & Planters Bank   )

New Orleans Sept: 11th. 1812

Desirous of obtaining *on the Credit* & for the use of the State of Louisiana, a loan of twenty thousand Dollars, I request to be informed, whether you can accommodate me, with the whole or any part of that Sum, & upon what Terms.

A Copy of the Law, under which I act is herewith enclosed.—

I have the honor to be, &c@ &c@ &c@
(Signed)   W. C. C. Claiborne

―――― „ ―――― „ ――――

―――――――――

To William Eustis

New. Orleans Sept: 14th. 1812

Secy. at War.

―――― „ ――――

Sir,

The *Legislature of Louisiana* deeply impressed with the dangers to which this State is exposed, & solicitous to make the requisite arrangements to co-operate effectionally with the general Government, in opposing any attempt of the enemy against this Section of the Union, has made it my duty to make application to the President of the U: States for the loan of four thousand stand of Muskets, & four thousand sabres, & as many pieces of field Artillery, as may in my judg'ment be necessary for the use of the Militia of Louisiana.—

A Copy of the resolution on this subject, as adopted by the Legislature is herewith enclosed, which I pray you to lay before the President, & to express my readiness in the name of this State, to enter into any just stipulation respecting the safe keeping of these Arms & for their Redelivery.— If the President should deem proper to loan the Muskets & Sabres desired, I must ask the favour of you to direct them to be conveyed to the post of Baton Rouge, & I promise in behalf of the State to defray any expense attaching such conveyance to an amount not exceeding five thousand dollars.—

As relates to the *field Artillery,* I am of opinion that two 4 pounders, two light sixes & 2 eight pounders would for the present answer our purposes, & these or at least a part of them (together with the necessary apparatus including a small supply of Ball & Grape Shot) might I presume be spared, without inconvenience to the service, from the train of Artillery now at N. Orleans & Baton Rouge.—

I have the honor to be, &c@ &c@ &c@

(Signed)   W. C. C. Claiborne

——— ,, ——— ,, ———

———————

To James Wilkinson

New. Orleans Sept: 22d. 1812.

Commg. the U: S: Troops

SIR,

I have the honor to acknowledge the receipt of your letter of the 17th Instant. In accomplishing my wishes relative to the auxiliary force, which you requested on the 14th. Ultimo, I have found myself exposed to embarrassments which were not anticipated. The general Assembly of the State (being in session at that time) was invited so to annex the existing Laws, as to put it in the powers of the Executive, to array in defence of the State, its whole Militia or such part thereof as occasion might require;— & as an inducement to doing so, the two Houses were informed of the extent of your requisition.

A mandatory Act was proposed; But it contained provisions which the Executive could not approve, & the sessions of the general Assembly were finally closed, without Legislating on this interesting subject.— Hence in part arises the embarrassments to which I allude;— Confiding however in the patriotism of the State, I stil feel myself at liberty to promise a zealous co-operation in such defensive measures, as may from time to time become necessary.— If therefore you will state to me, what particular positions on the Lafourche & the Lake Barrataria, you would wish to assume, & shall on your part make the necessary arrangements for provisioning these posts, I will order each to be occupied by a Company of Militia, & will have the detachment in readiness "to be mustered & inspected by a regular officer," with all possible dispatch.— In like manner I will (if you should under the instructions of the President think proper to make the requisition) order into the service of the U: S: one or two Companies of Militia to take post on the Teche within the County of Attackapas, a point, which in my judgment, ought not to remain as it now is, wholly unprotected.— I will further hold in readiness for service within the City of New Orleans, a disposable force of five hundred men to act as Exegencies may demand, either to quell internal commotions, or to meet an invading foe; but not to be Considered as being in the pay of the U: S: until ordered to take the field. To effect however these views, and as an indispensible requisite, I must ask of you the loan of Arms (the Militia being for the most part without them) & of some necessary Camp equipage.—

    I am,
      Sir,
        With very great respect
         Your mo: ob: Sert.
       Signed/ W. C. C. Claiborne

To Gov. David Holmes

New Orleans 29th Sept: 1812

M. Territory.

Sir,

On the 9th. Ult: I had the honor to enclose you a letter from the Judge of the Parish of Biloxy communicating intelligence of Indian depredations, as also a Memorial addressed to me, by a Number of the Inhabitants on pearl River, expressive of their great apprehensions, & entreating me, to send into the Chactaw Nation Simon Favre, whose influence with the Indians, the Petitioners believed to be such, as to insure a continuance of Peace.— About the same time I received sundry letters from respectable Citizens of the parishes of St. Helena & St. Tammany within this State, informing me of the frequent menaces of the Chactaws, & requesting that measures might be taken for the safety of the settlements.— Desirious of ascertaining whether or not there was ground for this alarm, I addressed a Talk to the Chiefs of the Chactaws (of which a Copy has been transmitted to your Excellency & sent it by a Special Messenger, Mr. Simon Favre, who was particularly instructed, to inform Mr. Dinsmoor, Mr. Pilchylum, or any other agent of the U: S: whom he might meet in the Nation of the object of his visit.— Since Mr. Favre's departure, I have received from him two Letters, the first advised me of his arrival in the Nation, & of the favorable disposition towards the U: S: of a Chief who was the Bearer of his Communication; & the second announcing the arrest & detention of Mr. Favre as a prisoner by orders of Mr. Dinsmoor. I am persuaded this proceeding is the Act of a subordinate Agent, & that it is not approved by your Excellency.

At a period, when the emissaries of the English, are busily engaged in inciting the Savages to War against the U: S: the Citizen (acting under the orders of the Chief Majistrate of a State) whose sole object in visiting the Chactaws was to incline them to peace, did not merit the treatment Mr. Favre has received! and permit me to add Sir, that at a period, when the Indian Tomahawk was believed to be raised against the Frontier settlers of this State on Pearl River & elsewhere, I felt it a duty, to take immediate means to ascertain the extent of the danger; so as to be enabled to direct the corresponding measures.—

I knew that the Governors of Tennessee, in the vicinity of which State the Chickassaws are settled, are in the habit of addressing Talks *to their chiefs,* & it has (I believe) at no time been considered an interferance with the resident agent.— I have observed also, in the Newspapers, that not only Messages pass, but interviews take place between the Governor of Ohio & the Indians on the frontier of that State, nor have I understood, that any exception has been taken to the proceeding.—

I presume that Mr. Dinsmoor finding Mr. Favre in the Nation without your Excellency's passport, wishes to consider him an Intruder, & will I fear be disposed to subject that unoffending Citizen to much inconvenience. I therefore hasten to request in behalf of Mr. Favre, your Excellency's interference, & to recommend him as an honest Man & a worthy Citizen.[1]—

I am,

Sir, &c@ &c@ &c@

(Signed)   W. C. C. Claiborne

To James Monroe

New Orleans 28th Augst. 1812.

Secy of State

I have the honor to enclose you my account of the expenses incident to the taking possession of the Tract of Country East of the Mississippi & west of the Perdido

---

[1] Dinsmore was frequently arbitrary in his official acts. See affair with Andrew Jackson in Bassett's Life of Jackson.

River, in conformity to orders of the President of the U: S: under date of the 27th of October 1810. from it appears, that of the $20,000 placed at my disposition, I have only expended $4202. & 96 Cents, I felt a sincere desire to keep my expenditures within the Limits of the most prudent economy, and I persuade myself, you will not think, that these Limits have been exceeded.—

You will find enclosed, vouchers for all the Items except such as relate to my personal expences & the Sale of public horses;— These in the hurry of my journey, & in the midst of occupations of high importance, I omitted to obtain.— But I trust that a positive declaration on my part of the Correctness of the Account, in every respect, will be received in support of the Charges, for which vouchers are not exhibited.— I will add Sir, & will pledge my honor to the fact that as regards my extra personal expences, they exceeded the sum, which I have charged.— I pray you Sir, to have the goodness to lay these accounts before the President, to whom I presume they must necessarily be submitted, & to inform me of his decision thereon.—

With sentiments of respect & esteem

&c@ &c@·&c@

Signed   W. C. C. Claiborne

To Gov. Holmes

New. Orleans October 5th. 1812

M. T.

——— „ ———

I enclose you a Duplicate of my Letter under date of the 29th Ultimo & I beg leave to repeat my earnest entreaties that you would extend your protection to Mr. Simon Favre, & direct his release from Confinement.

A letter from Mr. Favre under date of the 26th of September, states that he was stil a prisoner under the order of Mr. Dinsmoor;— I repeat Sir, that Mr. Favre has committed no offence against the Laws of the U: S:; He went into the Nation under my orders, & if in this transaction there has been an improper interference with the high authorities & duties devolving upon Mr. Dinsmoor; I request that Mr. Favre may not be the sufferer.— The Citizens of the State, over which I have the honor to preside, being greatly exposed to Indian depredations, I should have been wanting in duty, not to have used my best efforts to incline the Chactaws to harmony & peace.— And it is Sir, a source of sincere regret to me, that the faithful Citizen, who has been my Agent on the occasion, should have been deemed by an Agent of the U: S: a public offender.—

I am, Sir &c@ &c@ &c@
(Signed)   W. C. C. Claiborne

———— „ ———— „ ————

To Antonio' Mendez

New Orleans October 6th. 1812

Sir,

On accepting your resignation as Judge of the Parish of S. Bernard, I beg leave to thank you for your faithful public services, & to offer you my best wishes for your health & happiness.

(Signed)   W. C. C. Claiborne

———— „ ———— „ ————

P. S. Mr. D. Harper is appointed your successor to whom, you will be pleased to deliver, the Records of the Parish.—

W. C. C. C.

———— „ ————

Dr " The United States in Acc. Curr. with W. C. C. Claiborne for Expences to the taking possession of the Tract of Country East of Mississippi & West of the Perdido River.) " Cr

To Amount due me for purchase of horses & as Pr. Account No. 1. . . .	$564.75	1810 Novr. 3. By my draft on the post master Genl. in favor of the post Master at Lexington)	$ 120.--
To Amount of sundry payment &c & as Pr. Account No. 2. . . .	$3638.21	Dec: 3. By my draft on the Secy. of State in favor of John Lang. . . .	$ 800.--
		" " By my draft on the Secy. of State in favor of David Wright. . . .	500.--
		1811 Jany. 22 By my draft on the Secy. of State in favor of Jos: Saul. . . .	2000.--
		Balce. due from the U: States. . .	782.96
Dolls. - - $4202.96		Dolls.-$ 4202.96	

ERRORS EXCEPTED.

New Orleans.

A Writ of Election.

WILLIAM C. C. CLAIBORNE
Governor of the State of Louisiana.

To Andrew Latour Judge of the Parish of St. Charles and Achille Trouard Judge of the Parish of St. John Baptist.—

WHEREAS P. B. St. Martin, & T. E. Arnauld who had been elected Representatives to the general Assembly of this State, from the County of German Coast, have resigned their Seats, & the same are now vacant;— I have thought proper to issue this my Proclamation hereby requiring & directing an election to be holden at the usual places of holding elections in the County aforesaid on the fourth Monday of this present month (October) & the two following days to supply the vacancy occasioned by the resignation of the said P. B. St. Martin and T. E. Arnauld, & that the said election be conducted to Law.—

> Given under my hand and the Seal of the State at New Orleans on the 6th of October, in the year 1812.—
> (Signed)   W. C. C. Claiborne
> ———— ,, ———— ,, ————

Major General   New Orleans 8th October 1812
  Thomas Posey
  Baton Rouge
My dear Sir,
  Confiding in your private and public virtues— Grateful for your past services to your Country, & assured of your devotion to the principles of Civil & religious free-

dom;— Believing also that you highly appreciate the government & union of these States, & that the present eventful Crisis, you will firmly support such measures as the honor, the safety, the Independence of the Nation advise, I take great pleasure, in transmitting you a Commission, by which you are appointed a Senator of the United States.[1]— It is a source of regret, that this nomination is only temporary.— But I nevertheless hope you will not on that account decline the service.— As Congress will be in session early in the ensuing Month, it is important that you repair to Washington, with all possible dispatch.

In the event of your acceptance, it only remains for me to express a fervent wish, that my choice may be confirmed by the Legislature of this State,— And to assure you, that,—

I am, &c@ &c@ &c@
(Signed)   W. C. C. Claiborne

——— ,, ——— ,, ———

By William C. C. Claiborne
Governor of the State of Louisiana

In the name & by authority of the State.

WHEREAS John Noel Destrehan who had been elected by the Legislature of the State of Louisiana, a Senator to the Congress of the United States, did by a letter bearing date the 1st. day of this present month October, & directed to the undersigned announce his resignation as a Member of the Senate of the United States, to which he had been elected as aforesaid;— And whereas the Legislature of the State, not being at this time in session,

---

[1] This appointment was made to fill a vacancy caused by the resignation of Destréhan, who was elected by the legislature.

a power devolves on the undersigned, under the Constitution of the U: States & the Law of the State, to make a temporary appointment of a Senator to the Congress of the United States, in place of the said John Noel Destrehan,— Now therefore be it known that I William C. C. Claiborne Governor of the State of Louisiana, reposing special Trust & Confidence in the Integrity, patriotism & abilities of Thomas Posey a Citizen of the U: States, & an Inhabitant of this State do nominate & appoint him a Senator from this State to the Congress of the U. States, & I do authorize & empower him to exercise all the powers, & to discharge all the duties incumbent on him, the said Thomas Posey, as a Member of the Senate of the U: States from & after the date hereof, until the "next meeting of the Legislature of Louisiana which "shall then fill the vacancy" which the resignation of the said John Nole Destrehan has occasioned in the Senate of the United States.—

In testimony whereof, I have caused these letters to be made Patent, & the Seal of the State to be hereunto affixed.

> Given under my hand on the
> 8th day of October, in the year
> 1812., & in the 37th year of the
> Independence of the United States.
> Signed/ W. C. C. Claiborne

———— ,, ———— ,, ————

To James Wilkinson

New Orleans 12th Oct: 1812.

New Orleans

———— ,, ————

Sir,

I have the honor to transmit to you a letter addressed to me by the acting collector of this District, accompanied with a disposition, announcing a serious opposition to the

Revenue Laws, by an armed Banditti on the Lake Barataria. The Collector requests Military aid in enforcing the Laws, which I trust you will be enabled to afford & he suggests the expediency of your placing the armed force under the Command of Captain Ballenger, who has received a Special Commission as Inspector of the Revenue.— After perusing the letter of the Colector & the deposition refered to, I will thank you to return them to me.—

I am, Sir,

Sigd. W. C. C. Claiborne

———— ,, ———— ,, ————

To Col. Tousard

New Orleans 13th Oct. 1812

French Consul
New Orleans.

Sir,

Having understod, that several persons, inhabitants of this City, declare themselves to be Citizens of France, & on that ground claim exemption from Militia service, I deem it proper to inform you that every Individual, who was residing in this State at the period of our admission into the Union, (& who is not particularly exempted by the Law) is considered by me, as subject to the operation of the Militia Laws, & must conform to the same.—

I am, Sir,

(Signed)   W. C. C. Claiborne

———— ,, ———— ,, ————

To Judge Steele

New Orleans 13th October 1812

Baton Rouge.

The Legislature having directed by law, that there should be appointed for the Town of Baton Rouge, a Notary Public, & an auctioneer, I have the honor to inform you that I have named M. Charles Tessier to the first office & Christoval de Armas to the office of Auctioneer.— These officers, are vested with the same powers, & are entitled to the same emoluments, as are allowed by Law to the Notaries and Auctioneers appointed for the City of New Orleans.

Mr. Destrehan having resigned his Seat in the Senate of the United States, I have appointed Gen. Thomas Posey (temporarily) to fill the vacancy. I hope this nomination will be pleasing to my fellow Citizens of the County of Filiciana, & that their Senators & Representatives to the General Assembly, will at the ensuing session of the Legislature, unite in confirming the same.— I have always considered the Soldiers & patriots of Seventy six, as the fathers of our Country, & that their services should never be forgotten by a grateful people.— Of Genl. Posey's private virtues, all who know him can bear testimony, & of his faithful public services every one acquainted with American History, must have a knowledge.—

> I am,
> > Sir,
> > > With esteem
> > > > Your Hum. Sevt.
> > > > Signed/ W. C. C. Claiborne

———— „ ———— „ ————

Copy of a Letter from James Madison, President of the U: S. to His Excy. Gov. Claiborne.

Dear Sir

I have reecived your favor of the 2 Ulto. and very sincerely congratulate you on the high proof given you of the Confidence & affection of your fellow Citizens of Louisiana. The event is important in several political views, as well as gratifying to your personal friends. To myself it is a source of unfeigned pleasure.

I say nothing on public affairs: because I could say nothing which will not reach you with more certainty, & probably in less time than this letter, through printed vihitcles.

Accept my sincere esteem & friendly regards.—

Signed *James Madison*

Gov. Claiborne—

To James Wilkinson

New Orleans 16th Oct. 1812.

New Orleans

——— ,, ———

Sir,

From the enclosed return of the strength & State of the Detachment drawn from the Militia of this City which I propose to hold in readiness for acting duty & to order into the service of the U: States whenever it is deemed necessary for the safety of this Capitol or of the State, you will observe that to place it in a situation to act with effect there is wanting Muskets and Cartridge Boxes.— Permit me, Sir, to request of you the loan from the Stores of the U: States of the above number of Muskets & Catridges Boxes;— I will give you my receipt for the same, & will cause them to returned, whenever, they shall be required by yourself, of the officer Commanding the Troops of the U: States in this State.—

I hope to be enabled to render this Detachment of Militia a respectable Corps, & I persuade myself if the occasion demands, it will zealously & effectually Co-operate with the regular force against the enemy.

I am,

Sir, &c@

Signed/ W. C. C. Claiborne

——— ,, ——— ,, ———

To Diego Murphy

Comml. Agent   New. Orleans 20th Oct. 1812
New. Orleans
——— „ ———

Sir,

I have received your letter of yesterday giving information, that one hundred men, recruited in this City, were about marching to Nacogdoches with hostile intentions towards the Government of Spain.—

No person is authorized within the Territory or jurisdiction of the U: S:, to begin or set on foot or provide or propose the means for any Military expedition or enterprise to be carried on from thence, against the Territory or Dominions of any foreign Prince or State with whom the U: S: are at peace.'' Whatever information therefore, you may be in possession of, relative to a contemplated expedition from this City, or elsewhere within this State against the Dominions of Spain, you will be pleased to communicate on Oath, to the Honorable Judge Hall of the District Court of Louisiana, & such measures will be ordered by that Majestrate, as Justice shall dictate, & the Laws warrant.—

I am,
Sir,
Your obedt Servt.
(Signed)   W. C. C. Claiborne
——— „ ——— „ ———

By WILLIAM CHARLES, COLE, CLAIBORNE
Governor of the State of Louisiana.

A Proclamation.

WHEREAS, Considerations of public Interest, render an early Session of the Legislature of this State necessary, I have thought proper by virtue of the powers in

VI—13

me vested, to issue this my Proclamation, hereby conven-
ing "the General Assembly at the Seat of Government,"
on Monday the 23d. day of November next, & requiring
each & every member of the Senate & House of Representatives, to be punctual in his attendance on the day aforesaid.—

In testimony whereof, I have caused
these letters to be made patent, & the
Seal of the State to be hereunto annexed.

Given under my hand at the City
of New. Orleans, on the 20th. day
of October, in the year of our
Lord, one thousand eight hundred & Twelve, & in the thirty
seventh year of the Independence of the U. States of America

By the Governor   Signed/   W. C. C. Claiborne
    L. B. Macarty   ——— ,, ——— ,, ———
    Secy. of State.

———

To the Honble.
    The President of   State of Louisiana
        The Senate of the U: S:

                        New. Orleans 25 Octber 1812.
SIR,
    The Honorable John Noel Destrehan who had been
elected by the Legislature of Louisiana, a Senator of the
United States, having notified me of his resignation, &
the Legislature not being at this time in Session, it has become my duty under the powers vested in the Executive
of the State, to fill the vacancy by a temporary appointment.— To General Posey, a Citizen of the United
States, & an Inhabitant of Louisiana is confided the Im-

portant Trust, and I now have the honor to enclose you
a Duplicate Copy of his Credentials.—

> I am, Sir, &c@ &c@ &c@
> (Signed) W. C. C. Claiborne

———— „ ———— „ ————

To James Neilson

New Orleans 6 November 1812

Manshac
Dear Sir

I have the honor to enclose you a Commission for Mr.
John Devenport as a Justice of the Peace, which you
will be pleased to deliver to him, & I take great pleasure
in transmitting to yourself, a Commission as Sheriff of
the Parish of East Baton Rouge, in the place of your
son, who has resigned.—

Present my best wishes to your lady & family

> Your friend
> Signed/ W. C. C. Claiborne

———— „ ———— „ ————

To Thomas B. Robertson

New Orleans 8 Novber. 1812

a Representative to Congress
SIR,

M. Dejan, will deliver you Copies of a Certificate of
your late election, attested in a manner, which in the
opinion of the Attorney General meets the views of the
Law.—

> I am, Sir, @&c @&c
> (Signed) W. C. C. Claiborne

———— „ ———— „ ————

P. S. I will thank you to deliver to Mr. Dejan, the Cer-
tificates with which you were first presented.—

By WILLIAM C. C. CLAIBORNE
Governor of the State of Louisiana.

To all who shall see these presents, & more particularly the Sheriff of the first Superior Court District.—

KNOW ye, that by virtue of the powers in me vested & upon the application of the Judge & freeholders who tried Orphie a Negro Man slave belonging to the reverend Father Thomas, who states that the said Orphie is an object of mercy,— I do hereby reprieve the sentence of death pronounced by the said Judge & freeholders against the said Orphie & respite the execution thereof until the 10th. day of December next ensuing the date of these presents.—

[S]

In Witness whereof I have hereunto set my hand and caused the Seal of the State of Louisiana to be affixed this tenth day of November in the year of our Lord, One thousand eight hundred & twelve.—

Signed/   William C. C. Claiborne

————— ,, ————— ,, —————

By the Governor
L. B. Cacarty,
Secy. of State

A Writ of Election.

William C. C. Claiborne
Governor of the State of Louisiana

TO Andrew Latour Judge of the Parish of St. Charles, & Achille Trouard Judge of the Parish of St. John Baptist.—

WHEREAS Alexander LaBranche & René Trudeau who had been elected Representatives to the general Assembly of this State, from the County of German Coast in the place of P. B. St. Martin & T. E. Arnauld heretofore resigned have declined to serve in that character; I have thought proper to issue this my Proclamation hereby requiring & directing an election to be holden on the first Monday in December next & the two following days, at the usual places of holding elections within the County of German Coast, to supply the vacancy occasioned by the resignation of the said P. B. St. Martin, & T. E. Arnauld, & the refusal to serve of the said Alexander LaBranche & Rene Trudeau, who had been elected as aforesaid.—

Given under my hand & the Seal of the State, at New Orleans on the 6th of Nevember in the year 1812.—

By the Govr.

L. B. Macarty   Signed/   William C. C. Claiborne
Secy of State

A Writ of Election.

WILLIAM C. C. CLAIBORNE
Governor of the State of Louisiana.

To Cartier D'Otremer Judge of the Parish of Ascension, & A. D. Tureaud Judge of the Parish of S. James within the County of Acadia.

WHEREAS I have received the resignation of Genezy Roussain who had been elected a Representative to the General Assembly of this State for the County of Acadia, it becomes my duty to issue this my Proclamation, hereby requiring & directing an election to be holden on the first Monday in December next, & the two following days at the usual places of holding elections within the County of Acadia, to supply the vacancy occasioned by the resignation of the said Genezy Roussain, & that the said election be conducted according to Law.—

> Given under my hand & the
> Seal of the State, at New.
> Orleans on the 12th day of November in the year one thousand
> eight hundred & Twelve

By the Govr.   Signed/   W. C. C. Claiborne
    L. B. Macarty   ———— ,, ———— ,, ————
      Secy. of State

A Writ of Election.

WILLIAM C. C. CLAIBORNE
Governor of the State of Louisiana

To L. Moreau Lislet Judge of the Parish of new. Orleans.

WHEREAS I have received the resignation of Lebreton Dischapelle who had been elected a Representative from the third Senatorial District to the General Assembly of this State, it becomes my duty to issue this my Proclamation hereby requiring & directing than an election be holden on Wednesday the 25th. of this present Month (November) and the two following days, at the usual places of holding elections within the said Senatorial District, to supply the vacancy occasioned by the resignation of the said Lebreton Dischapelle and that the same be conducted according to Law.—

> Given under my hand & the Seal
> of the State, at New. Orleans on
> the 13th day of November in the
> year 1812. & in the 37th year of
> Independence of the United

By the Govr.   States.—
    L. B. Macarty   Signed/   William C C. Claiborne
      Secy. of State.

To Benj. Morgan

New Orleans Novber. 13th 1812.

New. Orleans.

Dear Sir

Previous to the receipt of your letter of the Morning (& for which I thank you) Mr. Crowdson had informed me of the events to which you allude.— I lost no time, in confering on the subject with the Military & Naval Commanders at present in *New Orleans,* & measures are in train, to enforce the Law:— Boats, Men, & Arms will be furnished the Collector, & if Mr. Crowdson should be fortunate in the selection of an officer to direct the expedition I hope we shall be enabled to bring the violators of the Law to Justice.—

With Esteem

(Signed)   W. C. C. Claiborne

———— ,, ———— ,, ————

To Paul Hamilton

New. Orleans Novr. 14th. 1812

Secy. of the Navy

Dear Sir,

I am entreated by the friends of Mr. Marchand a Native of this City who has been appointed by Commodore Shaw an Acting Midshipman in the Navy to recommend him to your patronage, & which I now do, with the sincerest pleasure, since I am assured, that, he is a young Man of great integrity of Character, the nicest sense of honor, & an excellent Seaman.— M. Marchand, who has been bred to the Sea, desirous to continue in the Naval service, is a Candidate for the honor of a Midshipman's warrant & founds his prospects for future promotion, on his own personal merits.—

> With sentiments of the greatest
> respect & esteem,—
> I am, Dr. Sir,
> Signed/   William C. C. Claiborne

——— ,, ——— ,, ———

To Dr. John Sibley

New Orleans 16th. November 1812

Natchitoches

——— ,, ———

I enclose you a Commission by which M. Manuel de Soto of Bayou Pierre, is appointed a Justice of the Peace for the Parish of Natchitoches.— As it is essential to the public interest, that the Commission be speedily received by Mr. Soto, I must ask the favour of you to forward it to him, by the earliest occasion.—

> I am,
> Dr. Sr.
> Your obedt. Sevt.
> Signed/   W. C. C. Claiborne

——— ,, ——— ,, ———

To Simon Favre

New. Orleans 16th. Novber. 1812

Pearl River
    Parish of Biloxy.

Sir, I have received & read with attention your interesting report under date of the 30th Ulto.— Your conduct in the course of the mission confided to you is approved, & to an expression of regret for the injury done you, by an Agent of the United States Government, permit me too add the assurance of my sincere disposition to be just & friendly towards you.— I have long thought, that the appointment of an Indian Agent for Indian affairs to reside on Pearl River, & who might be specially instructed to be the organ of Communication between the Governor of this State & the Chactaws was essential to the public Interest, & I know of no one more worthy of the public Confidence than yourself.— If therefore you will consent to Act in that Character, I will entreat the President of the United States to confer on you, such an Agency;— But on this & other subjects, I wish to converse freely, & hope you may find it convenient to visit this City, in the course of the next month.— We may then, fix upon a Sum also, which will remunerate you the expences incurred during your late mission, & be at the same time a reasonable Compensation for your trouble.— I am, Sir, &c@ &c@ &c@

Signed/ W. C. C. Claiborne

To J. R. Fitzgerald

New. Orleans 20th Novber. 1812.

Cashier of the Louisiana,
Sir,
    Desirous to avail myself of the disposition, (as expressed in your answer to my letter of the 11th of September last) on the part of the President & Directors of the Louisiana Bank to loan me (for the use & on the Credit of the State of Louisiana the sum of $20,000 on the usual Bank Interest, I have requested the Treasurer of the State, to call upon you, in order to obtain a form of such Note or instrument of writing as the Directors

may require me to sign, and to learn on what day the amount can be paid.—

I am, Sir, &c@ &c@ &c@
(Signed)   W. C. C. Claiborne

——— ,, ——— ,, ———

To Judge Warner

(private)

New. Orleans 15 decber 1812
Parish of St. Tammany

Dear Sir,

I have declined giving a decisive answer to your enquiries as to the extent of your present powers, because no opinion of mine, can or ought to be binding;— But taking into view, the great uncertainty as to the duration of the Parish Courts, & the probability that the Legislature now in session, will speedily introduce an entire change in our Judicial system, I would advise that you issue no process, but such as is essential to the preservation of good order or to prevent a Creditor from sustaining loss by his debtor removing without the State.—

I am, Sir, &c@ &c@ &c@
(Signed)   W. C. C. Claiborne

——— ,, ——— ,, ———

New Orleans Decbr 15th. 1812

Mr. Bringier the Father accompanied by his second Son, paid me a visit on this Morning, & in the course of Conversation, recommended to my patronage a Mr. Bourcier, who held a Commission as a Captain of Militia;

he spoke of Bourcier as a deserving Man, & the head of a large & distressed family;— In proof of Mr. Bourcier's integrity, he gave me in Confidence the following annecdote.— That he M. Bourcier, had in possession, my signature to a piece of paper for which one *of my enemys* had offered him six thousand Dollars & which he refused. — I enquired with great eagerness, to what instrument the signature was annexed, & why it was deemed so valuable.— Mr. Bringier replied, the *signature* was to the Commission.— But was so affixed that several lines might be written above it.—I asked Mr. Bringier the name of the person, who had offered for the signature six thousand Dollars; he could not tell, Mr. Bourcier had but informed him of the fact & exhibited the paper, & that he Mr. Bourcier had made the communication to put me on my guard for the future.— Mr. George W. Morgan Sheriff of the first Superior Court District, & Major of the 4th Regiment, informed me some Weeks since, that I did not observe a sufficiency of caution in signing Militia Commissions— that he had noticed several in which, there was vacant space sufficient, above the signature, to write a note or anything else, that would do me injury, & that he had heard several persons speak of the facility with which my enemies (provided they were base enough to do so) holding Militia Commissions, or could obtain them, might injure me.— I have committed these circumstances to writing & requested Mr. Dejan my private Secretary to enter them in my official Journal.

(Signed)   W. C. C. Claiborne

——— ,, ——— ,, ———

To James M. Bradford

New. Orleans 22d Dec: 1812.

Atty. at Law
    St. Francisville
Sir,
    Your letter of the   Instant has been received &
read with respectful attention.— I regret it is not in my
power to make of Judge Hampton the request you intimate, since his resignation has already been noticed in a
Message to the Legislature.— I will however take the
liberty to place your letter in the hands of some of the
Members, & it will I hope be an additional motive for
them, to adopt some permanent Judicial System.— A
measure which cannot be longer delayed without serious
injury to the people.

I am, Sir, &c@ &c@ &c@
(Signed)   W. C. C. Claiborne

——— ,, ——— ,, ———

To James Wilkinson

on the evening of the
New Orleans 28 Decbr. 1812
    /private/

Dear Sir,
    I have received your letter of this date, advising me,
that you "had been warned by Government to be prepared for the defence of this City against an attack from
the enemy," & requesting that the Battalion of free people of Color, may be placed under your orders.— I shall
reply on tomorrow or next day, & hope to be enabled
to meet your wishes in relation to the Battalion.— meantime however it is desirable, that you address me a Communication respecting the probability of an attack, which
might be submitted in Cofidence to the Legislature.— It

would I think, induce that body, to vest me with the necessary powers to call to your aid an Auxiliary Militia force.— Perhaps it will answer my purposes to lay before the Legislature the first paragraph of your letter, & with your permission I will do so.—The paragraph alluded to, is as follows, "I am warned by Government &c."—

If however you should think proper, & the information before you admits, I could wish to speak with more precision as to the extent of the danger to be apprehended. Your letter would be sent to the Legislature in entire Confidence, & if they did act upon it, as a love of Country should dictate, we shall have done our duty.— It is with the sincerest regret, I inform you that my present Militia powers do not enable me to co-operate with promptitude & effect in the defence of the State.—

I am, &c@ &c@ &@

(Signed)   W. C. C. Claiborne

" . "

To Albert Gallatin

New Orleans 29th Dec: 1812.

Secy of the Treasury
Dear Sir

I have received your letter advising me of the removal from office of Doctor Barnwell late surgeon to the Marine Hospital of this City, & that Mr. Williams (the Collector) had been instructed to consult with me as to a suitable person to fill the vacancy.— My impression is, that to separate the duties of Surgeon & physician, will favour the Interests of the Institution, & I hope Mr. Williams may feel himself at liberty to make such disposition.

On a former occasion, I took the liberty to mention to you, Mr. Peter L. B. Duplessis the Marshal of this District, as an Intelligent faithful officer, & a suitable charac-

ter to instruct the collection of such War Taxes in this
State, as Congress may impose.— My opinion of Mr.
Duplessis remains unchanged. Permit me also to name
to you, Mr. Thomas B. Johnson the present Post-Master
at New Orleans; as among the most prudent & promising
young Men in this State; he also might safely be in-
trusted with the Collection of the public revenue, nor do
I doubt but such a Confidence as you may repose in him,
will be faithfully discharged. The Collector of the District of Lafourche Mr. Wrenn, having resigned I beg
leave to recommend William Goforth of this State, as a
suitable person to fill the vacancy; Mr. Goforth is a native of New York, and late of the State of Ohio; By profession a physician & an honest amiable Man.—

I learn with sincerest pleasure the re-election of Mr.
Madison to the Presidency; It is the just reward of virtue, & he will serve to convince the world, that an American Statesman, whose course is honorable, & whose sole
object is his Country's good has nothing to fear from intrigue & Calumny.— In this State or rather in *New Orleans,* the Clintonians were numerous & active;— they
addressed themselves to the Interest of the Sugar & Cot-
ton planters, & spoke of the return of peace & lucrative
Sales, as the certain Consequences of Mr. Clinton's ele-
vation;— These arguments made some impression, & the
strongest hopes of success were indulged.— But the good
sense of the Legislature prevailed, & the vote of the State
of Louisiana has been such as reason, justice & gratitude
would dictate.—

I do not know, who will succeed Mr. Magruder;— He
will not be re-elected— General Posy is talked of— But
the circumstances which lately operated to his injury,
will again be brought forward.— It is contended, that
his family is in Kentucky, & that he has no fixed residence
in Louisiana.— Some Citizens, whose native language is
french, will be chosen perhaps Mr. Fromentin.—

Present me respectfully & affectionately to Mrs. Gallatin.—

(Signed)   W. C. C. Claiborne

———— „ ———— „ ————

To James Brown

New. Orleans Jan. 21st 1813

A Senator of the U: S:
Washington City.

Dear Sir,

Among the buildings in this City which in the year 1803. the Commisary of France delivered to the Commissioners of the United States, as public property, is one fronting on the Levee, commonly called the priests house. — It has been appropriated, under the Spanish Government for the residence of the *Vicar General of Louisiana,* in whose possession it was when the Country was delivered over to the Spanish authorities.   But during the short administration of the Colonial Prefect, (Mr. Laussat) he was dispossessed.   On assuming the Government of Louisiana in the name of the United States, the Vicar General entreated me, to reinstate him in possession of a building, which from long occupancy, he considered as the property of the Church; The request was acceded to, as well from Considerations of justice as policy, & to this moment, it has remained in the use & occupancy of the person claiming to be the head of the Catholick Church in Louisiana.— During the Territorial Government, I informed the Executive of the United States, of the *claim* of the Vicar General and recommended it for Confirmation.— I new beg leave to request your attention to this subject & to recommend to your protection, the claim of the Church to the building in question; It rests I believe on the same ground, as the titles of most of the parishes in the interior of the State, to the Houses & Lots in possession of the several parish priests— long & uninterrupted occupancy.— Since the election of M. Fromentin to the Senate of the United States, nothing of importance has been done by the Legislature.— A Judicial system is under discussion in the House of Representatives;— It provides for the establishment of seven circuit Courts & curtails the power of parish Tribunals;— It will probably pass the House of Representatives;— But will, I think, be rejected in the Senate.— We have just received some confused accounts from the Army under Command of General Alexander Smyth;— From present appearances it would seem, we were again disgraced on the Canada frontier, & that the President had been greatly unfortunate in the selection of his Military Chiefs.—

I am, Dr. Sir,

With great respect Your ob. Servt.

(Signed)   W. C. C. Claiborne

——— ,, ——— ,, ———

———

To Mr. Magruder

A Member of the Senate

New. Orleans 25th. Jany. 1812

Dear Sir,

I acknowledge receipt of several interesting letters from you, & for which you have my sincere thanks.— The view you take of public affairs is certainly correct & I accord in opinion that a determined & vigorous prosecution of the War is essential to the honor—the safety—nay the existence of the Nation.

Your communications to me have from time to time been shown to Members of the Assembly & other Citizens, who cannot but be sensible, of the deep Interest you take, in whatever relates to the welfare of Louisiana.— You have heard of the election of Mr. Fromentin to the Senate;— He received the united vote of every Member of the Legislature (except two), whose native language was french, & obtained on the first Ballot a decided Majority. — The course of popular opinion, always uncertain, is particularly so in this new State, & until the politicks of Louisiana are more firmly established, no public agent ought or can calculate, with any certainty on public support.— The Legislature remains in session, a Bill organizing a Supreme Court to consist of three Judges, & dividing the State into seven Districts & providing for the appointment of a Judge for each District has passed the House of Representatives; It will meet much opposition in the Senate, but there is, (I believe) a Majority, (perhaps of one only) in its favour.—

My young friend Mr. Joseph Basque, a creole of Louisiana, & a young Man of good conduct, wishes to enter the service of the United States; Will you do me the favour to extend to him your patronage; He would prefer an appointment in the Corps of Marines or Artillery — But if this cannot be obtained, he would willing serve in the Infantry.— Mr. Basque is 18 years of age & has been well educated;— He is at this time studying the English language, & will with a little practise, speak it correctly.—

I am Dr. Sir, &c@ &c@ &c@
(Signed)   W. C. C. Claiborne
——— ,, ——— ,, ———

To Genl. Posey
New. Orleans Jany. 25th. 1812.
A Senator of the U: S:
   Washington City
My dear Sir,
   Attribute not my long silence to a want of friendship or respect, but rather to the mortification I have experienced at the unjust course, which the Legislature of Lou-

VI—14

isiana pursued towards you, & the wish I had, that the information should first reach you, thro' another Channel.— Previous to Conferring on you, the temporary appointment, I had made my calculations;— With the support of the Florida representation, I was certain of your Confirmation, & without it, I entertained much doubt as to result.—If my memory serves me right I wrote you to that effect,— & I believe you left Baton Rouge under the impression that the Members from Florida, would to a Man give you their suffrage.— In that opinion I had also indulged myself;— But we were both disappointed;— Messrs. Carpenter & Hicky were your friends— the others supported on the first Ballot Skipwith, & on the second Ballot, (if I am correctly informed) voted to a Man for Brown.— Among the Members who were most decided in their opposition to you, were Genl. Thomas, Caldwell & Dent. the election for a successor to Mr. Magruder your name was again brought forward, I wished it withdrawn, because I foresaw we could not be successful. — The Members from Florida, on the last occasion, (with the exception of Thomas) supported you;— But the French who in opposition to Brown had supported you, were now for Fromentin, & they were joined by Thomas Caldwell & Dent, & I believe Mr. Olliver of Rapide— Had two of these Gentlemen voted for you, Mr. Fromentin would not have been elected on the first Ballot, & on the second, there was strong grounds of belief, you would have obtained a Majority:— But I learn General Thomas & Mr. Caldwell were fixed in their opposition;— they did justice to you as a Man & a Soldier— they acknowledged your integrity & faithful public services— But objected to your want of residence in the State, & to your political Tenets, which they thought were federal.— Of the ground of Dent's opposition, I am not informed, nor is it of any importance that you should know;— He is one of those persons, whose friendship if you have it not, will do you no injury.— Several letters from you, have reached me, & I sincerely thank you for information they contain.— A determined & vigorous support of the War is essential to the honor, the safety— nay the existence of this Nation!— The President has been truly unfortunate in the selection of some of his Military Chiefs.— From the view of Smyth's Conduct as presented in the papers, he has disgraced himself & humiliated the Nation. The recall of General Wilkinson from the Command at New Orleans, might prove injurious to the service in this quarter— But I think with you, his Military knowledge & experience might redeem the honor of our Arms, so seriously affected on the Canada frontier.—

A Judicial Bill providing for a Supreme & Circuit Courts has passed the House of Representatives of this State, & will probably be approved by the Senate.— as to the right of nominating to office, it is believed a small majority in the Senate, is in favour of the executive; But the minority on that question, are violent in their opposition to me, & make my administration arduous & unpleasant;— I hope however to go thro' without much injury.— Difficulties have always been in my way & I am not in the habit of shrinking.— It is reported here, that you are called to the Armies with rank of General, & will command in this quarter; I sincerely wish this may be true.— In any event, I indulge the hope of speedily seeing you in this State.

I am &c@ &c@ &c@
(Signed) W. C. C. Claiborne

New. Orleans Jany. 28th 1813

To the President & Directors)
of the Louisiana, Orleans, &)
Planetr's Banks. . . . . .)

Gentlemen,
The undersigned, being requested by the Senate &
House of Representatives of the State of Louisiana, to
ascertain on what terms a loan of fifty thousand Dollars
for one year can be negociated, has the honor to address
himself to the President & Directors of the Louisiana
Bank, & to enquire of them, whether they will loan, on
the Credit & for the use of this State, the whole or any
part of the above sum, & upon what conditions.—
(Signed)   W. C. C. Claiborne
——— ,, ——— ,, ———

To James Monroe

New. Orleans 2d March 1813

Secy of State
Sir,
The office of Judge of the District of Louisiana having
become vacant by the appointment of Mr. Dominick A.
Hall as a Judge of the Supreme Court of the State of
Louisiana, we beg leave to recommend Mr. John Dawson
of Virginia as a fit person to fill the vacancy.—
We have the pleasure of a long & intimate acquaintance with Mr. Dawson, & believe him eminently qualified
to discharge the duties of Judge of the District of Louisiana.   Although Mr. Dawson is not personally known to
the Citizens of this State, yet many of them, are informed
of the high standing of his long & faithful public services
have given him & justly appreciate the deep Interest, he

has invariably taken in whatever regarded the welfare
of this Section of the Union.—
                    We have the honor to be
                        Sir
                            Very respectfully
                                Your obd. Sevts.
                                    W. C. C. Claiborne
                            _____ " _____
                            Julian Poydras
                        _____ ,, _____

                To Andrew Jackson.

                            New. Orleans 15th March 1813
My dear Sir,
    I received some time since your agreeable favour, ad-
vising me of your approach to this Capitol, with two
thousand Tennessee Volunteers & enclosing your letters
of advice to the Assistant Quarter Master, & Contractors
Agent which were immediately delivered.— I need not
express to you the satisfaction your Communication afforded me;— At this perilous Crisis so respectable a reinforcement composed of men whose patriotism and valour are so well established would have given security to
this exposed Section of the Union, from all attacks from
without, & commanded from the savages in our vicinity
an adherence to the most pacific course;— Your safe arrival at Natchez with your Command was known to me, &
I was awaiting with anxiety, the pleasure of welcoming
you within this State, when I learn that by order of the
government, your detachment is discharged from the
service of their Country.— To what cause, this sudden &
unexpected dissolution of a force so ardent in their Country's cause is attributable, I cannot tell! Is it the har-
binger of peace? Is Florida acquired by Treaty, or is it

determined to abandon the Volunteer System, & to rely intirely on regulars? Do satisfy my enquiries, & relieve me from the surprize, which the sudden dissolution of your army has excited![1]—

In this quarter, the preparations for defencive war are not in the least abated! Forts on the Mississippi & on the Margins of the Lakes are in great forwardness;— Most of the Mechanicks of the City are engaged in making Gun Carriages— Timber is preparing for building Block Ships to operate on the lakes & at the Mouth of the Mississippi, & the Volunteer system, meets from the Commanding General the most flattering encouragement.— It is impossible to say whether or not, the enemy will attack New. Orleans; but I have always, considered it, as an event so probable, that the Government would have been highly reprehensible, not to have provided in time, the most ample means of defence shall I have the happiness of seeing you in New. Orleans, previous to your return to Tennessee.— The friendship which I formed for you in early life, is still ardent & sincere, & my best wishes, have & will always, attend you.— Can you not obtain a Command in the Northern Army? Our affairs in that quarter are indeed in a most humiliating State! The arm of every Citizen should be raised, until the lost honor of our Country is restored.— The surrender of Hull— the Proclamation Attack of Smyth, & the disaster, which has recently befallen our old friend Winchester, are causes of great affliction to every American Heart.— For myself, I have but little knowledge of the theory or practice of War; but could I obtain a Command in the Northern Army, most willingly could I resign the post to which the Citizens of this State have called me, & repair to Canada.— But I trust, that others better calculated than I am

---

[1] See Jackson Papers in Manuscripts Division in the Library of Congress for Jackson's letters to Claiborne.

for Military Command will not escape the Notice of Government.—

The Legislature of Louisiana after a session of near four Months, will in a few days adjourn & I am so pressed with business, that I have only time again to express the happiness it would give me to see you in this City, and to subscribe myself with great respect.—

Your faithful frd.

W. C. C. Claiborne

To Albert Gallatin

New Orleans March 16th. 1813

Sec of the Treasury

SIR,

On looking over papers in my office, I find a Communication to you, which was prepared under date of the 30th of June 1812, & by some mistake, was not forwarded. It is now enclosed, & contains my Account for the Contingent expences of the late Territorial Government, during the second quarter of the year 1812. Your letter of the 25th of May 1812, instructing me to close my Accounts on the 30th of April did not reach me until late in June, as will appear from my letter of the 27" of that Month.— I in consequence exhibited no charges (subsequent to the last of April) against the Government, but such as were necessarily incured in bringing the business of the Department to a close;— of these the services of the Clerk (who had been in the office for several years) & of a Messenger were indispensable.— The several other Items in the Account are for expenditures previous to the last of April.—

I am,

Sir,

Your mo: ob Srt

(Sigd.) W. C. C. Claiborne

To James Wilkinson

New Orleans 17th March 1813

New Orleans

SIR,

In an official letter from Thomas H. Williams Collector of the District of Orleans, under date of the 13th. Inst:, I am advised that an organized plan, for introducing Slaves & Merchandize into this State illegally, was formed on Lake Barataria, & with such combinations as to render Military & Naval aid essential to a due execution of the Laws.— I further learn from various sources that the Association is composed of near three hundred individuals;— that they have already armed two or three Cruisers, & Captured several Vessels, the Cargoes of which were landed on an Island of the lake Barataria, from whence an illicit Trade is carried on with this City.— The Collector alluding to these transactions, says "they are enormities, which in point of open impudence, defiance to the Civil Authorities & in their tendency to destroy the moral Character of the Country, & to ruin the Revenue of the United States, have not their parallel in America."— Sincerely desirous to do whatever may depend upon me, to arrest such lawless Acts, & to bring the offenders to Justice, I issued on yesterday a Proclamation of which the enclosed is a Copy.— I do not expect, that the Proclamation will induce these lawless men to disperse & separate;— But I trust & believe, it may tend to excite the vigilance of the officers of this State & to prevent the Citizens from Countenancing such violations of the Laws. As regards the principal offenders, I am persuaded, that nothing short of the most vigorous measures, will put a stop to their evil practices & resort to force is in my opinion indispensable, & as you are vested with the Military & Naval Command on this Station, I hope you may find it convenient to the service to send without delay to Barataria, a detachment sufficiently strong, to disperse the

Banditti.— I am ready to Co-operate with you, in any manner that my powers as Governor of Louisiana will justify & with this object, I request the honor of an interview with you, in the Office of the Collector of the District at such time, as your Convenience will permit.—

I am,

Sir,

Yours &c@

(Signed) *W. C. C. Claiborne*

To Thomas H. Williams

New Orleans March 17th. 1813

Collector &c@

Sir,

Your letter of the 13th Inst: has been received, & I beg you to be assured of my disposition to do whatever may be in my power to suppress the lawless association to which you allude.— I have issued a Proclamation of which the enclosed is a Copy. It is designed more particularly, as precautionary advice to the Officers & Citizens of this State, & will I hope, excite the vigilance of the former, & induce the latter to avoid all participation in such violations of the Law, as regards the principal offenders, the most vigorous measures have become indispensable.— I have suggested in a Letter (of this date) to General Wilkinson, the expediency of resorting to force;— apprised him of my disposition to Co-operate in any way my powers may justify, & solicited an interview with him in your office, at such time as his convenience will permit.—

I am,

Sir,

Yours &c@

(Signed) *W. C. C. Claiborne*

To Louisiana Senators and Congressmen

Gentlemen,   Baton Rouge 19th may 1813

I regret (request) of you the goodness to lay in person before the president the enclosed Copy of a Resolution entered into by the general assembly of Louisiana and, which solicit a loan of arms from the General Government— It is proper to informe you, that this resolution was soon after its date transmitted by me to the late secretary at war Mr. Eustis, with a request that he would lay the same before the president;— the secretary in reply refered me by order of the president to general Wilkinson, who was instructed to deliver to me such number of arms for the use of the militia as his limited supply would permit.— On application to the General, he discovered every disposition to accomodate, but the state of the Arsenal did not permit him to loan the state more than six hundred musket, I am making every exertion to organize the militia & to place it on the best possible footing but the want of arms, and the impossibility of obtaining them, by private purchases, discourage officers & men, & check all military ardour.— If you can obtain from the President a loan to this state of three thousand four hundred stand of muskets, and four hundred sabres, It would be doing much towards the Surety of this Section of the union.— I should then be enabled to hold in readiness for service a strong detachment of the militia of Louisiana to act whenever the occasion demand, and there would no longer be a necessity to send to this quarter the militia of the western states, unless indeed our safety is serously threatened by the enemy and with a greater force than I had supposed (Consistent with views in Europe and the defence of Canada) Concentrate on the mississippy.— If the arms desired can be obtained from the Government it would be convenient that they be delivered within Louisiana to my order, without subjecting the state to the expence of transportation;— but if on this point there exists the smallest difficulty I could wish the arms to the transmitted hence at the expence of the state.— I have understood that the arms desired could be spared, without inconvenience to the service from the Arsenal at Harpers Ferry;— If so Gentlemen, and the President assents to the loan, may I trespass further, on your goodness & request you to contract for their prompt transportation and delivery to my order at Baton Rouge in good Condition, and to draw upon me for the expences attending the same to any amount not exceeding five thousand dollars

I am &c.
Signed/   William C. C. Claiborne

To the honorables, James Brown & Eliques Fromentin
    Senators from Louisiana to the Congress of the
    united States.

Baton Rouge May 1813.

Sir,
    I have the honor to enclose you a Resolution adopted by the senate and house of representatives of the state of Louisiana, and subscribe myself

With great respect
Your obt. Sert.
Signed/   William C. C. Claiborne

To the senators &
    Representatives in Congress

(Circulars to Pilots)

New Orleans June 10th 1813

Sir,
    If any of the deputy Pilots in your employ at the Balize should be British subjects, you are hereby instructed to dismiss them & to report their names to the

marshal of the ———— You will also dismiss from your
service every other person against whom there exists the
smallest suspicion of holding intercourse with the enemy,
& you will report to me by every mail, whether any &
what vessels of the enemy are to your knowledge or belief hovering on our Coast.

I am, Sir, &c
Signed/   W. C. C. Claiborne.

To Genl. Flournoy

New Orleans June 10th 1813

Dear sir,
    The Bearer Joseph Dupard, a free man of Colour
residing near the English turn, waits upon you for the
purpose of Complaining of certain depredations committed on his property by the soldiers stationed at the
English Turn & of his fears of further outrage unless
you would be pleased to extend your authority in his
behalf.

I am sir &. c. &c.
Signed/   Wm. C. C. Claiborne

General Flournoy.

To Louisiana Senators

New Orleans June 10th 1813

Gentlemen
    On my return to this city, I have learned with sin-
cere regret, that the third Regiment of the United States
Infantry had been ordered from this state; If it is intended to be immediately replaced by another regiment
of equal strength there can be no objection; But it is my
duty to state to you, & to urge you, Gentlemen to represent to the Government, that the regular Force in this
quarter, Cannot be deminished without endangering the
safety of the state.— The militia are not & cannot for
some time be made efficient the Want of Arms & muni-

tions of War, are sources of great embarrassment, and
I renew to you my entreaties to effect if possible from
the Government, the loan of three thousand four hundred muskets & four hundred sabres.— We have a report to Day, that the taking possession of *mobile,* has
excited among the spaniards great dissatisfaction, &
that an expedition is fitting out at Havana avowedly for
the purpose of retaking *it.*— Two English sloops of war
are near the Balize, & it is said another has been seen
off the bay of Mobille.

The Mississippi is unusually high; It has overflowed
its Banks in Several places & the prospect of many industrious Planters totally blasted.— the Parish of Concordia is nearly inundated & every farm in the Parish of
Plaquemine more or less injured. A crevasse at the
plantation of M″ Kener, will destroy his Crop & greatly
injure the Crops of his Neighbourgs, particular of Mr
Fortier & Trudeau.— A Crevasse near Mr S Martin's
on the opposite shore has already done much injury in
that quarter, but the waters are now at a stand & will
I trust retire in a few days; I have not understood that
the smallest injury has been as yet received to Mr.
Brown's Plantation or in its vicinity.

I am Gentlemen, &c.

Signed) Wm. C. C. Claiborne

The Honorable James Brown & Eliguis Fromentin
Senators from the state of Louisiana
to the Congress of the United States.—

To Commodore Shaw

Sir,   New. Orleans June 10th 1813

I have received the letter in which you inform me,
that several persons employed by the Branch Pilot at
the Balize, were British subjects, & strongly suspected
of holding Intercourse with the enemy.— I have in con-

sequence directed that all persons of the above description, be dismissed from service, & that their names be reported, in order that the necessary measures may be taken to remove them from the sea board.

I am Sir &c.

Signed) Wm. C. C. Claiborne.

Commodore shaw.

To Dr. Duhamuel

New Orleans June 11th 1813.

Dear Sir

I received the statement made by yourself, and several other of my fellow Citizens of Attackapas relative to the seizure by the Collector of the Districts of Teche of sundry merchandize.— Having no Controul over that officer it only remained for me to exhibit the statement, to the district attorney General, Mr. Grymes, & his letter to the collector, advising a release of the merchandise seized aforesaid, is herewith enclosed & which I request you to deliver.— I shall forward the statement of the citizens to our senators in Congress, & will suggest the expediency of making some express legislative provisions, as the surest means of Guarding against the like inconvenience & injury occuring in future.

I am Dear Sir, &c.

Doctor Duhamuel.   Signed/ Wm. C. C. Claiborne

Circular to Parish Judges.

Sir,   New Orleans 11th June 1813.

The Public Printer has this day sent to the department of State in a Pamphlet, the laws passed at the last session of the Legislature & the secretary of the state being confined by Indisposition I hasten to transmit to

you several copies for the use of yourself & the other
Civil officers of your Parish.— The delay in printing the
laws subjects to state some embarrassment; you will find
that the period particularly assigned for the discharge
of certain duties has— but it appears to me proper,
that these duties be now attended to & at the earliest
possible period.— To the law regulating the appointment of sheriffs & for other purposes I request your
particular attention, you acquaint me, by letter *addressed
to the secretary of State* wether or not the sheriff of
your Parish has given the bonds required. In event,
that the sheriff nominated for your Parish, shall have
Declined to Accept, or Cannot find the necessary securities;— Will you be pleased in your letter to the secretary of State to mention a Citizen qualified to act as
sheriff & who would be willing to accept of the office.—

I am Sir &c

Signed/   Wm. C. C. Claiborne.

To Eliguis Fromentin

New. Orleans June 16th 1813

Dear Sir

Colonel Hawkins informed me of the Arrival of
Yourself & Lady at the Creek Agency, and I trust that
long eer this, you have reached Washington.— The present is indeed a most interesting Crisis, and I feel much
solicitude to learn the *Course,* which the new Congress
are disposed to pursue.— It is certainly prudent to be
represented in Europe at this eventual Epoch— nor
could a more Judicious selection of ministers have been
made, than those recently embarked for St. Petersburg.
— I fear however that the Russian mediation Will not
eventuate as Speedily as seems to be anticipated in an
Accommodation with Great Britain; the pretension of
England to the "Rule of the seas" seem to be supported
with great unanimity in Parliament, and I fear those

pretensions will not be relinquished until the haughty Islanders are made severely to feel the pressure of the war. in a letter Directed to Mr. Brown & yourself I expressed my sincere regret at the withdrawing of the third Regiment unless it is intended to be replaced by another Corps of equal strength.— I seriously apprehended (if the war is Continued an attack on this state; — I do not believe that Peace will be maintained with Spain; the course of affairs in east Florida, the recent taking possession of Mobille, & the support which the Revolutions in Mexico receive from the American Citizens, have occasioned much excitement at Havana, & will not I presume be well received by the Cortes.

We have distressing (news) from the Upper Parishes;— Warren and Concordia are wholly inundated and the Crops totally lost— The levee above Point Coupeé is said today to be broken, I hope it may be incorrect, for in such event, not only the Crops of Point Coupeé would be lost, but the waters would do great injury in Attackappas.

I took the liberty some time since to recommend Charles Dutillet of this City, for a commission in the army;— Will you do me the favour (to give) this Young Gentleman your kind Patronage,— He is an amiable youth, about twenty years of age, a native of New Orleans, & the son of our mutual friend Colonel Francis Dutillet,— my young friend will accept an Ensigncy in a regiment of Infantry, and would I am sure make a valuable officer.— Young Basque in whose behalf I, in a former occasion sollicited your support has been appointed a Lieutenant of Artillery and will I am per-

suaded prove worthy of the honor confered.— Present
my respect to your lady.

     I am dear sir
      With sincere esteem &c. &c.
       Signed William C. C. Claiborne.
The Honorable
Eliguis Fromentin
a member of the senate of the
United States, Washington City.

Copy of General Flournoy's letter to the Governor.

        New Orleans 14th June 1813
Sir

 In hastely Glancing the militia act of this State which
you did me the Honor to send me, I find that by the 10th
section you have power in Case of invasion insurrection,
or When the danger shall be such that the Public safety
may require it to call forth such detachments of the
militia as you may judge necessary &c. &c.

 The exposed situation of this state at all times to the
inroads of an invading enemy, who will put to use
every means in their power to excite the states (slaves)
to take up (arms) against their masters in my opinion
renders it essentially necessary that you should without
delay adopt such measures for the public safety as will
enable you at a short warning to turn out any portion of
the militia that may be necessary on the happening of
either of the aforesaid Contingencies & to enable you in
the event of a Call from the president of the united
States for your quota of militia to satisfy the requisition
with that promptness, Zeal & patriotism which have
marked your Political Career. This becomes the more
necessary on account of the instructions I have received

  VI 15

to order the 3d Regiment of the regular troops to join the Northern Army and which has been done accordingly.

The whole regular force at my disposal, when this Regiment has left me will not exceed, 1,500 men, the volunteers in Service About equal in numbers. With this force, it is impossible that the District Can be defended. — aid, therefore from the state authority is indispensable to our safety.

I have the honor to be,

Obt Sert

Signed   Thos. Flournoy

Brigadier General Commg. 7th Mil. District

His Excellency
Governor Claiborne.

To General Flournoy

Sir   New Orleans 17th June 1813

A press of business has prevented me until this moment from Acknowledgeing the receipt of your letter of the 14th Instant.

I am very sensible of the dangers to which this state is exposed from within & from without, and the expediency of taking in time *precautionary measures!* Among *these* the holding in readiness for active service, a strong Detachment of militia, is Certainly of primary importance,— and orders to that effect shal be issued.— It is however with Concern, I inform you, that the militia of Louisiania, is for the present in a state of Great Derangement.— You will have observed by the militia Law (recently passed) that Captains & Subalterns are to be elected to the several Companies, and such has been the delay in making those elections, and forwarding the returns, that only a few Regiments are yet organized.— Hence Sir, it is not in my power (to) array an auxiliary force, as promptly as I would wish;— But you may be assured that to effect the object I shall use all my Authority & best exertions.

I regret that at this eventful crisis the third Regiment should have been ordered from this district.— The force which remains at your Disposition, is certainly inadequate to our protection, and therefore I shall be solicitous so to arrange the militia, as to give you *in time of need,* all the aid which the population and resources of Louisiana will admit.

I have the honor to be
Sir
Very respectfully
Your most humble Servt.
Signed/   William C. C. Claiborne.
General Flournoy
Commanding the Troops of the U. S.
on the mississippy District.

———————

New Orleans June 21st 1813
Dear Sir,

The third Regiment is still here, and I entertain strong hopes that the orders for their ascending the Mississippy may be countermanded— from the information before me, I am persuaded, that occupancy of Mobille, has given great dissatisfaction to the Spanish Authorities, and that a Force is in readiness at Havana for some district service. Indeed it is confidently stated to me, that this force is designed by the Captain General of Cuba, to attempt the recapture of Mobile, and was on the point of sailing;— But that the Captain General was advised by a Council of War to await further operations untill the Regency of Spain was advised upon the subject and that a fast sailing Vesel had been dispached to Cadiz whose return to Havana, was expected with great anxiety.— General Flournoy has very properly augmented our forces on the Mobile Station;— The volunteers recently at Baton Rouge have been ordered to Mobille, and will give, with the troops already in that vicinity, an aggregate number of from 12. to 1500 men, under the command of Brigadier General Claiborn who will I trust be enabled to defend the Country. the movements in the Neighbouring Province of Texas, Deserve the attention of Government. The Revolutionists have got possession of the Capitol of their Province, St. Antonio and are likely for the present to maintain their possession.— Their Chiefs manifest no disposition to be Dependent upon the American Government, or to grant any peculiar privileges to the American people;— their objects seem to be, to encourage emoration (emigration) to fill their armies with adventurers from all Nations, & to set up for themselves;— They may become useful Neighbours,— but as we have no certainty of it, I wish sincerely, it comported with the Policy of the American Government to take possession of the country as far as the River Grande.— Under the Louisiana Convention, we claim the tract extending from the Sabine to the River Grande, or River Bravo, as it is some times Called. — During Mr. Jefferson's administration, our Claim was often avowed, and I have now on my Journals, sundry official letters addressed by me as governor of the Territory of Orleans (in Conformity to instructions) to the spanish Agents, remonstrating against their assuming any new military positions upon the Bay of St. *Bernard* or elsewhere within tract of Country Claimed by the United States.— the Bay S″ Bernard is west of the Sabine— The River Mississippy is beginning to fall, But another rise is apprehended as it is believed the Waters of the Missoury, have not yet come down.— The breaking of the big levee above Point Coupeé has done much injury in that Parish, and inundated a considerable portion of the Counties of Attackapas and Opelousas.— I believe your Plantation remains secure, unless indeed, you may have received some little injury from the back Water of the Crevasse at Mr. Kenner's, which I learn today extends far as the former Plantation of Colonel Andris.

A Young friend of mine M" Charles Dutillet, a son of Colonel Dutillet of this city, is anxious to enter the Army of the United States and would willingly accept of the Appointment of an Ensign. may I take the liberty to recommend him to your patronage; he is a promising Youth & will

(a *leaf cut out here*)

By William Charles Cole Claiborne,
Governor of the State of Louisiana, & Commander
in Chief of the Militia thereof.—

A Proclamation[1]

WHEREAS I have received information that a number of persons are combining in a project to invade the Dominions of Spain, a State in amity with the United States, and for that purpose assembling at or near Natchitoches, within the limits & Jurisdiction of Louisiana, it becomes my duty to issue this my Proclamation, hereby solemnly cautioning the Citizens of this State against entering into, or in any manner countenancing the project aforesaid;— and that no one may remain unadvised of the Consequences, which await the parties concerned, I do now make it known that by an Act of the Congress of the United States, passed on the fifth day of June, 1794, it is declared that "if any person shall within the

---

[1] Beginning of Volume IX.

"Territory or Jurisdiction of the United States, begin,
"or set on foot, or provide or prepare the means for any
"Military expedition or enterprise to be carried on from
"thence against the Territory or Dominions of any
"Prince or State with whom the United States are at
"peace, every such person so offending shall upon con-
"viction, be adjudged guilty of a high misdemeanor, and
"shall suffer fine and imprisonment at the discretion of
"the Court, in which the Conviction shall be had, so as
"that such fine shall not exceed three thousand Dollars,
"nor the term of imprisonment be more than three
years."—

And I do enjoin and require all officers Civil and Military of the State to be vigilant in the maintenance of
order and the preservation of the Laws.—

> Given under my hand & private Seal
> (there being no Seal for the State yet
> provided) at New. Orleans, on the 11th
> day of August 1812.— and in the 37th
> year of the Independence of the United
> States of America.—
>
> (Signed)   Wm. C. C. Claiborne

———— ,, ———— ,, ————

———————

New Orleans 9 January 1813.

To His Excellency, the Governor,
    & Captn Genl of the Island of Cuba
The Undersigned the Governor of the State of Louisiana, being informed that Antoine Laporte, a Citizen of
the United States, and Commanding officer of a privateer,
fitted out at New:Orleans, and duly commissioned by the
American Government to cruise against its enemies, having landed within the Island of Cuba, for the purpose of

obtaining some necessary supplies, was arrested, the papers of his Vessel detained and himself committed to prison, deems it his duty to ask of his Excellency the Governor and Captain General of the Island of Cuba an explanation of a transaction apparently so much opposed to that friendly understanding believed to exist between our two Nations.— The undersigned has further to request that if the said Antoine Laporte be still in confinement, he be released therefrom and such remuneration made him for his sufferings, as justice shall dictate.—

The undersigned tenders to his Excellency the Governor and Captain General of Cuba the assurances of his great respect and high consideration.—

(Signed)   William C. C. Claiborne

——— „ ——— „ ———

A Message from the Governor to the Legislature.

Gentlemen of the Senate & of the House of Representatives.—

I lay before you in Confidence a Copy of a Letter which in conformity to a Resolution passed at the last session of the Legislature I addressed to the Secretary at War, soliciting of the executive of the United States, a loan of arms, together with the Secretary's answer referring me to General Wilkinson, who was instructed to furnish such as his supplies will admit.— On application to General Wilkinson, I have received from the public arsenals between *six* & *seven* hundred stand of Muskets, which have been distributed among the several Militia Corps of New:Orleans.— It is proper to add that the General manifests a great desire to accommodate the Militia of the State.— But his supplies of arms are at present too limited to admit of the loan desired, he can furnish me with no Sabres, nor can he at this time state with certainty what further number of Muskets may be spared from the public stores.— Several Corps of Volunteers are raising in this State and in the Mississippi Territory destined for the service of the United States who will require the use of public arms;— But the General presumes, that without inconvenience he will in a short time be enabled to make me another loan of from five to six hundred Muskets & two or three pieces of field artillery.— New. Orleans January 14th. 1813

(signed)   William C. C. Claiborne.

By William Charles Cole Claiborne
Governor of the State of Louisiana, and Commander
in Chief of the Militia thereof.—

A PROCLAMATION.

WHEREAS I have received information that upon or near the shores of Lake Barataria, within the limits and Jurisdiction of this State, a considerable Banditti composed of Individuals of different nations, have armed and equiped several Vessels for the avowed purpose of cruising on the high Seas, and committing depredations and piracies on the Vessels of Nations at peace with the United States, and carrying on an illicit trade in goods, Wares and Merchandize with the Inhabitants of this State, in opposition to the Laws of the United States, and to the great injury of the fair trade of the Public Revenue;— And whereas there is reasonable ground to fear that the parties thus waging lawless War, will cease to respect the persons and property of the good Citizens of this State;— I have thought proper to issue this my Proclamation hereby Commanding the persons engaged as aforesaid, in such unlawful acts to cease therefrom and forthwith to disperse and separate;— And I do

charge and require all officers civil and Military in this
State, each within his respective District, to be vigilant
and active in apprehending and securing every Individual
engaged as aforesaid in the violation of the Laws;— And
I do caution the people of this State, against holding any
kind of intercourse, or being in any manner concerned
with such high offenders;— And I do also earnestly ex-
hort each and every good Citizen to afford, help, protection and support to the officers in suppressing a combina-
tion so destructive to the Interests of the United States
and of this State in particular, and to rescue Louisiana
from the foul reproach which would attach to its character should her shores afford an assylum or her Citizens
countenance, to an association of Individuals, whose
practices are so subversive of all Laws human and di-
vine, & of whose ill begotten treasure, no Man can par-
take, without being forever dishonored, and exposing
himself to the severest punishment.[1]—

> Given under my hand, & the Seal
> of the State at New Orleans on the
> 15th day of March in the year 1813,
> and in the 37th of the Independ-
> ence of America.—
> (Signed)   William C. C. Claiborne

———— ,, ———— ,, ————

——————

New. Orleans 14th April 1813—

General Armstrong)
Secretary at War.   )
Dear Sir,

Within the limits of the State of Louisiana, many
families of Chactaw Indians have taken up their residence and many vaggabonds of the same tribe frequently

---

[1] This refers to the Lafette brothers. For a good account of their
operations, see Walker's "Jackson and New Orleans," pp. 31_61.

visit this City & the adjoining settlements.— These people all acknowledge the authority of the Chiefs residing in the nation, and were there some convenient mode of my communicating with the Chiefs, we probably should not be so often troubled with Indian visits, and that whilst here, their conduct would be more orderly.— Several Parishes within this State, for instance St. Tammany, St. Helena, and Baton Rouge are much exposed to Indian depredations;— In the course of the last year, their safety was seriously threatened, so much so, that several farms were abandoned, and the frontier settlers fled to the interior for surety.— I sent a special Messenger to the Chactaw Nation with a Talk to the Chiefs;— My Messenger was arrested by the resident Agent Mr. Dinsmoor, and ordered out of the Nation.   I exhibit no charge against Mr. Dinsmoor;— As far as I know he is a vigilant officer, and my Messenger not being furnish (ed) with the passport superintendent of Indian affairs, for the Southern Department, I presume Mr. Dinsmoor had supposed it his duty to arrest him;— but I do hope that taking into view, the peculiar situation of this State, the Government will appoint an additional agent for the Chactaws, and that such agent be instructed to correspond with the Governor of Louisiana, and to communicate to the Chiefs such Talks and Messages as the Governor may forward to him.— I will recommend as this additional agent, Colonel Simon Favre who resides on Pearl River, not very far from the Chactaw boundary. — Colonel Simon Favre was agent for the Chactaws under the Spanish Government, and has more influence with these Indians than any man in existence.   Mr. Dinsmoor resides some where on the route leading from Natchez to Nashville, and so remote from New. Orleans, that a Correspondence between the Governor of this State & that Agent would be useless.— for further particulars as to the expediency of appointing an additional Agent,

and for the character of Mr. Favre I beg leave to refer
you to Mr. Fromentin of the Senate, who will do me the
favor to deliver this letter in person.—
                    I am, Sir, &c@ &c@ &c@
                 (signed)   William C. C. Claiborne.

To James Madison
President of the United States

                                New Orleans July 9th 1813.
Dear Sir,
    I sincerely wish the mediation of Russia may eventu-
ate in an early and honorable adjustment of differences
between the United States and Great Britain;— But I
much fear England has not yet sufficiently felt the pressure of the War to induce her to be just;— I trust however that the valor and interprise of our Naval Heroes,
will soon be equalled by our land forces and that the fall
of Canada will convince the enemy that he may loose
much and gain little, by a continuance of the War.—
    In this quarter we hitherto have only felt the effects
of the War on Commerce and agriculture.— But I entertain great apprehensions that a strong *force* and a judicious disposition of *it* may soon be necessary for our
security.— The Agents of Spain at Havanna & Pensacola express considerable dissatisfaction at the late occupancy of Mobille by the Troops of the United States,
an *an* expedition is fitting out at Havanna avowedly (as
it is stated) for the re-capture of that post.   Indeed it is
confidently reported the expedition was on the point of
sailing but that the Captain General of Cuba was advised
by a "Council of War," to await further operations until the Supreme Government of Spain could be consulted.
In the mean time the Governor of Pensacola has in a letter to the officer commanding at Mobille complained of

the taking possession of that post, as also of Baton Rouge as *Acts* of aggression and requires their immediate evacuation.— I further learn that the Spanish authorities have of late been unusually attentive to the Creek & Chactaw Indians & had made them considerable presents. How far this course of conduct may be dictated by the *enemy,* time will unfold;— But my impression has always been that *he* would not force Spain to break with the United States, until it became his policy to attack Louisiana and that *then,* all the power and the supposed influence of Spain in Louisiana would be inlisted against us.—The War on the Continent will afford ample employment for the French armies and it is probably that their Veteran Troops, will be withdrawn from the Peninsula; This will lead to a diminution of the British *force,* in that quarter, and a part of *it* may be ordered to Spanish America, as well with a view to menace Louisiana, as to preserve the Mexican Provinces.— An attack on Louisiana will necessarily divide the American forces, and may perhaps protract the conquest of Lower Canada.— The Spanish Mexican Provinces involved in all the horrors of Civil War will soon cease to be useful to Spain or her allies, unless a "force that can lood down all opposition" shall speedily arrive. But to enlarge is unnecessary.— your means of information will enable you to anticipate the enemy at every point, nor do I doubt but this Section of the Union, will, when the occasion demands, receive as ample support as your means will permit. In speaking of the Mexican Provinces it seems to me, that the movements of the revolutionists in Texas, are of great concern to our Country.— It is true the Capitol of the Province *St. Antoine,* has been taken, and that the revolutionists have hitherto met with little opposition.— But the savage and imprudent conduct of the Chiefs have already indisposed & disgusted the people.— Bernado the leader has all the qualities of a Tyrant,— *Weak, Cowardly* and

Cruel. After the Capture of St. Antonio, he rested from his labours, & gave time for the Royalists again to embody nor has he taken measures to organize a Government or to provide permanently for the support of his Army.— Anarchy prevails, and an arbitrary destruction of life Character & property is the order of the day.—It is rumoured that Bernado is deposed and a General Toledo (last from Philadelphia) called to the Supreme Command. But the Change is too late.— A regular *force* of three thousand men (the greater part from Vera Cruix) is certainly advancing towards St. Antonio, and will in all probability *drive the Revolutionists back on Louisiana.* *In such event* I fear some disorders on our frontiers will be committed, and I am not without apprehensions, that these disorders may be followed by Acts of hostility on the part of the Royalists.—

General Flournoy is providing for the defence of Mobille and has sent thitherto strong reinforcements.— He is exclusively devoted to his Military duties, and seems to me, to have made a most judicious disposition of his command.

I have given orders today for a Regiment of Militia drawn from the first Brigade (by draft) to be held in readiness for service, and so soon as the Militia of the more distant Counties can be organized in conformity to the provisions of a late Law, I shall add three other Regiments to this disposable force. I add with regret, that it has not been, and I fear will not be, for some time in my power to render the Militia of Louisiana efficient:— The heteregenious mass of which our population is composed;— The contrariety of language spoken the dispersed situation of our settlements & the want of arms present serious embarrassment.— I however shall not be wanting in exertion, & will in time of need, give to the General Government all possible aid in the defence of the State.—

It is believed that vast sums of money have been recently expended in providing for the safety of Louisiana; How far these sums have been judiciously expended, time will evince.— But from my knowledge of the Country, and the means of approaching it, I feel no hesitation in saying that a water defence is not only the most economical. but the safest that could be resorted to. The block ship destined (I learn) for the Lakes is in great forwardness and will with a few Gun Boats, be a formidable defence in that quarter. Two large Block Ships with a few look out Boats on the Mississippi, and one Block Ship and five or six Gun Boats on the Mobille would *give greater security,* than all the fortifications that could be erected.—

In speaking of fortifications, it is understood that several recently commenced, are left in an unfinished state, the proper officers being without means of completing them, nor can they procure them, since the protest of a number of the Bills of Colonel Shamburg the deputy Quarter Master General, has greatly affected the Credit of the War department.— Indeed Sir, the General Distrust of the Bills of the Quarter Master & Pay Master of the Army have already created much embarrassment, & will I fear, seriously injure the service.

Mr. Fulwar Skipwith has been here for some days, without being enabled to obtain a passage to his port of destination;— He has vested a Mr. William Taylor of this State with special powers, & this Gentleman departs hence for the Havanna in a few days, in hopes of obtaining a passage from thence to the port of St. Domingo. Mr. Skipwith did me the honor to apprise me of the nature of his mission, and to consult me as to the course proper to be pursued.— It seemed to me imprudent for him who I knew was obnoxious to, would excite the suspicion of the Spanish authorities to venture himself at Havanna. As regards Mr. Taylor I believe him to be a

discreet, honest, capable young man, & will execute the
trust reposed with great fidelity.—
I do not recollect ever to have seen the Mississippi as
high as the present year, and really, the *effects* have been
most distressing.— The loss of Cattle, Hogs &c@ have
been considerable, Crops that would have sold at half a
Million Dollars have been destroyed, and the injury done
to the houses, Fences, Levees & lands would not be repaired for that sum. But a stil greater misfortune is
apprehended, a prevalence of disease (one of the effects
of high waters) thro'out the State, and the death of many
valuable Citizens.
I request you to present my best wishes to your
amiable lady, & to permit me to subscribe myself.—
> With sentiments of the great respect &c
> (signed)   William C. C. Claiborne
> ——— ,, ——— ,, ———

To Vincent Gray

New Orleans July 14th. 1813

Merchant
   Havanna
Sir,
I avail myself of the present favorable opportunity
again to solicit your kind services in favor of the unfortunate Hargrove, & has fellow Captives.— The Governor of East Florida, has recently published a decree of
the Cortez, which accords a free pardon, to all persons,
concerned, in the rebellion (as it is termed) in East &
West Florida.— I have not by me a Copy of this publication, but the Decree to which it alludes, is understood to
be, what it purports, an Act of the Cortez, and many of
the party in East Florida styled patriots, have, I learn
availed themselves of the same, I have thought Sir, that
this decree of the Cortez, embraced the case of Har

grove & his unfortunate Companions, and I am some
what surprised, that they have not been restored to their
Liberty.—

Enclosed is a letter from Mrs. Hargrove to her husband which I request you to have conveyed to him; The
affectionate regards manifested by this unfortunate
woman, for her unfortunate husband & her continued in-
tercessions in his behalf, keep alive my warmest sympa-
thies & will I am sure induce you to renew your efforts
in the cause of suffering humanity.—

I am, Sir, &c@ &c@ &c@
(Signed)   William C. C. Claiborne

——— ,, ——— ,, ———

Extract of a private letter from Governor Claiborne to
M. Gray, dated July 14th 1813.—

My letter to you relative Hargrove & his Companions
is so expressed as to be shewn to the Captain General,
if you think advisable.— In the event, these unfortunate
Men should be liberated, I am persuaded that any expences you might incur in obtaining for them a passage
to New Orleans, would be remunerated you by the General Government.— I am the more certain on this point,
since, during the period of my acting as Governor of the
late Territory of Orleans, I was instructed by the Secretary of State to continue my efforts to effect the release of Hargrove & his fellow Captives.— After manifesting so direct an Interest in the fate of these Men,
it is not to be supposed, the Government would refuse
to pay the expences attending their return to the United
States, provided the same should not exceed the limits
of a prudent œconomy.—

I am, Sir, &c@ &c@ &c@
(Signed)   William C. C. Claiborne

——— ,, ——— ,, ———

To Mr. Fromentin

New Orleans July 15th. 1813

a Senator in Congress

Sir,

The third United States Regiment commenced its ascent of the Mississippi a few days since;— I much fear, this Regiment will be considerably reduced, previous to his arrival at Cincinati.— The recent overflowings of the *River* have left on its *margin,* an immense mass of vegetable matter which under the influence of a hot Summers Sun, will soon be in a State of putrifaction, and must render the Atmosphere greatly insalubrious.— The departure of the third Regiment has diminished one half the Regular force in this quarter, & leaves us much exposed.— I have issued orders for holding in a State of requisition a strong detachment of Militia, to take the field in case of Insurrection, Invasion or eminent danger of Invasion;— But the arraying of this force will necessarily be attended with delay, and to General want of discipline, will be added a Scarcity of arms unless the loan of Muskets desired, can be obtained from the General Government and speedily forwarded.—

The non payment of the Bills drawn by Colonel Shaumburg on the Secretary at War, has seriously affected the Credit of the War Department, in this State, & will I fear much injure the service. Colonel Shaumburg's Bills in many cases fell into the hands of private *individuals whom* their rejection *subjects* to serious embarrassments, I learn also, that the claims of my Citizens for labour done, or material furnished, at the different fortifications remain for the want of funds, unliquidated.— It is not for me to enquire, how far the monies expended in this State under the authority of the War Department, have been judiciously appropriated.— But I sincerely regret, that so many persons, relying on the Credit & good faith of Government and its officers, should have sustained injury.

The Mississippi is retiring within its Banks; every Parish on the River has sustained injury *more* or *less,* & many inhabitants, particularly those of Warren, Concordia, & Plaquemine are ruined.   The Citizens also on the Lafourche in Attackappas, the lower part of Opelousas and in Ouachittas has sustained much loss.   I fear the people will feel great inconvenience in meeting the public taxes; But the Legislature will be in session in time, to extend to them every indulgence, which the general interest will advise.—

Present me Respectfully to your lady, and believe me to be,

With sincere Esteem Yours &c@ &c@ &c@

(signed)   William C. C. Claiborne

—— ,, —— ,, ——

From Secretary of War

War Department June 22d 1813.

Sir,

I have the honor to acknowledge the receipt of your Excellencys letter of May 19th inclosing a Resolution of the General Assembly of Louisiana and requesting a loan of Arms for that State, in addition to those before received from the Commanding General at New Orleans.

The State of the public arsenals will not justify so great a supply of arms to any one State at this time, as you have requested.   Two thousand stands will be deposited with the deputy Quarter Master General at Pittsburg subject to your Excellency's order conformably to the provision of the Act of April 23d 1808, for arming the whole body of the Militia, for which duplicate receipt will be required.

It is not deemed expedient to loan arms to States or individuals, and your Excellency will please to transmit a receipt for those which have been landed by General Wilkinson.— This measure will supercede the accountability of your Excellency to this Department and the Arms will be charged to the State as part of her portion under the Act aforesaid.—

I beg you to accept assurneces of the great respect & Consideration with which I have the honor to be your Excellency's most obt. Servt.

(Signed)   John Armstrong

———— ,, ————

————————

To John Armstrong

New. Orleans July 22nd 1813.

Secretary at War

Sir,

I am honored with the receipt of your letter of the 22. June, informing me "That two thousand Stands of Arms, "will be deposited with the deputy quarter Master Gen- "eral at Pittsburg, and subject to my orders, conform- "ably to the provisions of the Act of April 23d. 1808. "for arming the whole body of the Militia for which "duplicate receipts will be required."— This supply of Arms will be a great acquisition to Louisiana, & I have only to regret the delay which must necessarily attend their transportation to New Orleans.— This State would be much accomodated if you would supply her also with 150 Sabres;— The service of Cavalry is best adapted to the Climate of Louisiana, and in many parts of this State (in the Western prairies for example) are the only troops that could act with advantage.— The want of swords & the impossibility of procuring them by private purchase, has delayed the organization of several Companies of

Cavalry, & in those Counties too, where they would have been most useful.

For the Arms delivered to me by the Commanding General, for the use of the State, I will, by the ensuing Mail, transmit you duplicate receipts, and for the arms to be delivered at Pittsburg to my order, I will authorize *both or either of the Senators* from Louisiana to the Congress of the United States, to *receipt.—*

I have the honor to be, Sir &c@ &c@ &c@

(Signed)   William C. C. Claiborne

———— „ ———— „ ————

To James Brown

New. Orleans July 22d 1813.

a Senator in Congress

Sir,

I have received your letter of the 22nd Ulto. and am thankful for the attention paid by yourself & Colleague to the Resolution of the Legislature requesting a loan of arms.— By a communication from the Secretary at War of the same date with yours, I am advised that two thousand stand of Arms will be deposited with the Deputy Quarter Master General at Pittsburg, subject to my order. These Arms will be a great acquisition to the State, & I regret that their transportation hither from the approaching low State of the Waters will necessarily be attended with so much delay.— I wish sincerely you could prevail upon the Secretary at War, to supply the State, with 150 Sabres;— Cavalry are the Troops best fitted for the Climate of Louisiana; and in many parts of the State, could act with the greatest advantage.— The want of swords and the impossibility of obtaining them by private purchase, has prevented the organization of several troops of Cavalry, in Counties where they are most wanting.

We have nothing new or interesting in this quarter, late accounts from St. Antoine, left the Revolutionists with fair prospects;— The Royalists having a second time been defeated, & Bernado acquiring daily an increase of numbers.—

I do not learn that the City is at this time unhealthy but serious apprehensions are entertained that fevers, will soon be prevalent.—

I am, Sir, &c@ &c@ &c@

(Signed)   William C. C. Claiborne

———— ,, ———— ,, ————

To James Brown

New. Orleans July 27th 1813.

a Senator in Congress

Dear Sir,

The mail of yesterday brought me your letter of the 29th Ultimo. I am pleased with the arrangement you have made for the transportation of the Arms, & any expences attending the same shall be immediately paid to your order.— I wish sincerely, you could obtain from the Secretary at War 150 Sabres, more would be desirable, but I presume a greater number could not be conveniently furnished us.— Louisiana I fear is in greater danger than the Secretary at War apprehends.— If the object of the enemy be *to prevent,* or *delay* the *conquest of Canada,* he will not fail to make a deversion *in this quarter;* for should he obtain a foothold here, it would require the whole of the *North Western Army and other of our forces which now menace Canada* to dislodge him.— It is probable during the sickly season, we may remain undisturbed; But I apprehend serious difficulties in the fall, & shall be prepared with all my means (feeble at best) to Co-operate with the Troops of the United States.— I have used & shall continue to use my best exertions to render the Militia efficient; But my prospects are far from being flattering.— The menaces of the Spanish Agents at Pensacola, & the apparent unfriendly disposition of the Creek Indians, have induced General Flournoy to concentrate most of the Regular force in this District, on the other side of the lakes.— The Creek will not for the present (I believe) commence hostilities, unless urged by the English;— But should Louisiana be invaded, the Creeks & Chactaws will unquestionably be enlisted against us.— As regards the Spaniards their course will dictated by England.— I am, Sir &c@ &c@ &c@

(Signed)   William C. C. Claiborne

———— ,, ———— ,, ————

P. S.   In the event that a Regiment should be raised, may I take the liberty, to request your support of Alexander Laneuville as one of the Majors.— This Gentleman served for seven years as a Lieutenant in the first Regiment of the United States Artillerists & left the service, in order to accept the office of Adjutant General of the Militia of this State, which he stil holds, & discharges the duties in a manner honorable to himself & very satisfactory to be.— Laneuville is a Soldier by profession;— He is a brave virtuous man, & has the advantage of a liberal education.— May I also recommend to your patronage Major Charles Tessier of the Militia, at present of Baton Rouge, as a Captain in the Louisiana Regiment.— Major Tessier is doubtless known to you. He is a native of Louisiana, of polished manners, & general information. The imprudencies of his youth seem to be corrected, & he enjoys now, & I believe very deservedly the confidence & best wishes of this society.—

(Signed)   W. C. C. C.

———— ,, ————

To Wm. C. C. Claiborne Esqr.
    Governor of the State of Louisiana

                    Philadelphia May 31st 1813.
Sir,
    Being about to publish an edition of the elementary
Military discipline established by authority of the United
States Army, & to which the Militia of the States are required to conform, I take the liberty upon the recommendation of Adjutant General Duane, the author of the
work, to advise you that a new edition is now at press,
in order, as the Legislature is now in Session, that should
you think proper to order any for the use of the Militia
of your State, you may do me the favor of intimating the
number which you may wish to be furnished with.— The
work being assigned to me by the author, a reduction in
the price will be made in proportion to the number.
Pennsylvania has taken 2000 Copies at $112½ Cents.
                    (signed)   W. L. Andrews

                    ———— ,, ————

            To W. L. Andrews

                    New. Orleans July 28th. 1813
    Philadelphia.
Sir,
    I have received your letter of the 31st of May adver-
tising me, of your intended publication of the "Element-
"ary Military Discipline established by authority of the
"United States Army to which the Militia of the States
"are required to conform."— I shall take pleasure in
recommending this work to the patronage of the Legislature of Louisiana at their next session and shall ask for
authority in behalf of the State to subscribe for four or
five hundred Copies.—
            I am, Sir, &c@ &c@ &c@
                (signed)   William C. C. Claiborne

            ———— ,, ———— ,, ————

New. Orleans July 28th 1813.

Dear Sir,

You have no doubt, heard *my orders,* directing a Detachment of Militia, from German Coast, to be holden in readiness for service, much investigated, and perhaps censured.— I trust however that my fellow Citizens will very generally approve the measure.— Pending the War in which our Country is involved the safety of Louisiana may always be considered as in danger.— We know that the enemy has the power & the disposition to do the United States great injury; We cannot tell the moment, when he may turn his attention to this State, and I cannot too early take my measures of precaution. If Louisiana, should, as I hope in God she, may remain undisturbed, my fellow Citizens will not be called from their homes;— But in case of insurrection, invasion, or emiment danger of invasion I shall order into the field a Militia force, & the Citizens drafted, or to be drafted under my late orders, will be the first to march.— On a former occasion in a case of insurrection there was not as speedy a movement on the part of the Militia, as was desired, and New Orleans presented a Scene of confusion which to me was very painful.— My late orders are designed to prevent this confusion and to insure in the hour of peril a speedy movement.— As regards German Coast, I know its exposed situation, and so far from weakening it, if the occasion demands, an auxiliary force, shall be sent to your aid.— The prejudice of the people against a draft, seems to me to be very unfounded; It is nothing more, than determining by lot on whom the first tour of duty shall fall.—

We have no late intelligence from Washington.— The President of the United States had been ill of a fever but was on the recovery.— There are no rumours of peace & at present no prospect of so desirable event.— The Creek Indians manifest a very unfriendly disposition towards

the United States, & had in considerable numbers repaired to Pensacola, and demanded of the Spanish Governor arms & ammunition which was refused them.— It
may be that Louisiana may remain tranquil; But I much
fear in the course of next Winter, we shall have our difficulties.— I design leaving New Orleans in a few days
on a visit to the interior Parishes, in order to acquit myself of a constitutional duty; To hasten the organization
of the Militia, & to cause to be holden in readiness for
service a disposable force from each Brigade.—

The United States troops, now in Louisiana are inadequate to our defence in case of attack, & it becomes my
sacred duty, to make such arrangements, as will enable
me, in time of danger, to call speedily to the field a respectable Militia detachment.—

I am, Sir, &c@ &c@ &c@
(signed)   William C. C. Claiborne

To James Monroe

New. Orleans August 1st 1813.

Secretary of State
Dear Sir,

Our last accounts from Washington left the President
dangerously indisposed, and the mail which is due on tomorrow is consequently expected with increased solicitude.— The death of an individual so eminently distinguished for his public & private worth, would at any time
be cause of universal regret; But at a Crisis so interesting as the present, it would be a heavy national Calamity.— I hope I attach more consequence to the uniform
opposition of Massachusetts to the general Government
than it deserves, but it really seems to me, if the men
who now direct the affairs of that State, are not checked
in their career, the ties which bind together the States

will soon be loosened.— The Resolution proposed by Quincy respecting the Navy is monstrous;— But it plainly shews, what are the ultimate views of his party.— The doctrine next avowed, will be, that as the War in the opinion of Massachusetts is unjust she ought not and will not contribute to its support, & therefore must resist taxation;— "peacably if she can, forcibly if she must."

That such a project exists I have little doubt & that it will be soon avowed, unless the American Congress, & the State authorities, by some strong expressions of disapprobation should convince these turbulent men that the Nation has the power and the disposition to preserve inviolate the American Union, & to enforce obedience to the Acts of Government.— We have been much cheered in this quarter, by the recent victories in Canada, and I trust our views of Conquest in that quarter, will be pursued with increase energies.— I have myself thought that the enemy with a design to embarrass our operations to the North, would make a deversion in this quarter.— An attack on Louisiana would necessarily weaken our Northern armies.— If the attack was made at this time, our means of defence are so limited, that I should entertain *great* fears for the safety of this Capitol and were the enemy to obtain possession, it would require the whole of the North Western Army, and perhaps the forces which now menace Canada, to dislodge him. The Creek Indians have commenced hostilities— 700 of their warriors are said to have crossed the Perdido, and the inhabitants are seeking an asylum in the fort of Mobile.— General Flournoy with a detachment of Regulars and General Clairborne with a Regiment of Volunteers, are on the waters of the Mobile, & will I trust speedily meet & disperse the invaders. I fear however, these poor, deluded people, are set on by the English, and who will also command the Co-operation of the Spaniards.— I recently issued orders for holding a detachment of Militia in readiness for service & directed the same to be obtained by draft if it became necessary.— In this City the order has been executed, & shall be enforced in the interior parishes.— In the City some men have been clamorous against the measure declaring it to be unnecessary and contrary to the laws.— But in the Country I anticipate less opposition.— I observe that a Bill is on its passage in Congress establishing a District Court at Mobile.— May I take the liberty to ask you, to make favorable mention to the President of Major Richard Clairborne of this State, as a Candidate for the office of Marshall for the Mobile District.— Major Claiborne was a meritourious officer during the Revolutionary War and has subsequently rendered public service in several civil employments.— He is now poor, dependant and in the vale of life;— But in the enjoyment of great activity of mind & body & fully competent to the discharge of the duties of Marchall.— I feel no delicacy in pressing the claims of Major Claiborne;— The connection between us, by *consanguinity,* if there be any, is so remote that neither can trace it & I speak of him with no *bias,* but that which a knowledge of his integrity his former faithful services, & his present dependant situation *has* excited. Before I conclude this letter, may I also recommend to your patronage Mr. Thomas B. Johnson the present Post Master at New. Orleans.— During six years of his residence in this City I have witnessed with pleasure his examplary deportment; His modest unassuming manners & the purity of his morals, united to a faithful, zealous & honest discharge of public duties, have secured him my esteem and best wishes.— I regret that the climate of Louisiana, should prove so unfavorable to M. Johnson's constitution;— of late his health is so often interrupted, as to induce him to wish a more Northern residence.— He informs me he has a great desire to obtain a Consulate for some European port.— His education & habits

admirably fit him for such a trust. To a general acquaintance with Belle letters, he has added a knowledge
of the French & Spanish languages, & to correct moral
conduct, he unites the most unremitted attention to business.—

I am, Dear Sir, &c'' &c'' &c''

(Signed)   William C. C. Claiborne

———— ,, ———— ,, ————

————————

To John Armstrong

New. Orleans August 13th 1813

Secretary of War.

Sir,

Having understood, that it was the intention of Government to raise a Regiment in Louisiana, & to station
the same permanently at New. Orleans, may I take the
liberty to recommend Alexander Laneuville for a Majority in said Regiment.— This Gentleman (a native of
France) was an inhabitant of Louisiana in the year 1803.
and was in 1805 appointed a Lieutenant in the first United
States Regiment of Artillerists, & continued in service,
until January 1812, when he resigned for the purpose of
accepting the office of Adjutant General of the State
which he now holds; and discharges in a manner honorable to himself and highly satisfactory to me.— Laneuville is a Soldier by profession; possessing an enlightened
mind, and evidencing on all occasions, the greatest integrity, firmness & independence of character.— May I
also recommend to your patronage Major Charles Tessier
of Baton Rouge;— This Gentleman is a native of Louisiana, and a member of an extensive & influential family
his education has been respectable, & he has acquired by
traveling a considerable knowledge of the man and of
things.— To a very commanding graceful person he

unites the most polished manners, and altho' his partiality for the ladies may have betrayed him into some imprudencies, his deportment has been so conciliatory, & his integrity, bravery and honor so well established that his acquaintance hold him in very high estimation.— Tessier during the Territorial Government was one of my aids, and is now a Major in the Militia of the State.— I think him worthy a like Commission in the Regular service;— But if this cannot be obtained I recommend him for a Captaincy.— I present no candidates for the offices of Colonel & Lieutenant Colonel of the Louisiana Regiment.—No doubt suitable characters will be recommended by the Senators & Representatives from this State, & these Gentlemen will I am persuaded agree with me in opinion that in appointing field officers for a Regiment to be raised and stationed in Louisiana, it would be inexpedient wholly to overlook the French and Creole inhabitants, who compose so great a portion of the population of the State.

I am, Sir, &c@ &c@ &c@
(Signed)   William C. C. Claiborne

—— ,, —— ,, ——

P. S. It may be proper to add, that the Adjutant General Laneuville and Major Tessier, are well acquainted with the English, French and Spanish languages.—

W. C. C. C.

—— ,, ——

Batture in front of the Suburg St. Mary.

The City Council of New. Orleans, having solicited the Governor to assist at their deliberations on the subject of the Batture, he attended at the City Hall on the 9th of August 1813. and addressed the Council as follows.—

Mr. Recorder and Gentlemen of the Council,—

Had my health permitted, I should have availed myself of the honor of your invitation, and been present at the sessions of the Council on Saturday last.— The question as to the right of property to the Batture in front of the Suburg St. Mary, is of very general concern.— That the public right should be maintained against the claims of individuals, is not only interesting to the City but to the State, and the whole Western Country.   To this end therefore, *any measure which the laws authorize* will meet my best wishes, and Zealous Co-operation.— A decision of the honorable the District Court of Louisiana, in the suit brought by Mr. Livingston against Mr. Dorgenoy late Marshall of the District, declares the removal of Mr. Livingston from the Batture, by order of Mr. Jefferson late President of the United States, illegal, and directs the plaintiff to be restored to his possession.— I am sorry the defendant has declined appealing from this decision to the Supreme Court of the United States; The high standing of the officer whose authority is denied, the importance of the Stake, and of the principles involved, make it desirable (for the satisfaction of all parties) that the case should have been carried before the highest Juducial Tribunal of this Nation.— I believe however, there is no way of obtaining an appeal but thro' the agency of Mr. Dorgency, and that the arreté of this Council, which proposes an appeal in the name of the City Council & the Governor of the State will be imperative.— Neither the one nor the other are parties to the Suit, and it is understood to be an established Rule, that a party can alone take an appeal.— The operation of this Rule, in the present case, is unfortunate, Since M. Dorgenoy has in fact been only *an Agent* & his personal *Interest much less, than that of the Public* envoloved in the issue.— The title of Mr. Livingston is not embraced by the decision of the Honorable the District Court. These (This) title however, has long been the subject of private and public discussion.— My *opinions,* formed at an early period of this discussion, were (as my duty enjoined) fully and freely expressed in my official Correspondence with the General Government, whilst I acted as Governor of the late Territory of Orleans.— From what I have seen, the Batture can only be considered a Shoal of the Mississippi;— a part of the port of New. Orleans, covered with water from four to five & six months in every year.— And the spot where boats and barges coming from the upper Country, can lie and land with greatest convenience and Safety.— From what I have heard, no doubt exists in my mind, but the Batture at low Water, has from the foundation of the City (with the extent it had from time to time) been used as a public landing & common, where Boats were landed and unload, and where the Inhabitants of New: Orleans obtaining earth for building and for raising the Streets and court yards, and that the French and Spanish Governors of Louisiana had invariably prevented the exercise of individual owner Ship over the same, and removed all intruders.— should the Batture be reclaimed, from my own observations on the Mississippi, and the information of much older Settlers than myself, I verily believe, it would change the current of the river in front of the City to the great injury of the port of New: Orleans and the lower Suburbs and plantations.— Such have been, and such are still my impressions.— perhaps they are erroneous.— contrary sentiments are entertained by others, and it is contended that the Batture is alluvion land, susceptible of private ownership & the property of M. Livingston.— The laws must ultimately decide, & to maintain the public right, we must alone resort to the means, which *these* permit.—

Considering the Batture as a part of the Bed of the Mississippi, it is an object of enquiry, what measures ought or can be taken by the State authorities, to prevent obstructions on that *Great highway,* the free use of which as well to the inhabitants of this State, as of all the other States, is made one of the Conditions upon which Louisiana was admitted into the American Union.— The subject has been submitted to the Consideration of the Attorney General, the Constitutional adviser of the Executive, and the result of his enquiries, shall be communicated to you.— As far as the laws and the principles of the Government authorize my immediate agency or give me a Controul over the public functionaries, whose province it may be to interfere, you may be assured of a prompt and faithful discharge of duty.— But if upon examination the powers of the State authorities, should on the present occasion, be found incompetent, we must speedily & respectfully solicit the further interference & support of the General Government. *More we cannot do.*— To proceed further than the laws justify, would furnish an example of evil tendency, & injure the best of causes.—

(Signed)   William C. C. Claiborne

New. Orleans Augst. 9th 1813.

To. M. Girod

New. Orleans Augst. 9th. 1813

Mayor of New. Orleans
Sir,

I have received your letter enclosing me a Decree of the City Council of this date, by which the Governor of the State is requested to concur with the Council of the City and to pray on his part also an appeal in his quality as first Majistrate of Louisiana to the Supreme Court of the United States from a late decision of the Judge of the District of Louisiana in the case of Edward Livingston against LeBreton Dorgenoy cidivant Marshall of the District of Orleans.— As this decision relates to a question of much interest, to the State, & involves principles of high importance, it seems to me desirable, that the case should be brought before the supreme Judiciary of the nation.— As neither the City Council nor the Governor were parties to the cause, I much doubt, whether an appeal on their application will be deemed admissible; I nevertheless have instructed the Attorney General of the State to unite with the Attorney for the City in support of the application, and should it succeed, there will not be the smallest objection on my part, in my official character, to be a party in this appeal.—

I am, Sir &c@ &c@ &c@

(Signed)   William C. C. Claiborne

To Thos. B. Robertson

New. Orleans Augst. 11th 1813.

a Representative in Congress
   Washington City
Sir,

A decision of the Honorable the District Court of Louisiana in the suit of Livingston Vs Dorgenoy, declares the interference of Mr. Jefferson in the case of the Batture illegal & directs the claimant to be reinstated in the possession.— If my memory serves me right, your opinion was always favorable to the Public claim to the Batture, & therefore I shall take the more pleasure in corresponding with you on a subject, so interesting to the City of New: Orleans, and to the State you have the honor to represent. The decision of the Court (altho' the title is not embraced) has occasioned much agitation in this City. The public sentiment is evidently wounded, & the public feeling greatly excited.— The enclosure marked *A* is a Copy of an Arreté of the City Council on the subject; The marked *B* of an address from myself to the City Council, & the paper marked *C* of a second arretté, advising an appeal in the name of the Governor & City Council, which I consider will be wholly inopperative, unless to show our perseverance in support of the public claim. I shall keep you advised of the progress of this affair;— In the mean time, as far as may depend upon my precepts & example, the public claim shall only be maintained by such means as the Laws justify, & in the further interference and support of the General Government should be found necessary I shall deem it my duty in behalf of the *State,* to address myself to you, as her Congressional Representative.—

The Creek Indians have commenced hostilities.— It is hoped immediate & active operations will be directed against them as the only means of rescuing our frontiers from great distresses.— We feel here very sensibly for the wrongs, *the more than Savage brutality of the enemy towards the people of Hampton.*— These transactions should warm every heart & strengthen every arm in his Country's cause.—

I am, Sir, &c@ &c@ &c@

(signed)   William C. C. Claiborne

———— ,, ———— ,, ————

To Thomas Jefferson

New. Orleans Augst. 14th. 1813

Dear Sir,

In the suit brought by Edward Livingston against LeBreton D'Orgeois late Marshall of the District of Orleans, the Honorable Mr. Hall, Judge of the District of Louisiana, has decided, the dispossessing of Mr. Liv-

ingston of the Batture, by order of the late President to
be illegal, & he directs the Plaintiff to be reinstated in
his possession.— The public sentiment on this occasion
is evidently wounded, & the public feeling greatly excited.— The enclosures *A.* & *B.* are Copies of the two
arretés of the City Council, and the paper marked *C.* of
a short address which I made to the Council.— Considering the Batture as a part of the Bed of the Mississippi
and included within the port of New. Orleans, I shall have
recourse to our States Courts, to enjoin Mr. Livingston
against exercising any acts of ownership over the same,
or in any manner obstructing the Navigation of the Mississippi, which is declared to be a great highway, and the
free use of which, as well to the inhabitants of this State,
as of the other States, is one of the conditions on which
Louisiana was admitted into the Union.— How far I shall
be enabled to succeed is impossible to say.— Mr. Livingston has found means either to neutralize or to make
active partizans of most of the lawyers in the State. The
people however, are fortunate in receiving the support
of the Attorney General Mr. F. X. Martin & of Messrs.
Moreau Lislet & Fielding Turner, three distinguished
lawyers, and I entertain strong hopes that we may yet be
enabled, to maintain the rights of the public.—
      The Creek Nation of Indians have commenced hostili-
ties & the Frontiers of the Mississippi Territory are
much exposed; We shall soon however have in that quarter, a respectable force, & I trust our Troops will be ordered to march immediately into the Nation, as the surest
means of punishing & puting down these faithless people. In a letter I received from my Brother General
Claiborne of the Mississippi Territory dated Fort Stoddert 3d. of August 1813. he says— ''I arrived at this post
''on the 30″ Ultimo and found the Country in great con-
''fusion and alarm.— The Creeks are making every prep-
''aration to attack us and on my part, I have, & shall

"make every arrangement for the protection of our fron-
"tier.— General Flournoy promised in case of a rupture,
, "to reinforce me, with the 7th Regiment, should he do
"this, & will authorize me, I shall march into the nation,
"& shall enter it with sanguine hopes of success.— The
"Indians are unquestionably supplied with arms & am-
"munition by the Governor of Pensacola.— A party on
"their return from that place with ammunition &c. were
"attacked by a party of Militia under Colonel Collier, &
"must have been defeated, but for the conduct of some
"of the Militia officers. Colonel Collier behaved bravely,
"he is missing & is supposed to have been killed on the
"retreat."

Louisiana has hitherto been fortunately exempt from
the immediate horrors of the War;— But I am not without apprehensions, that in the course of the ensuing Winter, we shall be called upon to repel an invasion, & to
meet an event of the kind, I shall make all the preparations, which my powers and the resources of the State
(feeble at best will admit.—

I am, Dear Sir, &c@' &c@ &c@

(Signed)   William C. C. Claiborne

"   "

EXTRACT of a Letter from Governor Claiborne to
Julien Poydras, dated New. Orleans August 16th 1813 /.

Dear Sir,

You will have heard of the decision of Judge Hall in
the suit brought by Livingston Vs. LeBreton D'Orgenoy.
The interference of Mr. Jefferson is declared illegal, and
the Plaintiff is to be restored to his possession. Enclosed
are two arretés of the City Council upon the subject, and
a short address upon the occasion, from me.— We are
doing all in our power to support the public claim.—

Messrs. Martin, Moreau Lislet and Turner, are employed
to prevent all intrusion upon the Batture, & to this end,
application has been made to Judge Pitot, to enjoin Mr.
Livingston against evercising any act of ownership over
the same or erecting thereon any kind of works, upon the
ground, that it is a part of the Bed of the Mississippi, included within the Port of New. Orleans, and no individual
ought or can be permitted to obstruct the navigation.
(Signed)   William C. C. Claiborne

——— ,, ——— ,, ———

To Thos. B. Robertson

New. Orleans Augst. 21st. 1813.
A Representative in Congress
Dear Sir,
Since my letter of the 13. Instant, it has been deemed
expedient to proceed against Mr. Livingston before the
Parish Court of New. Orleans, by way of *information* and
of which a Copy is herewith enclosed.— Mr. Livingston &
his friends (I learn) are clamorous on the occasion; They
represent the procedure as unprecedented, and affect to
consider it as a wicked (but feeble) attempt, to justify
opposition to the Tribunals of the United States.— But
to me the subject presents a very different aspect;— The
care of our Rivers and ports, appertain exclusively to
the State authority, and the means resorted to, seem to
me the best calculated to preserve the Public rights.—
The case is to be argued on the 24th Instant and the result is anxiously awaited.—
I have the honor to be &c@ &c@ &c@
(Signed)   William C. C. Claiborne

——— ,, ——— ,, ———

To James Brown

New. Orleans August 25th 1813.

a Senator in Congress

Sir,

The last Mail brought us, the state of the vote in the Senate, on the nomination of Mr. Gallatin to the Russian Embassy.— Your vote on the occasion, has given very great satisfaction to the friends of the administration in this City & will I am certain, be highly approved thro' out the State.— When the Embassy to Russia was announced my impression was, that the measure had been adopted not so much from the proffered mediation, as with a view, of insuring the United States an able representation in Europe at a period, when the great Belligerants wearied with the toil, and the distresses of War, might be disposed to sheath the sword.— The proposed Congress, for an adjustment of a general peace, is one of the events which the administration seem to have contemplated, when the envoys to Russia were selected, and surely a more judicious selection could not have been made.— Mr. Gallatin was certainly the most efficient member of the Mission; I take pleasure in acknowledging the merits of Messrs. Adams & Bayard;— But I do not hesitate to say, that no man in America is better acquainted with the interests of the United States commercial & political than *Mr. Gallatin,* nor do I know an individual as well enabled as *he* is, to support that interest in a *Congress* composed of Delegates from the several warring nations, *where* the debates and the proceedings will (probably) be wholly conducted in the French language.— The objection to Mr. Gallatin, that he was *Secretary of the Treasury* might have been waved— His *presence* in the United States, can better be dispensed with (since the duties may be discharged by another) than *that* of a Chief Justice & yet we find, that Genl. Washington and afterwards Mr. Adams nominated a

Chief Justice of the United States an Envoy extraordinary and in each case, the Senate sanctioned the nomination.—

I do not learn: that the Creeks have done much mischief.— We have on the Mobile frontier, a respectable force, which seems to be so judiciously disposed of, as effectually to cover our settlements.— The conduct of the Spanish Governor at Pensacola in supplying the Creeks with munitions of War, is highly reprehensible;— I doubt, whether this is not such an act of hostility, as to justify the American Government in directing Pensacola, to be immediately taken possession of;— I must confess, an order to that effect, would afford me the sincerest pleasure, for I have always considered the possession of Pensacola (and more specially during the present War) essential to the safety of Louisiana.—

   I am, Sir, &c@ &c@ &c@
          (signed)   William C. C. Claiborne
——————— ,, ——————— ,, ———————

EXTRACT of a letter from Governor Claiborne, to General Claiborne Commanding officer at Fort Stoddert dated
                    New. Orleans August 25th 1813.

I thank you for your several communications by Lieutenant Colo. Ross.— Your command is an important one, and I trust, you will be enabled to make such disposition of your force as effectually to cover our settlements.—

The Spanish Governor at Pensacola, in supplying the Creeks with munitions of War, has subjected himself to a serious responsibility;— The Creeks avowed an intention to commence hostilities against the United States, and the Governor by furnishing them with the means, has been himself a party.— We shall soon learn the view our Government will take of this transaction;— for myself, I shall be disappointed, if it does not lead to the occupancy of Pensacola, by American Troops, unless the act of the Governor be speedily disavowed by his superiors, & a just atonement offered for the outrage.— I must entreat you to keep me advised of events in your quarter, & more particularly as to the disposition of the Chactaws, to whose depredations (should they become hostile) several parishes of this State, would be much exposed.—

To Thos. B. Robertson

New. Orleans Sept. 4th 1813.

a Representative in Congress
Sir,

On consideration of the information filed by the Attorney General against Mr. Livingston in the case of the Batture, the Judge of the Parish, Mr. Pitot, thought proper to dessolve the injunction, which he had previously awarded;— It seems the Judge was under an impression; that until Mr. Livingston, had done some act to deprive the Citizens of the use of the Batture, or erected some works thereon, which might obstruct the Navigation of the Mississippi, the interference of the Court was premature and improper.— Thus the case rests for the present, nor has Mr. Livingston yet thought proper to prosecute the Mayor of New Orleans, or the inhabitants who are in the habit of taking as formerly *Dirt* from the Batture;— I am extremely desirous to have the right to tittle to the Batture finally settled; But feel some difficulty in determining the best manner of bringing the question fairly before our Courts.— The subject however is submitted to the consideration of the Attorney General (Mr. Martin) and the course he advises will be pursued;— It is believed, that the Indian War on the Mobille Frontier, will soon terminate; The Regular force ordered to that quarter, aided by the Militia of the Mississippi Territory if permitted to act offensively will in one Campaign, destroy or drive beyond the Mississippi, the whole of the War party.— The friends of the administration in this City sincerely regret the objection of Mr. Gallatin by the Senate and much admire your vote on the Question of the Embargo.—

I am, Sir, &c@ &c@ &c@

(signed)   William C. C. Claiborne

———— „ ———— „ ————

CIRCULAR TO COLONELS OF MILITIA

New. Orleans Septber 8th 1813.

SIR,

The War with the Creek Indians assumes a serious aspect; A Fort twenty five Miles distant from Mobile, has been taken, & 350 Men, Women, & children cruelly massacred.[1]— It is confidently reported that many slaves have escaped from their Masters and joined the Indians, and it is feared, the Chactaws if they have not already will soon become hostile. Hence the necessity of vigilance thro' out the State, and I enjoin it on you, to use your best exertion, to render your Regiment an efficient Corps.—

For the present I have only to instruct you, to cause regular Militia patrols within the limits of your command, & to recommend to the Citizens, to maintain a proper discipline among their Slaves.

I am, Sir, &c@ &c@ &c@

(signed)   William C. C. Claiborne

———— „ ———— „ ————

[1] Massacre of Fort Mines. See Encyclopedia of Mississippi History, Vol. 1, p. 732.

New. Orleans Septbr. 8th 1813.

Benjamin Morgan Esqr.
    New. Orleans
Sir,
    I request you to have the goodness to engage a Vessel to proceed to Maddisonville, & to be in readiness to sail tomorrow forenoon. I wish the Vessel, to be sufficiently large in addition to other Cargo, To take on board three horses.— Will you also be pleased to cause to be purchased on account of the State in the course of this day, one hundred pound of powder, and four hundred pound of Lead, & have the same put on board of the Vessel, you may engage as aforesaid.— These articles with one hundred Stand of Muskets, in boxes & a case of flints for which I will give you an order this afternoon, constitute the Cargo, I desire to strip for Madisonville, I enclose you a Check on the Bank for one hundred & eighty Dollars, which you will enter to the Credit of the State.—
                    I am, Sir, &c@ &c@ &c@
                        (signed)   William C. C. Claiborne
            —————— ,, —————— ,, ——————

            ——————

                    To Genl. Thomas

                New. Orleans Sept: 10th 1813.

    Baton Rouge.
Dear Sir,
    I enclose for your perusal a Copy of a circular letter, which I have addressed to the several Colonels of Regiments, and I take this occasion to inform you, that by a general order of the sixth instant, I have ordered Detachments of Militia from the several Brigades, of your devision to be holden in readiness for service.—

I set out for St. Tammany on tomorrow and will endeavor, previous to my return to New Orleans, to visit Baton Rouge.—We are surrounded by dangers and we must unite our best efforts to place the Militia of the State on the best possible footing.—

> I am,
>> Dear Sir,
>>> With Esteem
>>>> (Signed) William C. C. Claiborne

——— ,, ——— ,, ———

To Judge Toulmin

Parish of St. Tammany Sept: 16th 1813

Dear Sir,

Enclosed is a letter from the unfortunate Hargrove to his wife, which I beg you to give a safe conveyance. All my exertions to relieve Hargrove and his Companions in misfortune have hitherto failed of success;— Mr. Gray however, encourages me to hope, that on the *interference direct* of the President of the United States the Spanish authorities might be disposed to accommodate. I shall solicit this interference, and trust it will not be withholden.— I feel sensibly for the distress of your frontier; The object of my present visit to this Parish is to take some measures for the safety of the Inhabitants, which will be seriously menaced in the event of the Choctaws joined the Creeks, which seems to me highly probable.—

> I am, Dear Sir, &c@ &c@ &c@
>> (signed) William C. C. Claiborne

——— ,, ——— ,, ———

To Thomas Flournoy

Brigadier General
 of the 7th M: District
  Parish of St. Tammany Sept: 17th 1813

Dear Sir,

 I have received your letter of the 12th Instant, with its enclosures. General Claiborne gives me an interesting detail of the misfortunes attending the garrison of Fort Mims. The loss is seriously to be regretted; But the gallant defence which was made, & the consequent suffering of the enemy afford great consolation.— I experienced much solicitude for the personal safety of my Brother, but stil more for his Military fame. The misfortune however is not attributable to any neglect or inattention on his part, and I trust an opportunity may be offered him to avenge the death of so many brave men.

 The fifteen hundred Muskets reported to be furnished Louisiana were at the date of my last accounts in the Arsenal at Pittsburg.— I have urged their transportation to Baton Rouge, with all possible dispatch but from the low state of the Ohio I fear these arms will not reach me in less than two or three Months.—

 I obtained for Captain McQuean a translation of the letter from the Governor of Pensacola, & which I pursued with great interest.— There can be no doubt of the hostile disposition of the Spanish authorities towards the United States, and that they await only a fit occasion to act offensively. I am aware of the magnitude of the trust committed to you, & sincerely regret your limited means.— We must hope for better support, for surely the Government, cannot & will not be so perilous a crisis leave unprotected so interesting and exposed Section of the Union.— You have done right in ordering the 3d Regiment to Fort Stoddert, & it must & will be approved.—

I came in this parish, with a view of taking some measures for the safety of the Inhabitants which will be greatly endangered, in the event of the Chactaws joining the Creeks, which is not improbable.— On tomorrow I proceed to Baton Rouge by the way of St. Helena.— I wish much to visit the western parishes of this State; But I doubt, whether, my return to New. Orleans, may not become necessary.— If the English should hazard an attack against that Capitol, I should be happy to contribute in person against its defence.   I am not without apprehensions that the hostilities of the Creeks are designed by the English to withdraw our forces from the Mississippi, and leave New Orleans which they contemplate attacking unprotected.

I beg you to keep advised of all occurrences which interest our safety.— I need not assure you of my Zealous Co-operation.— Were my means equal to my wishes, you would find a prompt & firm supporter, but with an unarmed, & undisciplined Militia, I can only offer you partial aid.— You must have heard of the opposition in New. Orleans, to my orders for holding in readiness for service a detachment of Militia; I know that this opposition *originated* with a few individuals, of whose disaffection to our Country I have long been convinced, and it only remains for me to regret, that such Men should have influenced the opinions of many well disposed Citizens.— Any letters you may direct to me under cover to L. B. Macarty Esqr. Secretary of the State of Louisiana, will be duly forward.— Accept my best wishes.—

I am, Dear Sir, &c@ &c@ &c@

(signed)   William C. C. Claiborne

——— ,, ——— ,, ———

To Eliguis Fromentin

a Senator of the U : S :
Washington City.

Parish of St. Tammany Sept: 17th 1813

Dear Sir,

You will have heard of the Capture and destruction of the Garrison of Fort Mims by the Creek Indians, and the distresses of our fellow Citizens on the Mobile.— I have visited this exposed part of Louisiana, with a view, of taking measures, for the safety of the inhabitants, which will be greatly endangered, should the Chactaws join the Creeks;— an event *by no means* improbable.— I pray you Sir, by letter to your friend at Pittsburg, to urge him, if the arms for this State should still be there, to provide for their transportation to Baton Rouge, with all possible dispatch.— I repeat that the expense attending such transportation will be promptly paid on the Bills of Mr. Brown & yourself jointly, or individually.— The fifteen hundred Muskets promised will be great acquisition, & to which I should be much gratified, if two, three or four hundred Sabres, and as many pair of pistols could be added.— The Creoles of this Country are very partial to Cavalry service, and in some parts of our State, particularly the Western District they are the kind of Troops, that could act with greatest advantage. The great body of the Militia of Louisiana, are, I persuade myself disposed to unite hand & heart in the defence of our Country, but they are greatly deficient in Arms.

I am, Dear Sir, &c@ &c@ &c@

(Signed)   William C. C. Claiborne

———— ,, ———— ,, ————

To Thomas Flournoy

Lafourche Sept: 29th 1813.

Brigadier General
  of the 7th M. District

Sir,

 I have received your interesting letter of the 19 Instant with its enclosures.— The movements of Spaniards on our Western frontier commands my serious attention.— I persuade myself no offence will be offered to Louisiana.— But I am not without serious apprehensions, that they will be disposed to advance as far as the Arroya Honda, (now within the Jurisdiction of this State) which the Spanish agents contend to be the Eastern limit of the province of Texas.— I trust the force you now have on the Mobile will not only enable you to cover that frontier, but to disperse the hostile Indians.

 The people of the several parishes of St. Tammany, S. Helena, Feliciana and Baton Rouge seem disposed to rally, *at the first call,* among the standard of their Country, and I shall be disappointed if the people of the Western parishes, (whom I mean also to visit) do not feel and evidence the like patriotism.— At Baton Rouge, the people are repairing the Fortifications, and erecting Block houses. I pray you to have the goodness to suffer to remain at that post all the small pieces of Cannon & Shuch powder & Ball as may be now there. The people are much in want of munitions of War & such as are left at Baton Rouge would I am sure in case of emergency, be used with advantage & effect by the Militia.— I feel much for the safety of New Orleans during the ensuing Winter,— At present it could offer but little resistance to an attack from without.— I am making every effort to organize in the interior of the State a disposable Militia force, & my prospects are flattering. I shall return to

New. Orleans, about the last of October & earlier if my
presence becomes necessary.
                I am, Sir, &c@ &c@ &c@
                    (signed)   William C. C. Claiborne

                    ————— ,, ————— ,, —————

                    To Capt. Dubuclet
                        Attackapas October 4th 1813.
        Attackapas.
SIR,
    I learn with pleasure, that the Corps of Cavalry un-
der your Command, is completely organized and wants
only a few Sabres, to become efficient.—I have recently
given orders, for the purchase at New. Orleans of 150
Sabres, and if my agent should be enabled to procure
them, I will on my return to the City, furnish you the
number wanted.—It is expected, you will hold your Company in readiness to march;— If Louisiana should remain unassailed by the enemy, my fellow Citizens will not
be called from their pursuits;— But in the event that the
safety of our Homes & families should be menaced I shall
calculate on your Company's repairing with promptitude
& Pleasure to their Country's Standard.—
                I am, Sir, &c@ &c@ &c@
                    (signed)   William C. C. Claiborne.

                    ————— ,, ————— ,, —————

                    To L. B. Macarty
                        Nachitoches October 16th 1813
    Secretary of State
    of Louisiana.
Dear Sir,
    The defeat of the Revolutionists near St. Antoine, and
the entire ascendancy of the Royalists in the Province of
Texas, have thrown upon this frontier, many distressed

Spanish families. I have not been enabled to ascertain the precise number, but it is believed, at least twelve hundred persons have crossed the Sabine, most of whom are wholly destitute of the comforts, & the necessaries of life. — I learn however with pleasure, that the Citizens of this & the adjoining parishes have extended to these strangers much hospitality and supplied with a generous hand, their immediate wants.— It is reported here, that a Colonel Elisondo, the Second in Command of the Royalists, had sent to the fugitives a verbal Message to the following effect.— "That the unfortunate inhabitants of "Nacogdoches, and even the Rebels of St. Antonio would "be pardoned, provided they presented themselves at his "Head Quarters within fifty days." But it is said few, if any, are disposed to accept of the proffered Boon being apprehensive that the Colonel benevolent intentions would not be approved by his superiors, and that were they approved their existance would nevertheless be precarious, since having already become objects of suspicion, their lives, in the event of further attempts on the part of the Revolutionists might be in jeopardy. The Royalists under the command of Elisondo, had advanced to the Trinity distant 180 Miles from this post, and contemplated proceeding on to the Sabine, but it is said were very unexpectedly by two successive Couriers recalled to St. Antoine. It is stated upon the authority of a Spanish Deserter, & several fugitive inhabitants, that the retrogade movement was occasioned by a Revolutionary army from the Interior advancing towards Texas, and in such force as to menace St. Antonio.— Of the Revolutionists, who were taken by Colonel Elisando on his march to the Trinity, the Spanish subjects were immediately shot;— But the Americans, & some native Frenchmen experienced the greatest lenity;— passports to retire from the province & provisions were furnished to the whole, &

to the wounded, Horses were given.   Whether this len-
ient course, is attributable to the policy of the local Government or to the generous dispositions of Colonel Elisondo is not ascertained;— But the prisoners, who were
liberated, speak in grateful terms of the very kind, & humane treatment they received from that officer.— Among
the Strangers who in consequence of the recent events in
Texas, have been brought to this frontier are a nation of
Indians, called the *Lapans or Cances*.   They had taken
a decided stand in favour of the Revolutionists, assisted
at all their battles, & seem disposed to follow their fortunes.— This tribe, can bring into the field about five hundred men, and are represented to be brave & war-like;—
At the date of the last accounts, they were with their
families;— on this side of the Trinity & moving on towards the Sabine.   These Indians, will I trust be inclined as all the Tribes in this vicinity now are, to live in
peace & friendship with the United States.—The Agent
for the Government, at this post Doctor Sibley discharges with great fidelity, the trust committed to him;
—He has recently holden interesting conferences with the
Chiefs of the Caddoes, Couchattas & other tribes and
finds them all favorably disposed.— It seems War talks
had recently been sent to these Indians by the Creeks,
but had made no other effect than to induce them to inform Doctor Sibley of their willingness, to take up arms,
in defence of their American Brothers, whenever their
services were required.— I shall leave this post in two
days, for Rapides from whence I design to proceed by
Catahoula to Concordia, & hope to be in New Orleans between the 6th & 10th of November.—

I am, Sir, &c@ &c@ &c@
(Signed)   William C. C. Claiborne

A TALK from William Charles Cole Claiborne
Governor of the State of Louisiana, and Commander
in Chief of the Militia thereof, to the great Chief
of the Caddo Nation.— Nachitoches 18th October 1813.

Friend & Brother! I arrived at this Post three sleeps
past, and learn from our friend Doctor Sibley that you
had only left it last month. I should rejoice to have met
you here, that we might have shaken hands in friendship,
and smoaked & conversed under the shade of the same
tree. Seven years ago, Brother, we had a conference
at this place, Natchitoches, and mutually promised to
keep the path between our two nations white. We have
been both long in authority, and know from experience
the blessing of peace. We will endeavor to keep the
chain bright, and the Chiefs who follow us, may I hope,
so strengthen it that our children will live together as
neighbors and friends.

Brother, The United States are like the oak of the for-
est. A great body with many branches. The people of
the United States are composed of eighteen families.—
Each family has a chief, but the great beloved Man of all
is your father, the President, who stands in the place of
the great Washington. Our friend Doctor Sibley is the
agent of the President, and whatever he says in his name,
you must receive as his own words. I have seen brother
and highly approve the Talk you gave out, when you
was last in Council at this post. The advice you have
given to your own people, and to all red men with whom
you have influence, is that of a father to his children. I
hope they will hold it fast and live in constant peace with
the white people.

Brother! Seven years ago you told me your nation
had but one enemy. The Osages, and I am sorry to learn
you are still at War with those people. I have often
heard of the Osages. In the vast hunting grounds where

the great Spirit has placed a sufficiency of Buffaloe, Bear and Deer for all the red men, the Osages, I hear have already robbed the hunters of all nations, and their Chiefs wage War to acquire more Skins.   Among the white people, brother, there is also a nation of Osages.   Beyond the Sea, there lives a people called the English, who may really be considered white Osages.   On the big water, which the great Spirit made large enough for the use of all men, the English have already plundered every people, and their Chiefs direct a continuance of these outrages.   Many Americans peacefully navigating the big Water had their vessels and property taken from them. And others were compelled to serve on board of War canoes, and made to fight against their friends & Country Men.   But Brother such injuries could not be endured. The hearts of the Americans have become cross; They have raised the Tomahawk, & will not consent to bury it until the English are just towards them.   The warriors of your father, the President are marching into the Country of our enemy and the thunder of our great War canoes is heard on every Sea.

Brother!   The English unwilling to fight us man to man, have called upon the red people to assist them.— With tongues, as forked and as poisonous as a snake, they have told the Indians many lies, and made fair promises which they will not, and cannot fulfil.   Thus it is, many of the red men have been prevailed upon to throw away the Peace Talks of their father the President.— But the Americans have the power, and the will to punish all their enemies.   The other day, the Creeks, when it was supposed they were only quarreling among themselves, surprised one of our Forts, & spilled much innocent blood.— A fly you know brother may disturb. the sleeping lion— But our Warriors are now in arms against the Creeks, and it will not be in the power of their friends, the English to shield them against our vengeance.

I don't like many words, but there is something else on my heart which I must relate to you. I hear the Creeks have sent runners with War Talks, to the Conchattas and other tribes, your neighbours, but I hope all these people will look up to you, as an elder Brother, and hold fast your good advice. When your father was a Chief, the paths from your Towns to Natchitoches was clean, and if an Indian struck the people of Natchitoches — It was the same as to strike him. You now brother, stand in your father's place.— To a Chief, a Man and a Warrior, nothing could be more acceptable than a sword, but a suitable one could not be obtained at this place.— I have therefore directed, that a sword be purchased at New. Orleans, & forwarded to Doctor Sibley, who will present it to you in my name.—

Farewell brother! I pray the great Spirit to preserve you in health & happiness.

(Signed)   William C. C. Claiborne

——— ,, ——— ,, ———

To John Armstrong

Louisiana October 25th 1813.
County of Rapides.

Secretary at War
Dear Sir,

I am now on my return to New. Orleans, from a visit to the Western frontier of this State. Such of the Revolutionists of Texas, as survived their late defeat near St. Antonio, together with a number of distressed families have sought an asylum in this State. I thought it probable, the Royalists would advance to the Sabine, & perhaps to the Arroya Hundo, but it seems they have established their Head Quarters at St. Antonio, & design to suffer the County between that Post and the Sabine to remain a desert. The Caddo Nation of Indians, & other Tribes residing on or near the Waters of Red River are very friendly towards the United States;— War Talks had been sent to them by the Creeks.— But it seems, they cannot be shaken in their determination to remain at peace with the United States.— I have become acquainted in this Country with a very deserving young Man, who wishes a Commission in the Army, and who I beg leave to recommend to your patronage.— I allude to a Mr. Smith Gordon, a modest, unassuming, amiable youth, who seems much attached to Military life, & in his character as adjutant of a Militia Regiment, has by practice, and reading already acquired a tolerable knowledge of Tactics.— Mr. Gordon is nineteen years of age, and were he now honored with the Commission of a Lieutenant in the Louisiana or any (if his life should be spared) he will from his merit meet with rapid promotion.—

I am, Sir, &c@ &c@ &c@
(signed)   William C. C. Claiborne.

———— ,, ———— ,, ————

————————

To William Jones

Louisiana October 25th 1813.
Secretary of the Treasury
Dear Sir,

From the bottom of my heart, do I congratulate you, on our repeated naval victories. The affair between the Enterprize & the Boxer, is a brilliant one, but the triumph of Perry on Lake Erie, goes to establish our Naval Supremacy & gives to the War in Canada a new aspect.— What has become of the Frigates President Congress &

Essex? I pray God to preserve them, & to extend his
peculiar favours to their intrepid Commander. A youth
of great promise Mr. Henry Sibley the Son of my friend
Doctor Sibley of this State (is very desirous to enter the
Navy, and I take the liberty to recommend him to your
patronage: He is 18 years of age and were he now honored with a Midshipman's Warrant, I am sure he would
from his merit meet with rapid promotion.—

I am, Sir, &c@ &c@ &c@
(Signed)   William C. C. Claiborn

———— " ———— " ————

By WILLIAM CHARLES COLE CLAIBORNE
Governor of the State of Louisiana and Commander in
Chief of the Militia thereof.—

A PROCLAMATION.

WHEREAS the nefarious practice of running in Contraband Goods, which has hitherto prevailed in different
parts of this State, to the great injury of the fair trade,
and the dimunition of the Revenue of the United States
has of late much increased.— And Whereas, the violators
of the Law emboldened by the impunity of past tres-
passes, no longer conseal themselves from the view of the
honest part of the community but setting the Government
at defiance, in broad daylight, openly carry on their in-
famous traffic; and Whereas it has been officially known
to me that on the fourteenth of last Month a quantity of
contraband goods seized by Walker Gilbert, an officer of
the revenue of the United States, were forcibly taken
from him in open day at no great distance from the City
of New. Orelans by a party of armed Men, under the orders of a certain John Lafitte, who fired upon, and griev-
ously wounded one of the assistants of the said Walker
Gilbert; and although process has been issued for the ap-

prehension of him the said John Lafitte, yet such is the countenance and protection afforded him, or the terror excited by the treats of himself and his associates, that the same remains unexecuted.—

And Whereas the apathy of the good people of this State, in checking practices so opposed to morality, and to the Laws and interests of the United States, may impair the fair character which Louisiana maintains, and ought to preserve as a member of the American Union;

I have thought proper to issue this my Proclamation, hereby strictly charging and commanding all officers of the State, Civil or Military, in their respective departments, to the vigilant and active in preventing the violation of the Laws in the premises, and in apprehending and securing all persons offending therein: And I do solemnly caution all and singular the Citizens of the State, against giving any kind of succour, support on   to the said John Lafitte and his associates but to be aiding and abetting in arresting him & them, and all others in like manner offending, and I do further more, in the name of the State, offer a reward of five hundred Dollars which will be paid out of the Treasury, to any person delivering the said John Lafitte to the Sheriff of the Parish of New. Orleans, or to any other Sheriff in the State, so that he the said John Lafitte may be brought to Justice.—

In testimony whereof, I have caused the Seal of the State, to be hereunto affixed.—

Given under my hand at New Orleans on the 24th day of November 1813. & of the independence of the of the United States the thirty eighth.—

By the Governor
(Signed) L. B. Macarty)
Secy. of State)

(signed)   William C. C. Claiborne.

From Genl. Flournoy

New Orleans 6th Decber 1813.

Governor Claiborne

Sir,

I am induced to believe, that the report of a British force having been landed at Pensacola is not true, but think an attack on this City is meditated in the course of the early part of the Winter. The necessity thereof of having the Militia kept in a constant state of preparation, and discipline for the service is too obvious to require from me;— But will entreat your Excellency to take such steps as will enable you to order out the force of the City for its defence, at a moment's warning, and to furnish a portion of the Militia from the upper Country, in the event of a call being made upon you for an additional force.—

Enclosed is a proposition from a volunteer Corps of horse which is respectfully submitted for your Consideration.—

I have the honor to be Sir, &c

(signed)   Thos. Flournoy.

———— „ ————

To Mr. Brown

New. Orleans 11th December 1813.

a Senator in Congress

Dear Sir,

To my great mortification the General orders (a Copy of which, accompanied my letter of the 8th Instant) meet in this City, with much opposition; They are by some viewed to be illegal, and by others to be unnecessary.—

Already they are the object of attack by the News-papers, Scribbers, whose mischievous designs are the more to be regretted from the facility, with which *in this City* they produce discussion & discontent.— If indeed Louisiana should be attacked, the Regular Troops, are too few in number, to defend the avenue to New Orleans, & unless, the people should feel and act in unison & with great firmness the Country will for the moment be lost. It is not believed, that at present General Flournoy could conveniently concentrate at any one point, within this State, more than 700 Men, of his weakness, he has fully advised me, and has added, that the most prompt support from the State authorities, would in the hour of peril be essential to our safety.— I think it highly probable that the General will in a few days (make) such a requisition of me, for one thousand Men, and which I shall certainly comply with as fully & promptly as may be in my power. — In the patriotism of the Interior Counties of the State, I place great confidence & I persuade myself I shall be enabled to draw from *them* a respectable force for the defence of the Capitol.— I am not without hopes also, that as the dangers increase, the Citizens of New. Orleans, will more willingly than they now do, submit to privations, and unite hand and heart in all measures of defence.—

I pray you Sir, to keep me fully advised of the progress of the War, & more particularly of every occurrence which may indicate an intention of the enemy to attack Louisiana.— It is reported here, and credited that 1200 English Troops, have recently arrived at Burmudas; It is added that this detachment, with several black Regiments from Jamaica will in the course of the Winter, be landed at some point within Louisiana.— One thing is certain that the officer Commanding the English Fleet now on this Coast menaces us (in the course of the Winter) with black Troops, & that in the political circles of Pensacola a speedy arrival there of an English force is confidently spoken of.—

At the request of Doctor Shaw, I take the liberty to
enclose to you a recommendation in his favor, for a Captaincy in the army.— Permit me to add, Sir, that I always esteemed Doctor Shaw, as a correct Citizen & as deserving of private & public confidence.—

I am, Sir, &c@ &c@ &c@

(Signed)   William C. C. Claiborne.

————— ,, ————— ,, —————

To John Perkins.[1]

——————New Orleans October 21. 1814——————

Sir,———————————

————————————— I am indebted to you for several very
interesting letters and I have noticed with great pleasure
your zeal and activity at the present momentous Crisis.—
Too much attention cannot be paid to our Caddo and
other Indian friends.— At present the Cherokees, Chick-
asaws and Chactaws furnish General Jackson with as
great an Indian force as is desirable; but in the event of
an actual Invasion of Louisiana we shall probably need
the aid of our Western Indians, I pray you to keep them
prepared for a prompt Co-operation.— It would seem
by the information from Nachitoches, that the Spanish
Authorities of the province of Texas had made peace
with several Indian Tribes lately their enemies, and were
likely again to acquire an influence in their Councils, that
a column of 800 Spanish Regulars was advancing toward
Nacogdoches, and that it would probably be attempted
to occupy the post of Bayou Pierre; In this last event
Colonel Johnson of Rapides has ample instructions, and
I reply on his executing them with promptitude and de-

---

[1] Beginning of Volume X.

cision.—It may happen that you will in no manner be molested by your Spanish Neighbourgs, but in the present state of things I am unwilling any further to diminish our military force in your vicinity; I admire the motives which led Doctor Robinson to raise a volunteer Corps, and the Patriotic Spirit which induced him and them to make a tender of their services thro' me to the United States. I did not respond to this application from an unwillingness to damp the ardor of any American, who in this moment of peril, is ready to bare his bosom in his Country's Cause but since you press me on this point, I must say Sir, that as relates to Doctor Robinson I am delicately situated; he has been considered by the American Government, as lately engaged in enterprises which the Laws of the United States forbid and to my Knowledge a warrant against him has been issued by the districk Judge of Louisiana and which I believe remains unexecuted, under these Circumstances I could not consistent with my sense of duty Confer on Doctor Robinson a Commission.— In this Sir you will not perceive anything of a personal nature; It is not possible for me to be influenced, by any such Consideration;— On the Contrary the spirit of enterprise which has marked the Doctor's pursuits in life, his personal firmness, and the very excellent opinion entertained of his head and heart by my lamented friend General Pike lead me to regret the course my duty compels me to adopt.— I trust however that the Young men of Nachitoches will willingly join the Association, which Colonel Johnson has projected, and discovers such laudable zeal in completing;— should Louisiana be invaded on either hand this association would be enabled to render the State the most essential services, nor is there any doubt but under the guidance of their patriotic Leader every individual attached to it, would deserve well of his Country.— The American arms have met with the most brilliant successes to the north, nor has the enemy since his repulse at the Point of Mobile made any further attempt in this quarter.— We are however impressed with the opinion, that this Capitol will be attacked in the Course of the Winter, and are making every preparation for its defence.—

                I am, Sir, &c@ &c@ &c@
              (Signed)   Willm C. C. Claiborne
Doctr. Sibley.—

To Mr. Fromentin.

New Orleans 24" October October 1814.
Dear Sir._____

_____ I have the honor to acknowledge the receipt of your letter of the —— Ultimo and thank you for the information it Contains.— I have made, and am stil making every possible exertion to defend Louisiana against all attacks from within and from without.— I am zealously supported by Major Generals Villere, and Thomas, and have reason to be content with the patriotic Spirit which pervades the State.— there are indeed individuals, on whose friendly disposition towards the American Government, I cannot depend,— but I calculate with certainty on the fidelity of the great mass of the population;— There has unquestionably been of late a change in the public Opinion, and I see with pleasure, that the best informed citizens are perfectly convinced that the safety and welfare of Louisiana can alone be secured by an indissoluble Union with the American States.— The requisition from this State is nearly completed, and to which is added several Volunteer Corps of Cavalry and Riflemen.— In less than ten days, Regulars and Militia in the Service of the United States, there will be in this City, upwards of **two** thousand men, which the local Militia for

286 MISSISSIPPI TERRITORIAL ARCHIVES.

the most part well armed and well disposed would enable us to make a good defence.— Lafourche is well guarded and looks that post shall be speedily established on Barrataria, terre aux boeufs and the pass of Chef Menteur.— We shall not be surprised, and unless attacked by an overwhelming force you may fear nothing for our safety. General Jackson continues at Mobile, with a very respectable force; he enjoys the Confidence of the Louisianians, and well deserves it.— The joint letter of your's and Brown's to the Secretary at War is much approved here and we Calculate on its producing the desired effect.— The 1500 stand of arms to which you allude were received and have for the most part been delivered to the Militia now in actual service.— I pray you to write me often and to keep me fully apprised of occurrences.—On my part I will inform you of every thing interesting in this quarter, the Legislature is convened for the 10th of next Month.— I hope there will be Union, and but one opinion, in calling forth the energies of the State and giving to them patriotic direction.—

I am Dear Sir,_____

Signed / W. C. C. Claiborne_____

The Honble Mr. Fromentin_____

To James Monroe.

New Orleans October 24th 1814_____

Sir,_____

_____I have the pleasure to inform you that the requisition from this State for a thousand Militia Infantry is nearly completed, and to which has been added two troops of volunteer Cavalry and one Company of Volunteer Riflemen.— We shall in a few days have in this vicinity about two thousand troops, including the detached Militia, which with the local militia most of which are well armed and well disposed would enable me in case of an attack to make a good defence.— Major General Jackson continues at Mobile, and has I presume by this time been reinforced by a strong detachment of volunteers from Tennessee.—The last accounts from Pensacola, left the English in Possession of that Post, and in the daily expectation of the arrival of the Fleet, and many transports with troops.— We are extremely anxious to learn that Pensacola had been possession of by General Jackson, we are assured that gallant officer only awaits the Instructions of the Government to that effect and which it is hoped will not long be delayed.—Pensacola is in every sense of the word an enemy's Post.— It is there that the retreating Creeks found an assylum and were permitted to make avery preparation to renew the war against our frontiers;— It was there that the English land and naval forces made every necessary arrangement for the late attack against the Point of Mobile, and after their repulse they again retired to Pensacola where not only all their immediate wants were supplied but they have been permitted to recruit their forces.— with a knowledge of those facts, and that Pensacola is in every point of view the most elligible spot for the debarkment of an english force destined for the attack of Louisiana, I must confess Sir it would give me the sincerest pleasure to learn that General Jackson had been authorized to pursue to that point his beaten enemy, and to drive from hence him and his protectors the spaniards.— my apprehensions for the safety of New Orleans have of late greatly subsided.— I find that General Jackson has already a respectable army, and that every preparation has been made for further reinforcements from the Western States, I find also a very patriotic Spirit pervades this State and that the best informed Citizens seems to be convinced that the happiness and prosperity of Louisiana depend upan an indissoluble union with the western and atlantic States;— for the present, Sir, every precaution will be taken to guard against a surprise, and unless we are attacked with an overwhelming force I have every reason to hope we shall give a good account of the enemy, come when he may.—I must not however disguise from you the fact, that Louisiana must look for permanent safety to support of our gallant Western Brothers.

I am sir,_____

Signed   W. C. C. Claiborne_____

The Honble Mr. Monroe_____

To Andrew Jackson.

New Orleans October 24 1814_____

Sir, _____

_____Your address to the Louisianians is well received, and will make a favorable impression.— A feeble attempt has been made in a paper, called the Louisiana Gazette to take exception to its style and manner,— But I do not learn, that a single worthy citizen unites in opinion with the newspaper scribler.— The natives of Louisiana are for the most part a virtuous a gallant People; You have inspired them with Confidence, and I am proud in the belief, that in any event, they will prove faithful to the United States.— The Natives of the United States, residing in this State, have for the most part, manifested the most favorable disposition; but I have cause to be particularly satisfied with the Militia of the Baton Rouge district; Their quota of the requisition was furnished with the greatest promptitude; an excellent Company of volunteer Cavalry from that District are also in service, and a volunteer Company of Riflemen are expected in a few days.—An excellent Company of Cavalry Composed

of Creoles of Louisiana arrived on last evening from attackapas and about five hundred and fifty of the detached
militia Infantry are expected here in two or three days
from Baton Rouge.— Major General Villeré of the First
and Major General Thomas of the second devision of
militia have manifested the greatest zeal and I am much
indebted to them for the support they have given and
Continue to give me. I have also abundant reason to be
satisfied with the Conduct of Colonel McRea and the
Quarter Master General Colonel Pratt. I find these Gentlemen greatly disposed to promote the good of the service and to afford the militia every proper accommodation.
— Your address[1] sir to the Chosen men of Colour will
be printed on this day;— I will use my best efforts to promote your wishes, but I do not know with what success.—
I have already apprized of the distrust which exists here
against this Class of people;— I believe it ill founded but
its existence may, and I fear has in some degree indisposed them towards us.— The difficulty among the officers of the Battalion of Colour of which I informed you
is nearly arranged and I continue to think in the moment
of trial they will prove a meritorious Corps.[1]— Fort St.
Philippe at Plaquemine is in need (I learn) of reinforcements; if it meets your approbation I will detach to that
post a lieutenant and forty men of Colour.— _____
                              I am sir, &c. &c._____
                    Signed / Wm C. C. Claiborne_____
Major General Jackson._____

---

[1] In letters to Claiborne of Sept. 21, 1814, advises securing the co-
operation of free men of color, saying that distrust will make them
enemies, in Jackson Papers Book G, 152 Library of Congress MSS. Div.

To James Monroe.

New Orleans 25th October 1814_____

Sir, _____

_____ In my letter of yesterday, which was written in great haste, I was not sufficient explicit when speaking of the local militia; I meant to confine myself exclusively to the militia of the City and faux Bourgs, two thirds of which are armed with good muskets but the remaining third for the most part are without arms of any description except some fowling Pieces, which I have been occasionally brought on Parade.— The militia in the Interior of the State are almost wholly destitute of arms, they are very pressing in their demands on me, and it is with regret I find myself without the means of arming them.— Fifteen hundred stand of muskets have been furnished the State by the General Government, a thousand of which are in the hands of the detached militia, and the remaining five hundred are reserve for the use of such corps as are expected to volunteer their services.— I have convoked the Legislature for the tenth of next month, and one object of the Call is to invite them to make provisions for the purchase of *arms;* but should this be done, I fear they cannot be had in this City.— could the General Government loan to Louisiania two or three hundred Sabres, and of as many of horseman's Pistols, it would indeed be a great accommodation, and add more to our security, for on the event of insurrection among our slaves, Cavalry are the troops which can act with greatest advantage.

I am sir,_____

Signed   W. C. C. Claiborne_____

The Honble Mr Monroe_____
Secretary at War_____

To James Monroe.

New Orleans October 25th 1814_____

Sir,_____
_____You will have heard of the fortunate result of a joint attack by land and water under the orders of Colonel Ross of the 44 United States Regiment and Captain Patterson of the Navy against the Pirates and Smugglers of Barrataria.— of the Meritorious Conduct of Captain Patterson on that occasion I have borne testimony in a letter to the Secretary of the Navy and I now Sir take the liberty to express to you my approbation of the zeal and activity displayed by Colonel Ross.— It was at my particular request, that the Colonel detailed for the service, a detachment from his Regiment, and in commanding it in person, he gave additional proof of the patriotic feeling by which he was influenced.—These Pirates are at present dispersed, but to prevent their reassembling, a naval force on this station, in peace or in War, will be indispensable.[1]_____

I am sir &c_____
signed / W. C. C. Claiborne_____
The Honble _____
Mr. Monroe_____

To Col. McRae.

New Orleans October 25th 1814_____

Sir,_____
_____ I deem it proper to inform you that a Company of mounted Riflemen not more than 100 nor less than 60 Strong from St. Francisville under the Command

---

[1] For a good account of the expedition against the smugglers of Barrataria see Walker's account in Jackson and New Orleans. He refers to legal records on file in the U. S. Dist. Courts at New Orleans. Martin in his history of Louisiana states that Lafette's papers were taken and turned over to the court.

of Captain Griffith will reach this city in six or seven days for the purpose of being mustered in the service of the United States.— be good enough sir, to pass this information to the Contractors, and to order the proper officer to have prepared for them, the necessary Camp equipage_____

I am sir &c_____

_____ Signed/   W. C. C. Claiborne____

Coll. McRea_____

To. Col. Collins.

New Orleans October 28th 1814

Sir,_____

_____ It is proper that I should see you, in the course of the day, and if your health is not so much impaired, as to make it impracticable for you to repair to this city, I request you sir to accompany my aid Colonel LeBlanc who will deliver you this letter.—I am sorry that you did not think proper to come to town, on yesterday with Colonel Fortier, and I shall stil more regret if you do not find it convenient to comply with my request of this day._____

I am sir _____

_____ signed / W. C. C. Claiborne____

Col. F. Collins_____

To Andrew Jackson.

_____New Orleans October 28" 1814____

Dear Sir,_____

_____I am honored with the receipt of your letter of the 19th Instant.— It gives me pleasure to learn, that Lieutenant Basque, is continued in the

Army;— He possesses Talents, and a genius susceptible
of much further improvement.— But is young and I fear
imprudent.— The free men of Tennessee have acquired
the confidence and the esteem of the Union;— Their distinguished Patriotism is indeed an example for all the
states and no one of them has more occasion to profit
of it than Louisiana.— I shall use with discretion all the
information you give me, whatever is published relative to your movements will be in the form of editorial
intelligence, and always with caution.— I have reason
to believe, that you are correct in supposing the
enemy desirous to ascertain the extent of the force
declined for the defence of the lower Country;— It
has been given in a letter from a Colonel Colliel/ who
altho' a spanish officer, may from his long residence be
considered as an Inhabitant of Louisiana/ to a Captain
Moralez now in Pensacola.— The original letter is now
in my hands and you have been furnished with a Copy by
the Marshall, Mr. Duplessis. The letter has been submitted to the Attorney General of the State;— He thinks
the Judicial Authority cannot notice it;— but supposes
if the *Governor* thinks Colliel a dangerous Character *he*
may then, be sent away.— On yesterday Colonel Colliel
was requested by one of my aids, to attend me at the
Secretary's office; he was much indisposed, and beged
to be excused until this morning 11 o'clock, when he
promised with certainty to present himself. I shall give
him 48 hours to prepare for his departure for a Spanish
Post, and if force be necessary to send him away I shall
use it.— Colliel is an old man and the father in law of
Mr. Delacroix one of our wealthiest Sugar Planters, a director of the Bank, and a member of the Committee of
Safety.— The Chief of the Caddoes, is a man of great
merit, he is brave, sensible and prudent.— You may rely
on whatever he may say to you;— But I advise, that you
address a Talk immediately to the Chief, he is the most

influential indian on this side of the River Grande, and his friendship sir, will give much security to the Western Frontier of Louisiana.— It is right you should know that Doctor Sibley the Indian Agent at Nachitoches is a very unpopular man with the Inhabitants, he has some warm friends, but many bitter enemies.— I have myself found him, a zealous Faithful agent, and an ardent friend to the Government but for some cause to me unknown, he appears to have suffered in the opinion of the administration.— I have now in my possession a letter from the late Secretary at War, directing his dismission, and a letter of appointment for a successor, with authority to fill up the blanks with the name of such Citizen, as I supposed merited the trust;— To this moment I have not acted upon these letters, owing to the impossibility of finding here a suitable Character.— Sibley has no information from me of this authority, or rather instruction to remove him and I believe him wholly uninformed upon the subject.— What ought I to do?— Unless you can give me the name of some active intelligent faithful man, I must return the letters to the Government.—

A former Communication from me will have informed you of the delay which attended the receipt of your addresses to the Louisianians and to the free men of Colour.— each address has been published, the first has evidently made a favorable impression, and the effect of the latter, will be soon known.— I have always thought that the policy you propose is the proper policy to pursue towards the free men of Colour.— but sir my views on this respect, have not been seconded by other public functionaries of the State.— Lately sir there has been a great emigration to Cuba of free people of Colour, and many others are I am told to follow;— This circumstance will much operate against your plain, But it is nevertheless believed that several Companies may be raised;— I will write you more particularly hereafter.

— Receive my warmest congratulations on our successes by land and water.— We are once more a great united and gallant people.— Let the Invincibles of Wellington advance, and they find in free men in arms, a foe before whom their laurels acquired in europe will fade._____
I am sir,_____
Major General Jackson__Signed/ W. C. C. Claiborne__

To Andrew Jackson.

New Orleans October 28th 1814_____
Dear Sir,_____
_____I feel great solicitude for the welfare of Young Basque.— I fear his youth, inexperience, and warmth of disposition may lead him into imprudence,— It however is a pleasure to me to know that he is at present under your immediate Command, and I trust he may by his good conduct recommend himself to your esteem. — It seems, an american minister, A M. Irvine has been appointed to Spain,__ I fear this does not argue a design on the part of our administration to avenge the Injuries, which the Agents of the Government have endeavored to inflict upon us in this quarter.— On the 24th of this Month, I wrote to the Secretary at War /M Monroe/ what follows.— "Major General Jackson continues at "Mobile, and has I presume by this time been reinforced "by a strong detachment of volunteers from Tennessee. "— The last accounts from Pensacola left the english in "possession of that Post, and in the daily expectation of "the arrival of a Fleet, and many transports with troops. "— We are extremely anxious to learn, that Pensacola "is in every sense of the word, an *"enemy's Post,* It is "there that the retreating Creeks, found an assylum, and "were permitted to make every preparation to renew

"the War against our Frontiers;— It was there, that
"the English land a naval force made every arrange-
"ment for the attack against the Point of Mobile, and
"after their repulse they again retired to Pensacola,
"where not only all their immediate wants were sup-
"plied but they were permitted to recruit their broken
"forces.— with a knowledge of these facts, and that
"Pensacola in every Point of view, the most illigible
"spot for the debarkment of an English force destinced
"for the attack of Louisiana I must confess it would give
"me the sincerest pleasure to learn that General Jack-
"son had been authorized to pursue to that place his
"Beaten enemy and to drive out him, and his protec-
"tors." Such are the sentiments which I have not hesitated to avow to the Administration, and if you should
think without awaiting orders to pursue your beaten
enemy to Pensacola, you will stand Justify upon every
principle of policy, upon every principle of the Laws and
usages of Nations.------------------------------------

                    I am Dear sir,--------------------
            Signed/ W. C. Claiborne-------------
Major General Jackson--------------

_____

To Andrew Jackson.

            New Orleans October 28th 1814----------
Dear Sir,---------------
--------------The mail of this morning has brought me
your letter of the 15th Instant.— The same rumour concerning the gun Boats to which you allude has prevailed
here, but it proves untrue.— A Continuance of adverse
Winds must have retarded the Passage of Vessels from
hence to Pensacola or you would not remain uninformed
of the state of things in this quarter.— Since my recov-

ery from my late indisposition I have made you several
communications, and in one of them I mentioned the disposition which *until your further orders* would be made
of the Militia requisition of this State.— In pursuance
of this plan I have to inform, that one complete Company near a hundred strong, under Captain Hicks have
ascended the River to the Lafourche, where they will
soon be joined, by a detachment of one First Lieutenant
one second Lieutenant and Forty Privates raised in the
vicinity of Lafourche and which will be mustered into
the service of the United States.— Hicks is instructed to
assume an illigable position low down on the Lafourche,
to throw up a batterie for one 12 Pounder, which he has
with him, and to build a strong Block House, in case of
the approach of the enemy, he is to hasten information
to the commanding officer at New Orleans and to Brigadier General Hopkins of the second Brigade of Louisiana Militia, and this latter officer /who resides near the
Lafourche/ is directed without waiting further orders,
to turn out the whole or such part of his Brigade, as the
occasion may require, and to aid in repelling the enemy.
— Another Company near a hundred strong will leave
hence in a few days to watch some passes on the waters
of Barrataria with the double view of guarding a surprise by the enemy from that quarter, and to prevent
there assembling of the Pirates and Smugglers.— The
Feliciana and Attackapas Cavalry about a hundred
strong are stationed in this city and will be employed in
reconnoiting and aiding information between this city
and the English Turn, and terre aux Boeufs, and occasionally to Fort St. Philip, at Plaquemine and the Post
to be established on the Lafourche.— A Company of
mounted Riflemen, said to be a hundred strong from St.
Francisville, will be here probably in ten or twelve days.
— They will temporarily be stationed in this city, and
employed for the present on detachments occasionally

with the Cavalry but most generally as videttes in the vicinity of terre aux Boeufs and Chef Menteur.— The Cavalry and Riflemen, are the troops best calculated to act in case of Domestic Insurrection, and with a view of making on the negroes, the desired impression, I shall request that these Corps be occasionally marched in a body above and below the city for some distance. between four and five hundred Militia from Baton Rouge will arrive here probably in a few days, and as I informed you in a former letter will take post at the english turn.— You will observe sir that a thousand Militia Infantry in obedience to the requisition are not yet in the Field.— There are many defaulters among the drafted men,— some from long and Continued indisposition, but most I fear from a bare and wilful neglect of duty.— Enclosed sir is a general order issued on the occasion, you will notice that it applies only to the first and second Brigades, from the second division no special Report has yet been received it is believed however that the defaulters in that Part of the State, will not prove numerous;— I learn however that since the Militia were ordered from Baton Rouge there have been frequent desertions.— Colonel Johnson of Rapides has promised to send me 80 infantry, and with this and other Corps, which will probably offer themselves, I hope to excede the Requisition,— Tennessee I perceive is always herself.— Truly Sir, no State in the Union, is more conspicuous for real, practical patriotism.— her gallant Militia which are soon to be with you, to accomplish all your objects and to leave the Mobile Section in perfect security whilst you pay us a visit at New Orleans,— this visit is greatly desired, and by no one more than,

Dear Sir &c@ &c@_____

Signed/   W. C. C. Claiborne_____

Major General Jackson_____

To Col. Pratt.

New Orleans October 30th 1814----------

Sir,-------------------------
------------------------If the law makes provisions
for furnishing the army with straw I request you sir to
take the earliest occasion to purchase the necessary
Quantity for a Detachment of six hundred Louisiana
Militia in the service of the United States to be stationed
at the English Turn, and where they will arrive prob-
ably on Monday or Tuesday next.-------------------
I am Sir, &c &c
Signed/ W. C. C. Claiborne--------
Colonel Pratt.--------------

To Captain Humphreys.

New Orleans October 30th 1814--------

SIR,-------------------
----------------------The detachment of Militia from
Baton Rouge will early on Too-morrow be halted near
this city, for the purpose of refreshing themselves, pre-
vious to marching thro' Town.— Desirous that their ap-
pearance should be respectable, I wish you to deliver to
Captain Foelkel, the bearer 350 Cartridge Boxes for the
use of this detachment taking his receipt for the
same.--------------------------
Captain Humphrys.   I am sir &c &c--------------
Commissary of Military Stores----------
Signed W. C. Claiborne--------

To Col. Pratt.

SIR,_____   New Orleans October 30th 1814.____

_____The detachment from Baton Rouge
will early on Too-morrow be at Macarty's near to
this City, where they are ordered to halt and refresh
themselves, Previous to marching thro' Town.— I am
anxious to send out to them on To-morrow their Cartridge boxes, and if the Weather continues rainy a
few tents.— Will you be pleased to order one of the Public Waggons to receive such articles as Captain Foelkel
of the, who will deliver you this letter wish to convey
on the morrow to Macarty's for the use of the Mil-
itia._____
                    I am sir,_____
Colonel Pratt_____ Signed/   W. C. C. Claiborne

To Attorney General Rush.

                New Orleans October 30th 1814_____
Sir,_____
    You no doubt have heard that the late expedition to
Barrataria, had eventued in the entire dispersion of the
Pirates and Smugglers and the Capture of nearly all
their Cruisers.— It is greatly to be regretted that
neither the *General* nor *State Government* had not
sooner been able to put down this Banditti;— The length
of time they were permitted to continue their *evil Practices* added much to their strength and led the People
here, to view their course as less vicious.— Measures
tending to the prevention of crimes, can alone relieve us
from the distress of punishing them;— Had such measures in regard to the offences in question, been earlier

taken, we should not now have to lament the frequency of their commission— I have been at great pains to convince the people of this state, that Smuggling was a moral offence; But in this I have only partially succeeded.— There are Individuals here who in every other respect fulfil with exemplary integrity all the duties devolving upon them as Fathers of Families and as Citizens— But as regards Smuggling altho' they may not be personally concerned, they attach no censure to those who are.— It is the influence of education of habit of bad example.— Formerly under the Government of Spain Smuggling in Louisiana was universally practised, from the highest to the lower member of society.— To shew you the light in which it was then viewed, I will only observe, that occasionally in conversation with ladies, I have denounced Smuggling as dishonesty, and very generally a reply in substance as follows would be returned. — "That it is impossible for my Grand Father, or my Father or my husband, was under the Spanish Government a great Smuggler, and he was always esteemed an honest man.— It takes time to remove the Influences of prejudice of example of former habits. Much has already been done to reconcile the Louisianians to the Government, laws and usages of the United States, and more must yet be done to do away all traces of those improper feelings and sentiments which originated with and was fostered under the corrupt Government of Spain.— Prosecutions are now pending in the District Court against several of the Barataria offenders, and in the course of the investigation, it is probable that the number inplicated will probably be very Considerable. Justice demands that the more culpable be punished with severity.— but I see no good end to be attained by making the penalties of the law to fall extensively and heavily.— The example is not the less imposing by circumscribing the number of its victims, and the mercy which should dictate it, seldom fails to make a salutary and lasting impression.— Should the President think proper to instruct the attorney of the District of Louisiana, to select a few of the more hardened offenders of Barrataria for trial, and to forbear to prosecute all others concerned, I think such an act of Clemency will be well received, and be attended at the present moment with the best effects.— A Sympathy for these offenders is certainly more or less felt by *many of the Louisianians* with some it arises from national attachment; but with most, from their late trade and intercourse with them.— Should the Attorney for the District, be instructed not to prosecute the case of minor offenders, it is desirable that such instructions be accompanied with the opinion of the executive as to the offence of Smuggling and that publicity be given to the same.— Such a document would I am persuaded be productive of great good.— It may be I am in error.— Some of my Contrymen of talents and virtue think differently, but for myself, I have always thought, that as much may be done with the Louisianians by a mild policy, and the act of persuasion, as any People I ever knew.— which impression has always influenced my Public Conduct.— It is true I have often failed in my objects,— But a Chief Magistrate with more talents and discretion than I possess who should pursue such a course, could not fail to succeed.— do me the favour sir to submit this letter to the President and be good enough to inform me when your leisure permits how far he may approve the limits, which with the greatest deference I have taken the liberty to recommend.—

I am Sir &c &c._____

Signed W. C. C. Claiborne_____

THE HONORABLE MR. RUSH._____

Attorney General of the United States.__

___By WILLIAM CHARLES COLE CLAIBORNE.___

_____Governor of the State of Louisiana._____

_____WHEREAS official information has been given me that divers Disorderly and Turbulent Individuals have since the accession of Louis the 18th— to the crown of France, wantonly insulted the person, and in some instances offered violence to the House of the Chevalier de Toussard Consul of his most Christian Majesty, and altho' one of them has been apprehended and bound to his good behaviour, yet several others have of late renewed their attacks on the Consular House, and taken down, and carried away the arms of the king placed according to custom over the door of said house, and daily threaten further indignities to the said consul; — And whereas it is essential to the preservation of order and specially due to the good understanding, which happily exists between the Government of the United States and that of France, that such indecorous and unprovoked attacks and indignities should not be repeated or remain unpunished;— I have thought it my duty to issue this my Proclamation, notifying to the good Citizens, and other Inhabitants of this State that the Chevalier de Tousard is the accredited Consul of the King of France in Louisiana, and is to be respected as such; — And I do recommend it to the civil officers of the State to be active and vigilant in suppressing any attempts that may be made, to _ill-Treat_ or to insult the said Consul, or to offer any Indignity or violence to his Dwelling.— And I do further more offer a reward of Two Hundred dollars for the discovery and apprehension of the Person or Persons who forcibly took and carried away the arms of the Sovereign of France, which the

Consult, according to accustomed practice had placed over the door of his Dwelling._____

Given under my hand & the Seal of the State at New Orleans on the Second of November. Eighteen Hundred and Fourteen.

By the Governor_____

____L. B. Macarty____

_____Secretary of State.

_____Signed William C. C. Claiborne._____

To Pierre Lacoste.

New Orleans November 2nd 1814____

SIR,_____

_____Having been fully appraised of the assault made by an Indian in your vicinity on M″ Celestin, and the fate which the assailant so justly merited, it remains for me to take such measures, as may prevent the Comrades of the deceased, from resorting to the principle of retaliation, and sheding innocent blood.— To this end, I require you sir, without delay to exert yourself in assembling several of the Indian hunters which may be found in the Neighbourhood of Terre aux Boeufs, and if possible the Five Indians, who were with the deceased at the time he was shot, and in my name invite them to an audience with me at New Orleans. — In the discharge of the duty, I now impose upon the good Inhabitants of the Parish of St. Bernard, will I am sure give you every assistance.— It is possible, a friendly Conference with these Indians, may induce them to refrain from sheding blood._____

I am sir, &c &c_____

Major Pierre Lacoste_____

Signed/ William C. C. Claiborne_____

To Chevalier Toussard.

New Orleans November 2″ 1814_____
Sir_____

_____I have received your letter
of Yesterday, and sincerely regret the Insults and Indignities which have been offered to your Person and dwelling by some disorderly and Turbulent Individuals.— desirous to bring those offending to Justice and to prevent
any further outrages, I have prepared upon the Subject
a Proclamation, and of which, I enclose a Copy for your
perusal.— In the mean time I request you to believe that
the conduct of which you complain is not approved by
the good citizens of New Orleans, and that the Civil
Magistrates, will not be wanting in exertions to prevent
its repetition.—

I am sir, &c &c_____
Signed   W. C. C. Claiborne_____
Le Chevalier de Toussard_____
French Consul._____

To Andrew Jackson.

New Orleans November 4th— 1814—
Sir,_____
_____ Your communication of the 23rd Ultimo is
before me.— The Tennessean Volunteers under General
Coffy have no doubt reached you and the drafted men
under General Taylor will not I hope be long delayed.—
We are all solicitous to learn that affair in the Mobile
were arranged to your satisfaction, and that you pay this
section of your Military district an early visit.— The detachment you have ordered from Tennessee to New Or-

leans cannot arrive too soon.— The prospects of Peace
are at an end.— The Terms submitted by the English
Commissioners, would to a Conquered People, be vastly
humiliating.— But a *Nation* Great, Powerful and Free
could not consent *even* to consider them without com-
promitting its dignity and honor._____ Lest these
extraordinary propositions may not have reached you, I
enclose a paper containing them, I forbear to make any
comment; they will be read by every American, and excite
but one feeling, one opinion._____ I Consider our
Country now, as standing upon elevated and sure ground;
the People will be United, and the Enemy made to accede
to Just Conditions._____ I am sensible of the in-
expediency of dividing too much the *Forces in this State;*
My object has been, and still is, to concentrate the greater
Part of the disposable Militia Force near New Orleans.—
The settlement on the *Lafourche* was exposed, and as that
Bayou was one of the avenues by which New Orleans
could be approached it was deemed prudent to assume
and fortify a Position on the same, and I am happy it
meets your approbation;— The Detachment on Barrataria if the occasion requires may be recalled in Forty
eight hours; In the mean time, they serve as videttes on
one of the avenues of approach;— The Militia from
Baton Rouge are Posted at the English Turn, where
Colonel McRea contemplates throwing up a *Field* work,
behind which the Militia and other Troops, in the event
of an attack may Fight with more Confidence.— It is believed by many Persons / and myself among numbers /
that the Mississippi may probably be the avenue of approach selected by the Enemy;— If so and he comes in
force, the Fate of New Orleans will be decided at the
English Turn._____A wind with which a Fleet
might ascend from the Balize, will not serve thro' the
Turn;— Hence Batteries at the Turn could act to advantage, and the enemy to hasten his steps must make

his way by land._____ Colonel Shaumberg and **Mr.**
Benjamin Morgan descending since, to Fort Saint Philip,
were solicited to favour me with their opinion as to the
state of the defences on the Mississippi and of the scites
most proper to be occupied._____ I now take the
liberty to enclose their Original report, and to recommend it to your consideration._____ You will observe that Fort Saint Philip is represented to be deficient in men;_____ This I learn will be immediately remedied by Colonel McRea, who send on a reinforcement;— The Colonel had also previously determined
to complete the Fort at the English Turn alluded to in
the report, but how far that officer may feel himself
authorized to reoccupy the post at the Balize, I am not yet
fully informed.— You will observe sir, that this is deemed
by Colonel Shaumberg and M. Morgan, a most important
measure, and as absolutely essential to the security of
this City against all approaches by way of the Missis-
sippi._____ So far as regards the advised co-
operation on the part of the Navy in the defence of the
Balize and South West Pass, I have been informed by
Captain Patterson, that it cannot be given, without
abandoning the lakes, and leaving the Communication between New Orleans and Mobile wholly insecure._____
Captain Patterson complains much of the Want of Sailors.— The Brig Etna has not more than twenty six Persons on board;— the ship Louisiana is wholly without
nor can they be obtained; six Gun Boats and one
Schooner is Captain Patterson's effective force; he was
asked by me whether he had authority to purchase Vessels and answered, it had been expressly denied him, but
that nevertheless in case of exigency, he would purchase,
but thought it useless, as additional Sailors could not be
procured in this Station.— Captain Patterson seems disposed to co-operate with promptitude and zeal in such
manner as his *means* permit;— but is of opinion, that

these will not enable him for the Present to do more, than to guard the lakes and keep the Communication free between the Mobile and this City._____

In a late letter, I advised you of the Publication of your address to the Free men of Colour.— Its effects are beginning to be manifested;— A M. Bourgeois a French man by birth but who has resided here for several Years, and supports a very good Character, came to me today, and said he could raise a Company of a hundred men, provided he Could receive the commission of Captain. _____ I requested him to raise the same without delay, and promised to recommend him to the General commanding the District, who alone had the Power of commissioning him. _____ There are I am told two other Gentlemen, who desired to raise Companies, but they have not yet named the subject to me. _____ _____ You have been informed of the Contents of an intercepted letter written by Colonel Colliel a Spanish officer, to a Captain Morales of Pensacola; This letter was submitted for the opinion of the Attorney General of the State, as to the measures proper to be pursued against the writer. _____ The Attorney General was of opinion, that the Courts could take no cognizance of the same, but that the Governor might order the writer to leave the State, and in case of refusal to send him off by force._____ I accordingly Sir ordered Colonel Collier to take his departure in Forty eight hours for Pensacola and gave him the necessary Passports. I hope this measure may meet your approbation._____ It is a Just retaliation for the treatment locally observed by the Governor of Pensacola to some American Citizens, and may induce Spaniards residing among us to be less Communicative on subjects which relate to our Military mouvements. _____

_____ Mr. Abner L. Duncan who goes direct to Head Quarters will have the honor to deliver you this

letter;— You have long known him and therefore no recommendation from me is necessary.— Mr. Duncan feels a lively interest in all measures which promise to give security to our Country and as regards the present Condition of our Military preparations in this State, he can give you much useful Information. _____
I am, Sir, &@ &@
Signed/   Will"— C. C. Claiborne_____
Major General Jackson._____

To Col. McRae.

New Orleans November 4th 1814.____

Sir_____

_____ The News of the Morning leaves us no hope of peace, and every reason to believe that Louisiana will soon be attacked by the enemy. _____ It seems to be the opinion of many well informed Citizens that if invaded, the Mississippi, will be chosen as the avenue of approach, and indeed I apprehend myself, that the enemy will find that route the most convenient. _____ Under this impression, I learn with the sincerest pleasure your determination to strengthen the Garrison at Fort St. Philip and to repair and man the Battery at the English Turn. _____ May I call your attention also to the Balize which has always been as a Post, dependent upon New Orleans/ take the liberty to ask, how far you may be authorized to occupy and fortify that Position? It is believed that a few heavy Pieces mounted at the battery formerly erected at the Balize, Could keep a Fleet from passing the Bar, and in any event, a Detachment stationed in the vicinity of that Pass will give us early notice of the enemy's advance, which is all important._____ I take this occasion to inform you that a Company of

mounted Riflemen seventy strong, and destined for the
service of the United States will reach this City on this
afternoon._____

                    I am Sir,
                    Your humble Servant,
                signed / Willm C. C. Claiborne_____
Colonel MacRea_____

To Andrew Jackson.

                New Orleans November 5th. 1814_____
SIR_____
_____ I omitted to mention in my letter of Yesterday that a company of mounted riflemen from St.
Francisville Seventy Strong, had arrived and were for
the Present Quartered with the Feliciana Cavalry._____
_____ A Company of volunteer Infantry from Rapides
are stil expected and a Detachment of Fifty volunteers
have I believe joined Captain Hicks on the Lafourche.—
The requisition of a Thousand Militia Infantry will very
soon / I trust be Completed and to which the Cavalry
and Riflemen being added will give you from this State
an auxiliary Force of Twelve hundred men._____
In this City there are several uniformed Militia Corps
of much promise and my impression is, that on *these* with
other Companies of the Militia, much confidence may be
reposed in the moment of Trial.— There are Individuals
who believe otherwise; It may be, I am in error; but there
certainly has been a sensible change in the Public mind.
____ ____ There is not displayed by the Public at large
that enthusiastic ardor which is to be found in the Western States; But there is no symptom of opposition to the
Government and Laws._____ A Strong hatred is manifested towards the Enemy, and a determination expressed

to unite in the defence of the State._____ You will observe Sir, that I speak of the People at large;— I know there are some disaffected characters, and in this City are many vagabonds who if the occasion served, would be disposed for mischief.— The Legislature of the State will be in Session on the Tenth Instant, and their zealous support at this moment of danger, will confirm the Louisianians in their present good disposition._____ But if unfortunately a spirit any thing like that, which led the Legislature, the last winter to oppose a Militia requisition, should again prevail, I shall encounter great embarrassment and much opposition._____ But as I have already observed a great Change in the Public mind has apparently taken place; Many members of the Legislature, have always had American Feelings, and sentiments, & those whom I have lately seen profess the most patriotic Intentions, and all will I hope act a part, which the crisis advises and the security of the Country demands.— The Colonel Commanding the Detached Militia Alexander Declouet, is anxious to obtain a Furlong for three weeks, and begs me to be an applicant to you in his behalf for that Indulgence.— He has a mother labouring under a decease of which she cannot recover and a numerous Family whose Interest requires his presence for a few days in Attakapas.— Colo. Declouet is the Senior Colonel in the State;— He belongs to an ancient Creol Family, who were much patronized by the Spanish Government, and one of his Brothers is now an officer at Pensacola;— But in Colonel Declouet's fidelity, I place entire confidence;— he has on various occasions afforded proof of his attachment to the American and for the uniform and steady support he has given to me, I feel under personal obligations.— I have said thus much of Colonel

Declouet lest the feelings attributed to some of his family
may excite some suspicion as to him.—

I am Sir,
With great Respect
Your humble Servant
Signed/   William C. C. Claiborne.—

Major General Andrew Jackson
Commandg. the Seventh M. D.
Signed/   William C. C. Claiborne._____

_____ Extract from a letter from Major General Andrew Jackson to Governor Claiborne dated Head
Quarters Pierces Stockade October 31st 1814.——

Being desirous to place New Orleans and its vicinity
in a state of perfect security, I have ordered a force of
Five Thousand five hundred men from Tennessee and
Kentucky to proceed by forced Marches direct to your
city._____ Independent of this I have notified
Governor Holmes to hold the whole Militia of the Territory, in readiness to march at a moment's warning._____

Recent information from the most correct sources,
has been received of an expedition of Twelve or Fifteen
thousand men, sailing from Ireland early in September
intended to attempt the Conquest of Louisiana. You will
therefore see the necessity of preparing for Service, at
an hours of Notice the whole body of Louisiana Militia__
I rely on your Patriotism and activity and hope not to
be disappointed._____

To Genl. Morgan.

New Orleans November 17th 1814.____

Dear Sir,_____

_____ I did a few days since, say to you,
that taking into Consideration the fact that of the Louisiana detached Militia in the service of the United States
more than Two thirds had been drawn from the second
division, I have thought it just to take from that Division
the General of Brigade, which the orders of the Secretary
at War had called for, and in as much as you was the
senior Brigadier of the second Division the Command in
question was at your disposition, so soon as my intentions could be notified to Major General Jackson, and
time afforded him to give such orders as the appointments of a Brigadier General in this quarter would necessarily call for._____ I have since discovered from
conversing with Generals Hopkins and Labatus (?) of
the First Division of Militia that this arrangement is
considered by them as injurious to their military rights,
and that from their ideas of Justice, nothing could be
more correct, than to ascertain the Senior Brigadier of
the First Division, and to decide by lot whether the command of the Detachment shall devolve on you or him, it
has been intimated to me since my last interview with you
that this proposition is not disapproved even by yourself,
and that you are disposed to accede to it.— Upon this
Statement of Facts, I have only to observe that there is
nothing I more desire, than not only to act correctly on
this question, but that the generals interested should be
satisfied with my decision. If therefore sir, you should
wish the promise of Command which was made you a few
days since, to be Conclusive, *It shall be so;*— But if you
should be inclined to wave that promise and draw for
Command with the Senior Brigadier of the First Division, it shall take that course; Or if it be more agree-

able to all parties that the question as to the right of
Command should be left to the opinion of three Military
men, / not connected with the Militia / whom I will name
it shall be so directed._____ Whatever may be my
private partialities for Individuals, so far as regards the
rights of officers, I shall always endeavor to divest myself of personal Feelings;____ The consideration which
induced me to offer you the Command the other day,
speaks for itself, and whilst there may be some who may
disapprove, doubtless will others who will think it cor-
rect._____

I am Sir,_____
Your humble Servant_____
Signed/   William C. C. Claiborne_____
BRIGADIER GENERAL _____
David B. Morgan,
New Orleans.

To Genl. Jackson.

New Orleans November 17th 1814_____

Sir,_____
Your letters of the thirty First Ultimo are the last
which has reached.— The probable destination of the
Forces, which were to have sailed from Ireland in September last, makes me solicitous to hold in requisition all
the energies of this State, and if I am supported by the
Legislature, now in session, you may calculate with certainty on my efficient Co-operation._____ The enclosed Copy of my communication to the Two houses of
the Legislature, will shew you my sentiments as to our
national affairs and how ardently, I desire, that the Just
war in which we are engaged may be prosecuted with
union & vigour._____ It is certainly true that the

Louisianians have of late manifested the most Patriotic disposition, and that if the Spirit which exists be cherished and encouraged, we have every thing to hope from the great Majority of this Population._____ The Legislature have not as yet done any thing to damp the Public Ardour._____ I hope the body will be Justly impressed with the dangers to which we are exposed, and will warmly second all my efforts;_____ But I fear, I much fear they will not act with the promptitude and the energy which the Crisis demands._____

I am Sir,
With Great Respect,
Your humble Servant._____
Signed/ William C. C. Claiborne____

Major General Andrew Jackson._____
Commdg the Seventh Military District
    Mobile_____

To Col. McRae.

New Orleans November 18th 1814_____

Sir,_____

_____A few days since I stated to you that I should be desirous of sending some dispatches of Importance to Attakapas and requested of you the goodness to furnish me with a private of the Attakapas Cavalry to convey the same._____ These dispatches are will be ready on Too-morrow and you will oblige me, by ordering Captain Dubukely to detail a man, as an express to receive and to obey my orders._____

I am Sir
Your humble Servant,—
Signed/ William C. C. Claiborne—

Colonel McRea_____

To Gov. Blount.

New Orleans November 18th 1814

Dear Sir,------------

Since I last had the honor to address you, a great change has taken place in the Public mind in this Quarter, and a very Patriotic Spirit pervades the State.____ If the Legislature, now in session, should cherish and encourage this spirit we shall have every thing to hope for, from the great Majority of this Population; but if unfortunately, under an impression that the danger is not as great as has been apprehended, the Legislature should decline giving me a cordial support, Jealousy & distress will arise, and it will not be in my Power to co-operate as effectually as I could wish in defence of Louisiana._____ In any event however we shall be made secure by those brave and determined men who are hastening from Tennessee and Kentucky and I await their arrival with much anxiety.____

I am Sir,--------------

Your humble Servant

Signed/   Willm. C. C. Claiborne.____

His Excellency Governor Blont

Nashville.____ Tennessee.

To Andrew Jackson.

New Orleans November 18th 1814____

Sir,--------------

------------ Private accounts represent you to have entered Pensacola on or about the 8 Instant. I await with anxiety the Particulars, but I cannot for a moment delay offering you my congratulations on the event._____ It has given here the sincerest pleasure, and will I am

certain be highly approved thro' out the United States.
_____ You will certainly recollect that by the orders
of the Secretary at War making a requisition on the
several States for an auxiliary Militia Force, the Brigade to be drawn from Louisiana and the Mississippi Territory was entitled to one Brigadier General and one
Deputy Quarter Master General.— The latter officer has
been furnished by Governor Holmes, and the Brigadier
remains to be designated by me._____ The General of
Brigade in this state, are as you may suppose, solicitour
of this command, and I owe it to them to make a selection, but however an early nomination might interfere
with some of your arrangements, I have thought proper
previously to apprise you of my intentions._____ In a
few days I shall give you the name & character of the
Brigadier who will be ordered on duty and sincerely hope
he may prove worthy of your confidence._____

I am Sir &c &c

Signed/ Willm. C. C. Claiborne_____

Major General Jackson_____

To David Reese.

New Orleans November 19th 1814

Sir_____
_____ My last letters advised you how desirous I was to organize a Company of mounted Infantry
for the defence of Attakapas, and I again urge you to
second me with your best efforts.— As relates to the
muskets, they shall be forwarded by the first occasion,
after they shall have been informed that the company has
or will probably be raised.— In the mean time I have
only to urge you to maintain regular Militia Patrols, and

to keep me advised of all occurrences which interest the
Public Safety.------------------
I am Sir,-------------

Your humble Servant

--------Signed/   Willm. C. C. Claiborne
Major David Reese----------
Attakapas--------

To Capt. Hicks.

New Orleans November 19th 1814---
Sir,------------
You will have received from the Inspector General,
authority to muster into the service of the United States
the volunteers of Lafourche and such of drafted Militia
as may present themselves, all of which I will thank you
particularly to report to me.------------ Enclosed is a
Commission for Mr. David Randall, as a Second Lieutenant in which capacity you will be pleased to muster
him into the service.----------------
I am Sir &c &c

signed   Willm. C. C. Claiborne.—
Captain Hicks, Camp Hopkins
On the Lafourche.--------

To Capt. Patterson.

New Orleans 22nd November 1814—
Sir------------
------------ A Company of volunteer Cavalry from
Attakapas have been ordered into the service of the
United States, they are for the most part without Pis-

tols. nor can they be supplied either from the army store or by private purchase in this city.— You will therefore greatly promote the good of the service and much oblige me by the loan of thirty pair of Marine Pistols._____ They shall be returned the moment it shall be in my power to supply the Cavalry in another manner, in any event, when the Company shall be discharged, and sooner if you shall require it, if you cannot lend me thirty Pair, I will thank you for twenty, or as many as you can conveniently spare._____ I am sir

Your humble Servant

_____Signed/ Willm. C. C. Claiborne__

Captain Patterson
of the Navy_____

To David McGee.

New Orleans December 9th 1814____

Sir,_____

_____ I have read with much interest the letters you addressed me, and sincerely wish it were in my Power to furnish you with some Public employment._____ Vacancies for office seldom occur and when they do, you can readily anticipate the number of applicants which present themselves._____ At this moment, I do not know of a vacancy, which would suit your views, and if one should happen, as the Power of appointment is divided between the Executive and Senate, I could not promise success to any one applicant._____ As regards the literary work, you contemplate, I can assure you of its usefulness and desire its Completion._____ I fear however in this City, and State, useful as work would be to the Inhabitants, it would not meet with liberal encouragements._____ A love of letters has not ·

yet gained an ascendency in Louisiana, and I would advise you to seek for your productions the Patronage of some one of the Northern Citys._____ If however you will entrust me with a prospectus of the work, I will submit it to the Regents of the University of Orleans and if they should think useful to that institution, I think you may Calculate on their support._____ I am Sir_____

Your humble Servant_____

Signed/   Willm. C. C. Claiborne_____

David McGee Esq._____

To Eliguis Fromentin.

New Orleans December 9th 1814

Dear Sir,_____

_____ I write more to advise you of our anxiety to learn the news from Washington than to furnish you with any thing interesting from this quarter._____ General Jackson is with us, and the Tennessee Militia daily expected._____ It is not believed that the British are in Force any where in our vicinity, and the apprehensions of Invasion seems to have subsisted (Subsided). _____ I should regret however to see the smallest relaxation in our preparations for defence. _____ Messrs. Lewis of Attakapas, and Francis X. Martin have each been presented to the Senate as Judge of the Spreme Court and rejected._____ I do not know at present an Individual who could unite a Majority in the Senate;_____ Seven members have voted for Martin, and will I believe, be satisfied with no other Person._____ There are I think seven others who would prefer Mr. Joshua Lewis, and several members have expressed a wish that Mr. Robertson might be nominated. _____ The House of Representatives consume much time in debate and as yet the Legislature have *answered no one of the objects for which they were called.* I trust and hope however they will unite in some measures which the Interest and safety of the State imperiously demand._____

What is likely to result from the New England Convention?____for myself, I view this proceeding with much anxiety and inquietude._____ It surely presents an alarming aspect to the friends of the Union, and will not fail to encourage the enemy to attempt the overthrow of our Government._____

I am Sir,_____
Your humble Servant,_____
_____Signed/   Willm. C. C. Claiborne

The Honorable_____
Eliguis Fromentin._____

To James Monroe.

New Orleans December 9th 1814____

Sir,_____

_____ Major General Jackson arrived in this city on the First Instant, and has been received with all the respect to which his long and useful services so Justly entitle him._____ No officer who could have been assigned the Command of this District, would have been more generally approved than General Jackson, nor do I know one under whose orders in the Field, I would more cheerfully place myself. But in this event of General Jackson's Death, or absent from the District, it is not improbable but some contest may arise as to the right of Command._____

_____ At the last session of the

Legislature of the State by a Resolution of the Two Houses, I have been requested whenever the Militia of Louisiana were ordered into the Field, to Command in Person._____ In Consequence it has been and is stil my determination, whenever the danger of Invasion becomes eminent, to order out the whole, or such portion of the Militia of the State as circumstances shall render necessary, and to place myself at their head. It however is far from my wish to enterfer with the Command of General Jackson._____ On the contrary I have assured him that on receiving I will obey his orders._____ I however should be unwilling to acknowledge any other officer either of the Regular army or of the Militia, on duty in *this Station,* as my military superior._____ I do not know how far General Jackson may be inclined should I take the Field to consider me as his second, nor do I design at present to press a decision; it is not improbable, that the General would rather the President should determine, the rank to which a Governor of a State taking the Field was entitled and I would myself prefer that course._____ I observe if the News Papers are to be accredited, that Governor Tompkins of New York has been vested by the President with the Command of all the Forces within that State._____ I do not ask for a *like Command* within Louisiana; It has been committed to much abler hands and I should regret a change._____ But diffident as I am of my Military Talents, I must confess Sir, I should with extreme reluctance within my own State, submit to the Controul of any one of the Militia Generals in the service of the United States, who had no greater military experience than myself and less knowledge of the Country._____ I solicit therefore that whenever in case of Invasion or eminent danger of Invasion, I should in my character as Governor of Louisiana order out a portion of the Militia and place myself at their head, that General Jackson may be instructed to consider me as second in Command of the Forces to be employed within this State._____ Be good enough I pray you Sir, to bear this message of mine to the President and to inform me how far he may be disposed to grant it._____ I have read with much pleasure your plan for augmenting the army, and facilitating enlistments._____ In the event that the additional army of Forty Thousand men, be raised, I´should feel happy Sir to be honored with a Commission._____ The war in its commencement and progress has always had my support and in its vigorous prosecution at the present moment I see the only difficulty for our Independence._____ With these Sentiments I am unwilling to remain an inactive spectator of the Struggle._____ Like most of my Country men who have been called into service, I can claim, but a limited Knowledge of Military Affairs; I however hope you will not consider me as presuming too much in wishing the Command of a Brigade,— and

I am sir_____

Your humble Servant

Signed/   Wm. C. C. Claiborne

The Honorable_____

James Monroe,_____

Secretary at War_____

To Genl. Thomas.

New Orleans December 17th 1814

Sir,_____

_____ You have enclosed an extract from my General Orders of this day. Order out such guards as may be necessary to maintain a police among the slaves, and keep out Videtts towards the Arnette._____ My volunteers and Colonel Constant will soon be with you, and communicate my views and wishes in detail._____ I have no arms to lend you, let the Militia use such as they have or can procure._____ If you can spare one hundred and Fifty mounted Riflemen from the third Brigade hasten them on New Orleans._____

I am Sir, Yours, &c &c_____

Major General Thomas._____

Signed/   Wm. C. C. Claiborne_____

To the Barratariors.

HEAD QUARTERS, New Orleans December 17th 1814

_____ THE GOVERNOR of LOUISIANA informed that many Individuals, who may be, or are supposed to to be implicated in the offences hitherto committed against the United States at Barataria have for some time past concealed themselves on account of their inability to procure Bail, in case of an arrest, but who at the present Crisis, manifest a willingness to enroll themselves and to march against the Enemy he does hereby invite them to join the Standards of the United States, and he is authorized to say, should their conduct in the Field meet the approbation of Major General Jackson, that officer will unite with the Governor in a request to the President of the United States to extend to each and every Individual as aforesaid so marching and acting a Free and Full pardon._____

Signed/   Willm. C. C. Claiborne_____

Governor and Commanding the Militia.

To Louisiana Senators and Congressman.

New Orleans December 20th 1814.

Sir,_____

_____I have the honor to enclose you sundry Resolutions which have been adopted by the Legislature of the State._____ They will give you an idea of the

Spirit and Union, which at present happily exist, and the sincerity and zeal with which the State authorities are disposed to co-operate in the defence of Louisiana. I must call your attention particularly to the third and Fourth Resolutions & to add that you shall be duly advised of the *advances which,* in behalf of the State, I shall make for the completion of the Fortifications.— In the mean time I hope the Representation from Louisiana will make the necessary application to obtain for her the desired credit._____

_____ Since the Capture of our gun Vessels the Enemy has remained inactive on the Lakes; he was seen on Yesterday near the Rigolets Fifteen or Twenty sails in view; of his force at Ship Island we remain uninformed, as also at the Balize. We however feel ourselves secure, there is but one sentiment, one mind and old and Young are a like prepared to meet & Repel the Foe._____
Eligius Fromentin)
    and   )   of the Senate &_____
____James Brown)
                 I have the Honor
                    to be
                      Very Respectfully &c &c
               Signed   Willm. C. C. Claiborne_____
_____Thomas B. Robertson, of the House of
            Representatives.
_____Washington City

To Andrew Jackson.

           New Orleans December 20th 1814____
Sir,_____
    I have the honor to enclose you a return in part of the Militia of the State of Louisiana.[1] You would sooner have received it, but for causes which I could not Con-

---

[1] Jackson Papers, Military Papers, Vol. V, p. 78.

troul._____ The enclosure *A*. is a return of the Regular Militia, at present within the city and environs of New Orleans._____ Their numbers have been diminished by several Detachments heretofore ordered into the service of the United States, and by two or three Companies recently raised I learn under your authority, and of which description are the Detachments under Mess. Ogden & Jacques Viessire._____

The Enclosure *B*. will shew you the strength of the several Rifle, Marine and Veteran Corps of Cheveau's Troop of Cavalry and of the Fire Company._____ The Rifle Company is an Independent Corps organized under a particular Law._____ The Marines have recently been raised and consist for the most part of transient Persons. _____ The have been organized by me into a Batalion, and fully officered; They were inspected on this morning, and are anxious to be put on duty._____ The Veterans are comprised of men exempt by law from Militia Service, or incapable by age or bodily infirmaties of active Duty._____ Cheveau's Cavalry is an Independent Company, entitled by law to peculiar Privileges, one of which is to be more immediately under the orders of the Governor._____ The Fire Company is composed of Fathers of Families entitled by law to exemption from ordinary militia duty; But who at the present Crisis, have made a voluntary tender of service within the City.

_____

The enclosure *C*. will shew the strength of a voluntary Battalion of Free men of Colour, which I have recently organized, and officered, they have been inspected, and are armed with good muskets, Cartridge Boxes and Bayonets; Belts have not been furnished them, nor have I any at my disposition._____ This Battalion is solicitous to be put in activity, and if you think proper to make me the vehicle of conveying your wishes, it shall be ordered to any point you shall designate._____ I have

not accurate information as to the present Condition of
the Battalion of Uniform Militia /Planche's Command/
at present under your immediate orders; It has of late
been much added to by recruits from the Regular Militia,
and indeed the practise of having one company to join
another, has of late become so common, that to prevent
the total destruction of some Corps and much derangement to others,— I have deemed it proper to forbid it in
General Militia orders._____

The Return of the Battalion of chosen men of Colour,
ordered to the Chef Menteur has been mislaid; another,
will soon be furnished me, and Copy shall be forwarded
to you on Too-morrow if desired;_____ But I take it for
granted that of the strength of this Corps you are fully
informed._____

As regards the Militia of the State generally, I cannot give you full information, but I have ordered the Adjutant General to prepare a general Abstract from the
Returns last received, and which shall be transmitted to
you._____

I am Sir_____

With much Respect_____

Your humble Servant_____

Signed/   William C. C. Claiborn

Major General Andrew Jackson.
Commang. the seventh M. District_____

To James Monroe.

New Orleans December 20th 1814____

Sir_____

I have the honor to inform you, that in a Letter from
your predecessor General Armstrong, under date of the
12th of August. last, I was authorized to appoint an In-

dian Agent in the place of Doctr. Sibley._____ Knowing that the Caddo and other Indians west of the Mississippi were embodying at Natchitoches under the orders of General Jackson, I was desirous that the Agent should be a military man and in the entire confidence of the General._____ I in consequence consulted him as to a proper person, and with his approbation, I filled up the blank in the Commission entrusted me, with the name of Thomas Gales late Judge advocate of the Seventh Military District and made the Commission to bear date the 20th of August 1814. Mr. Gales is a young man of much promise; He is by profession a Lawyer, and was for some time past, attached to the suit of Major General Jackson, and by whom he has been appointed commander of the Caddoes and other Indians embodyed at Nachitoches.____

I am Sir_____

Your humble Servt.

Signed/   W. C. C. Claiborne

THE HONORABLE_____

_____James Munroe_____

_____Secretary at War, Washington City._____

New Orleans 30 December 1814____

Dear Sir,_____

The Enemy remains encamped, about seven miles below this City, within full view of our army under the command of General Jackson;_____ The Force of the Enemy is veriously stated from four to seven Thousand; _____ In an attack on the evening of the 23d Instant the enemy suffered considerably, and but the darkness of the night, which caused some little confusion in our ranks, the affair would have been decisive._____ We have lost some very brave men, and among the number, I am sorry to mention Two highly Esteemed officers of

your state, Colonel Henderson of the Rifle Corps and
Colonel Lauderdels of the Volunteers._____ The Tennessee Troops equal the high expectations which were
formed of them;— It is impossible for men to display
more patriotism, Firmness in battle or Composure under
fatigue and privations.— The Louisianians also deserve,
and will receive, the highest approbation, we are united
as one man, and a Spirit prevails which ensures our safety; We may have and calculate on having some hard
Fighting; But you need not fear for the result._____
The Commanding General inspires much confidence, and
all his Troops, Regulars, volunteers and Militia are in
high Spirits, and anxious to be led against the Enemy.
This will be done in due season;— The Kentucky Troops
are daily expected; until reinforced by them the General
has very prudently determined to maintain his present
position._____ A Position which completely covers the
City, and from which the enemy cannot dislodge him._____
The American army is drawn up in line from extending
the Mississippi to the Cypress Swamp, having in front a
wet ditch, and an entrenchment impenetrable against
musketry or smaller pieces of ordnance. The right flank
covered by the River and the Left by the Swamp, and
the whole defended by several pieces of Canon of various Calibre._____

_____ Your humble Servant _____
_____ Signed/ William C. C. Claiborne_____

To James Monroe.

New Orleans January 4th 1815.

Sir,_____
_____ The Enemy continues in our vicinity but
for the last ten days has been very quiet. on the first
of the month, he opened on our lines a heavy Fire of

Shels, Grape, Cannester and Rockets, which killed and wounded several of our brave Fellows, but his batteries were soon silenced, by a well directed Fire from our Twenty Four Pounders._____ Six privates have deserted from the enemy from their statement and that of some of the Prisoners, we are enabled to form an opinion as to the enemy's Force._____ He is represented to have eight Regiments, Two of which are black._____ Of these Regiments the Strongest is said to be eleven hundred, and the weakest Five hundred, but admitting that they average eight hundred which is probable, their number may be estimated at six thousand four hundred, with the addition of a Corps of Marines and some artillerists. _____ The enemy is now supplied with some heavy artillery and is strongly entrenched._____ The arrival on this Morning of the Kentucky reinforcements will probably enable the commanding General / JACKSON / to act on the offensive._____ It is asserted that some of the Enemy's Ships of war have entered the Mississippi;— But we have at Plaquemine and the English Turn /Two Important Points/ Strong Fortifications, which I hope and believe they cannot Pass._____ I stil feel assured of the safety of this city, In addition to the Kentucky Troops we have received reinforcements from the Interior of Louisiana._____ We have to lament for *the moment* a scarcity of arms, but are hourly in expectation of an Ample Supply which the General is informed has left Pittsburg some time since._____ The Regulars, the Militia and People are in high Spirits.____ _____

I am sir,_____

With the greatest Respect.._ ......_

Your humble Servant

Signed/ William C. C. Claiborne_____

His Excellency, Governor Blunt
Nashville, Tennessee.

To James Monroe.

New Orleans January 6th 1815____

Sir,_____

_____ Enclosed is a Duplicate Copy of my letter under date of the 23rd of December. Mr. Gales the Indian Agent has set out for Nachitoches, he was detained here longer than he had intended from the impossibility of obtaining funds for his necessary personal expences owing to the entire Stagnation of Trade, and the distresses of the times, he could not find a purchaser for his Bill on account of Salary on the War department, until I could borrow the amount, I felt some regret on the receipt of your letter mentioning Mr. Gauvin, that I had previously filled up the Blank, in the letter of appointment, I trust however that the selection will meet your approbation.— M. Gales is a well informed young man, and I am assured will deserve your Confidence; he resigned for the Agency, the office of Judge Advocate for the Seventh Military District, and I should learn with sincere regret, his being superceded in the agency._____

_____ I take it for granted that Major General Jackson keep you fully advised of all Military occurrences in this vicinity, and consequently shall only state, that the contending remain /this day/ quietly within their intrenched lines, that the arrival of General Adair with the Kentucky Troops has given additional security to this city, and that we hope soon to be enabled to drive off in the Invaders._____

I am sir _____

Your humble Servt.____

Signed /   William C. C. Claiborne____

The Honorable _____

_____ James Monroe_____

_____ Secretary at War._____

To James Monroe.

New Orleans January 9th 1815

Sir,_____

_____ Since I last addressed you nothing important occurred until yesterday the 8th Instant._____ At the dawn of day the enemy advanced in Columns the attack of our lines, protected by an incessant fire from all his batteries;— his primary efforts were directed against both our Flanks._____ The right supported by the River, and the left by a Cypress Swamp_____ This evinced an ardour which nothing could have overcome, but the steady firmness and well directed fire of our brave Troops._____

_____ At the commencement of the firing, I repaired to the scene of action and arrived there, before the battle was ended.— The officers and men, the Regulars, the Kentucky, Tennessee and Louisiana Militia seemed to me to be a like and determined._____ The fire of the Kentucky and Tennessee forces on the left was particularly fatal to the Enemy._____ They soon strewed the Field in their front with the dead and dying._____ The battle continued with vigour for near two hours, when the Enemy retired from the contest._____

_____ I cannot with any kind of certainty state their loss in Killed, Wounded and prisoners, it is however estimated at Twelve to Fifteen hundred Among the Killed are Colonel Raney, a Major Pringle, and many other officers; Among the Prisoners I have seen Fifteen or Sixteen officers, most of whom are wounded._____

_____ It is a matter of equal Joy and wonder that in a conflict, so long, so glorious to us and so fatal to the enemy our loss is astonishingly small. It is not believed to exceed in Killed and wounded, twenty-five or thirty among whom I have not heard of one officer._____

_____ The intrenchments protected our men

from the fire of the enemy and altho' their batteries poured forth a Shower of Shells, balls and Rockets, they did very little injury; for the most part overshooting the lines, and following harmless in the Field behind._____ _____ The Commanding General /Jackson/ will give to Government the particulars of a day no less honorable to him, than profitable to his country._____ He will do Justice to his brave Army and his distinguished brothers in arms, Generals Carrols, Adair and Coffy, and many others whose merits he can justly appreciate._____ _____ The victory of the American arms, would have been complete and Louisiana probably delivered at once from the Invading Foe, but the momentary success of the British on the opposite shore or west side of the Mississippi._____ _____ Batteries had been erected there to annoy the Enemy's lines, and under the brave Commodore Patterson, had gloriously contributed to our successes. _____ They were protected by a detachment of the Kentucky and Louisiana Militia, under Brigadier General Morgan of this State._____ Pending the attack on our lines a party of the enemy, the force of which is not correctly ascertained, but is supposed to be inconsiderable crossed the River, and owing to some cause not yet accounted for, our Troops speedily gave way, and the brave Commander was compelled to spike and abandon his cannon.— General Morgan is understood to have been cool and collected, and to have made many efforts to rally his men.— General Jackson was prompt in reinforcing him so, as to check the enemy's advance & we hope to day to hear of our batteries being reoccupied._____

I am Sir, &c &c _____

_____ Signed   Willm C. C. Claiborne._____

P.S.— Since writing the above, I have had the pleasure to learn that the enemy has abandoned our_batteries on the opposite shore, and recrossed the River, he has also suffered more in the action of the 8th than I at first imagined._____ Their Commander Lieutenant General Pickingham (Pakenham) is said to have been killed and his second Major General Keene badly wounded._____ I am very sure our own loss does not exceed the number stated._____Indeed I have reason to believe I have over rated it. _____

To James Madison.

New Orleans January 19th 1815____

Dear Sir._____

I congratulate you on the glorious issue of the contest in which was involved the safety of this section of the Union._____ It has this moment been officially announced to me by one of the aids de camp of Major General Jackson, "That the enemy evacuated their camp in "the course of last night, and that the State of Louisiana "is now probably Free from the presence of an Invader." I cannot on this occasion forbear to express the high sense I entertain, of the meritorious services of the Army and Navy.— In the former the Militia were alike conspicuous with the regular Troops, for their Zeal, Firmness and Forbearance under privations._____ Our Brethren of Tennessee, Kentucky and the Mississippi Territory deserve the thanks of the Union, for their effectual support in the preservation of one of its important members; and I glory in the opportunity which has afforded the people of Louisiana to prove that altho' the Youngest of the great American Family, they are not the least in valour and Patriotism._____

_____ I decline entering into details; They are reserved for the Commanding General who will do ample Justice to the brave men, who have contributed so much to his own and national Glory._____ I should however be unjust were I not again to bear testimony to the good conduct of the officers of our navy on this Station. _____ Although early deprived by an overwhelming force, of the few gun Boats which constituted the greater part, of our naval Strength, they stil found and improved the means of adding to the Luster of the naval Character of Columbia._____ Their Chief Commodore Patterson after furnishing with promptitude to the army and militia such supplies of arms and ammunition as could be spared from the naval Stores, or prepared by his marines, caused to be erected batteries on the western bank of the Mississippi opposite to the English Camp from which he continued a galling fire, greatly to the annoyance of the enemy, and to the support of our lines. _____ During a conflict so long and so obstinately maintained a great effusion of Blood might have been expected; The enemy have indeed lost their best Generals, and at last one third of their original force, But thanks to almighty God the loss on our side in killed and wounded from the commencement of the attack to the retreat of the foe, falls short of a hundred and fifty.__ _____ The oponents of the American Union will no longer I hope thank it easy to make an impression on its distant Sections and the friends of our common Country may hereafter look with calmness on any attempt which may be made to sever any of its members from the original Stock._____

I have the honor to be, Sir,
With great Respect &c &c
Signed   Wm C. C. Claiborne_____

JAMES MADISON_____
President of the United States_____

To Andrew Jackson.

New Orleans January 21st 1815.____

Sir,_____

I enclose for your perusal a letter addressed to me by General McCausland, and have to add that the Prisoners attended to, have reached this City;— The Privates have been deposited in the Jail, and the officers will remain at the Government house, until the Marshall /who is absence from his resident/ shall make some other disposition of them._____

I am Sir &c &c
Signed / Wm. C. C. Claiborne_____

Major General Jackson_____

To Andrew Jackson.

New Orleans January 25th 1815____

Sir,_____.___

_____ To complete the Fortification on the Gentilly road, I am advised by General Toledo who designed them will require the work of six carpenters for one week and of Fifty labourers for Fifteen or Sixteen days;_____ I have therefore to request of the Major General commanding, to direct the Quarter Master to engage these workmen and labourers;_____ General Toledo promise to return to the Fortification, and cause the m to be finished with all possible dispatch._____ The Plank, nails, &c for the platforms, the Quarter Master general has already been required to furnish, and a part has been transported to the Fortifications._____ A Letter from General McCausland dated on yesterday announces that many barges full of men were seen on the lake Borgne, Stearing towards the Rigolets._____

I am Sir, _____

_____ Your humble Servant,

Signed / W. C. C. Claiborne _____

Major General Jackson._____

To Andrew Jackson.

New Orleans 31st January 1815____

SIR,_____

Applications being hourly addressed to me by the Militia officers of the State to learn the disposition to be made of the various detachments now at this place, and finding a wish very General on the part of the citizens to return to their respective homes, I take the liberty to ask whether in your Judgment the services of the whole or what part of the Militia of this State now in the service of the United States can be disposed and with at what peirod._____ May I ask also whether since the date of your Letter upon the subject, you have heard anything further from the British Commanders respecting the negro slaves;——— You will excuse my solicitude upon a Subject so immediately interesting to many good Citizens of the State, and in whose behalf in any character as civil Governor I would wish to address a letter to the British Commanders, and to convey it by these distinguished citizens, if you should not already have effected the restoration of their property._____

I AM SIR._____

Your humble Servant

Signed /Will" C. C. Claiborne____

Major General.

_____Andrew Jackson._____

VI—22

To John Dick.

New Orleans February 11th 1815____

Sir,_____

Your Letter of the tenth Instant has been read with respectful attention.— I think with you, that the disposition of the President to exercise lenity towards the Individuals charged with Piracy and other offences at Barrataria as communicated to me in the letter of the Attorney General of the United States under date of the tenth of December last will be greatly increased by the good Conduct of these Individuals during the late Invasion of Louisiana, and the interest taken in their behalf by the Legislature of the State and the Commanding General of the Seventh Military District._____ Under this persuasion your entering Nolle Prosequis in all the cases you have named to me, where prosecutions have been commenced or presentments found, will meet my approbation._____

I am sir _____
signed / Willm C. C. Claiborne_____

John Dick Esqr._____
Atty Gen" for the Ls Dt____

To Stephen Marerceau.

_____New Orleans 24th February 1815____

Sir,_____

I find that the Martial Law which was proclaimed in the city of New Orleans by the general orders of the officer Commanding the Forces of the United States in the seventh Military District of which this State makes a part, continues to be enforced to the injury of our Fellow Citizens._____ If the liability of an American Citizen not the military service of the United States, to have his conduct tested by the arbitrary principles of Martial Law can ever exist, it cannot certainly be expected to be endured at another moment, than that of the actual Invasion of that part of the Country in which it is Proclaimed. _____ Yet although the enemy does not at this time occupy an inch of ground within this State, the capitol of Louisiana, the city of New Orleans and its environs continue to be the theatre of Military Dominion._____ The Plea of necessity under which alone this measure is said to be grounded, ceasing to give it any Justification, I can no longer remain a Silent Spectator of the prostration of the Laws._____ I therefore request you Sir, without loss of time to repair to this city, and resume your official duties; that you give your aid to the Civil Majistrates, particularly the Inferior ones, and on receiving information of any attempt of the Military to seize the person of any Private Citizen, not actually in the Military Service of the United States, you are specially instructed to take for his protection, and for avenging the Injured Laws of this State such measures as your knowledge of the Laws will point out._____

I am sir
Very Respectfully
Your humble Servant
Signed / Willm C. C. Claiborne.__

Stephen Marerceau Esqr._____
Attorney General, for the State of Louisiana_____ _

To General Adair.

New Orleans February 25th 1815.____

Sir,_____

To a soldier who has done his duty in all the conflicts, in which his country has been involved, from the war of Independence to the present moment, it must be matter

of great exaltation to notice the valour and firmness of
the children of his old friends; to be convinced, that they
are the true descendants of the original stock._____
That the young men of your Brigade should have looked
up to you in the hour of Battle as their guide, and their
Shield, is only a continuation of that Confidence which
their Fathers had in a Chief, whose arms had so often,
and so successfully been raised against the Foe._____
The Enclosed Resolution of the General Assembly of
Louisiana will shew you the high (esteem) which is entertained in this State, of your own services and of those
of your Brothers in arms._____ Be towards them the
vehicle of our sentiments and receive for yourself the assurances of my Respects and Best Wishes for health and
happiness._____

I am sir,_____
Your humble Servant,
Signed/ Willm C. C. Claiborne____
BRIGADIER GENERAL ADAIR.
of the Kentucky Troops._____

To General Carroll.

New Orleans February 26th 1815____
Sir,_____
I take great pleasure in communicating to you a Resolution of the General Assembly of this State expressive
of gratitude and thanks to you and your gallant Comrades for the Brilliant share, they have had in the defence of Louisiana, and the happy harmony they have
maintained with the inhabitants and Militia of this
State._____
Under a Leader Young in Years but old in deeds of
valour, our brethren of Tennessee hastened to our relief.

They arrived in time, to participate in the conflict with
the advancing foe, to thin by a well directed Fire his numerous Columns, and greatly to contribute to his final
overthrow._____ It must be pleasing to you to contemplate the present comparative security of Louisiana.
_____ It cost you and your brave associates some Toil-
some days and watchful Nights._____ But it is not to
the gratitude of this State only that you have acquired a
title._____ The whole Union must feel indebted to
those whose faithful services have conduced to the preservation of one of its important members._____

I tender to you Sir,
the assurances of my great
Regard and Esteem._____
Signed / William C. C. Claiborne._____

Major General Carroll.
of the Kentucky Troops.

To General Coffee.

New Orleans February 26th 1815.

Sir,____ _____

It affords me the greatest pleasure to enclose you a
Resolution of the General Assembly of Louisiana, acknowledging the Faithful and useful services of our
Western Brothers, and tendering their thanks to you
among their distinguished officers._____

The Love of Country which induced you to exchange
the calm of domestic life for the privations incident to a
camp is no less ardent in the brave volunteers whom you
lead than the gratitude which the People of Louisiana
bear towards you and them;_____ A Heroic Band
whose firmness in the Field has alike contributed to avert
from our settlements the horrors of Indian Warfare and

to the entire defeat and discomfiture of the Powerful Foe, who so arrogantly menaced the Safety of this great and growing city._____

Receive for yourself, and be towards your companions in arms, the organ of expressing my highest confidence and sincerest good will._____

Signed / Willm C. C. Claiborne_____
BRIGADIER GENERAL COFFEY.
of the Tennessee Volunteers._____

To Colonel Hines.

New Orleans February 26th 1815____

Sir,_____

The enclosed vote of thanks of the general assembly of Louisiana, which I now have the honor to transmit you brings to my recollection, the Satisfaction I experienced more than twelve years ago, on signing the Commission which ushered your military Talents into light. _____ At that early period of your life, the highest hopes of your future usefulness were entertained by your friends._____ And to them & to you, it must be alike pleasing to know, that these hopes have been fully realized._____ Your gallant Conduct, and that of the Corps you Command during the last Campaign, was indeed the astonishment of one army and the admiration of the other._____

It will be gratefully remembered by your Country, and has afforded for me an occasion to renew to you the assurances of my Respect and Esteem._____

Signed / Willm C. C. Claiborne____
COLONEL HINES,
Commanding the Mississippi Cavalry.

To General Thomas.

New Orleans February 25th 1815__

SIR,_____

I have the honor to enclose you a Resolution of the General Assembly of Louisiana from which you will perceive the grateful sense which is entertained of the services rendered to this state by " our brave brother Soldiers from Tennessee, Kentucky and the Mississippi Territory and their gallant Leaders._____

It is the pride of America to see her gallant defenders guide the Plough or front her Enemies as the National Interest and Safety shall advise._____ To such Citizen Soldiers do we chiefly commit the protection of our dearest rights. The defence of our beloved Country, and that we may continue to do so, and with confidence, the glorious termination of the Campaign in which you have borne so distinguished a part, affords a Pleasing Proof. _____ From the prospect now before us, we may be permitted to hope Sir, that the calm of Peace, will soon authorize you to rest from the toils of war and to lead back your Patriotic Division to their Families and Friends. _____ The best wishes of the Louisianians will adways accompany you and them._____ The Spirit of Union of mutual affection and confidence, which now happily exists between the people of this State, and their Brothers of the sister States, will I trust be forever cherished. _____ It is the surest pledge of our National Safety and glory._____ I tender to you Sir the assurances of my Respectful attachment._____

I am Sir,—

Your humble Servant

Signed / William C. C. Claiborne.

Major General Thomas
of the Kentucky Troops.

To James Monroe.

New Orleans February 10th 1815.—

Sir,------------

In my last letter, I enclosed you a Copy of the French Consul's letter to me relative to General Jackson's order for certain French Subjects to repair into the Interior of this State, and of the answer I had returned.-------- I now transmit you a Copy of a news paper publication on the subject which appeared on the Third Instant in the Louisiana Courier, and which Mr. Louillier, a distinguished member of the Legislature of this State avowed himself the author.[1]---------- On the Fifth of this month Mr. Louillier was arrested by order of General Jackson, and lodged in the Barracks. On the same day the Judge of the District / Mr. Hall on application directed a Writ of Habeas Corpus to issue; But before the Writ was served, Judge Hall was himself arrested and conducted under a Strong guard to the Barracks, where he remains confiled.-------- The orders which relate to the French Subjects, were on the Eighth Instant retracted or suspended at the request as is stated of the Orleans Battalion of volunteers; —But the French Consul Colonel Tousard, has been specially commanded to retire from without the limits of General Jackson's Camp and which he has done by leaving the city.— Two days since the United States district attorney /Mr. Dick/ applied in behalf of Judge Hall to Mr. Lewis, Judge of the First Judicial District of Louisiana for a writ of habeas corpus, which was issued and served on the General.-------- But the attorney was immediately arrested and lodged in the Barracks where he still remains. Orders were given for

---

[1] Louisiana Courier, Feby. 3, 1815. Fortiers' Louisiana Vol. III, p. 152.

the arrest of Judge Lewis; But they have been recalled. _____ I decline for the present making any comments on these proceedings, but I must request you Sir, to communicate them to the President, General Jackson has thought proper to declare the city and precents of New Orleans his camp, and to enforce in and over the same *Martial Law,* and to the entire prostration of the laws and civil authorities of this state and of the United States.[1]_____

We have for some days past been in expectation of receiving official information of the ratification of the Treaty of Peace;_____ But we are doomed stil longer to remain in a State of Suspense._____ The Official Messenger who left Washington on the 14th January either was not given the dispatch intended for him, or it has been lost, for it seems nothing satisfactory has reached General Jackson, and by me not a Line upon the Subject has been received._____ The mail of this morning brings us intelligence from Washington as late as the morning of the 14th of ———— at which time it is said the treaty was before the Senate, but the result of their deliberations not ascertained._____

I have the honor to be

Sir

With great Respect

Your humble Servant_____

Signed William C. C. Claiborne.____

THE HONORABLE

    The Secretary of State,_____

      for the United States_____

_____WASHINGTON CITY._____

P.S. Since writing the above I have obtained a copy of the last orders relating to the French Subjects and which you have herewith enclosed._____

---

[1] J. S. Bassett's Life of Andrew Jackson.

To Col. Declouet.

New Orleans.

Sir,------------

In the name and by the authority of the General Assembly, I have the honor to present to your Regiment a Stand of Colours.......... They will be borne to you by the Adjutant General and you will be pleased to receive them as evidence of the highest confidence in the Patriotism and valour of yourself and your companions in arms. ------ The Regiment under your Command is particularly distinguished, It composes the first Corps of Militia which Louisiana furnished for the service of the great family to which she is united by the indissoluble ties of interest, affection and gratitude.......... The occasion which called you into the field was of the greatest importance to your Country, nor could the zeal and promptitude with which the call was met escape the notice and approbation of your Government........... With these sentiments, I commit this Standard to the protection of your Regiment.......... When and where it shall be unfurled, let it awaken the most ardent love of Country.......... Let it animate every Heart and excite every mind to deeds of valour and virtue...........

Signed   William C. C. Claiborne.____

Colonel A. Declouet
of the drafted Militia.

New Orleans February   1815

------------CIRCULAR.------------

Dear Sir,_____

We (are) assured here on the authority of Admiral Cockran, that a treaty of Peace between the United States, and great Britain was signed at Ghent on the

26th of December last and which treaty being already ratified by the Prince Regent awaits only the sanction of the American Government to put an end to hostilities.— Taking it for granted that the conditions are such as neither to compromise the honor nor the Interest of the United States, I offer you my congratulations on an event so desirable to our Common Country._____

You will learn with regret, that an unfortunate misunderstanding exists between Major General Jackson, and the Legislature and *Executive* authorities of Louisiana against the *latter* of which I have reason to believe, his resentment is more immediately directed._____ With a Favorit and Victorious Chief whose gallantry and exploits have attracted so much *admiration*, I am well aware I can enter into no contest upon equal grounds._____There however is a Shield which a kind Providence furnishes the cause of Justice and truth, which resists present attacks and grows stronger with time.— On former trials, I have experienced the strength of this Shield, nor on the present can it fail to extend to me the most ample security._____ I acknowledge that General Jackson has rendered important services nor do I deny him the possession of some great qualities; But the violence of his character casts a Shade upon them all, and in this Capitol he has observed a Course of Conduct which cannot be easily excused, much less justified by those who feel a proper regard for the rights of others.[1]_____

I am Dear Sir,
With great Respect &c &c
signed/ Willm. C. C. Claiborne____

[1] Papers in West Florida Manuscripts Library Congress. Transcript of the case of the United States vs. Major Genl. Andrew Jackson.

To James Monroe.

New Orleans March   1815____

Sir,------------------

Mr. Louillier, whose case as particularly mentioned in my last letter being brought before a Court Martial denied its authority to try him; but the court is understood to have decided in favour of its competency, the prisoner refusing nevertheless to answer the plea of not guilty was entered by order of the Court._____ The decision of the Court was rendered I am told on yesterday, but is not yet promulgated;_____ In the mean time, Mr. Louillier remains in confinement.— The Honorable Judge Hall whose case I also stated in my last letter, was on this day removed from the Barracks, and escorted by a small guard of Cavalry about five miles above the city, beyond the point which the General Considers as the upper line of his Camp._____ We await with great solicitude intelligence of the ratification of the Treaty by the President and Senate._____

I am Sir

With great Respect

THE HONORABLE   Your obt. Servant.____

Signed/   Willm. C C. Claiborne_____

The Secretary of State,

_____for the United States,_____

To Col. Toussard.

New Orleans March 2nd 1815_____

Sir,--------------

I have had the honor to receive your communication of Yesterday with its enclosures, the executive of Louisiana has no controul over the acts of the officers Com-

manding the Military district within which it is included.
Whether or not the rights secured by Treaties and the
Laws of nations to the subjects of his Christian Majesty
residing within this State, are violated by the General
Order of which you complain is a question not for me to
determine._____ It properly belongs to the Judicial Power, and there can be no doubt but on proper
application, it will interpose its authority in such manner, as Justice and the Laws shall prescribe.

I am Sir,
With great Respect,

Colonel Toussard   Your humble Servant,
French Consul.   Signed/ Willm. C. C. Claiborne.

To James Monroe.

New Orleans March 2nd 1815.

Sir,_____

I have the honor to transmit you a translation of a
letter which was addressed to me on last evening by the
French Consul, together with a Copy of the answer which
I have this moment returned._____ I have
•had no conversation with General Jackson relative to the
orders of which the Consul complains, nor do I know
whether there be any reason for this measure, other than
the one expressed.— Under an impression that the treaty
of peace, said to have been concluded at Ghent contains
nothing derogatory to our national honor or Interests,
we await its ratification with great solicitude.___ That
union and mutual confidence which so recently pervaded
this whole community no longer exists;____ I persuade
myself however that if the people should again be called
upon to repel an advancing foe, it would be the signal for
reunion, and for the like display of Patriotism, valour

and firmness, which in a recent occasion did so much honor to the Louisianians and so greatly contributed to their safety.------------------

I am Sir

THE HONORABLE   Your humble Servant

Signed/ Willm. C. C. Claiborne

The Secretary of State
_____for the United States._____

To Toussard.

New Orleans March 14th 1815.

Sir,---------------

Your letter of the Eleventh Instant has been received. — The transactions to which you allude not falling within my province to notice I can only say that your communication shall be transmitted to the Secretary of State for the United States._____ In the mean time Sir, your return to this city will be agreeable to the executive of Louisiana, and as heretofore you shall be recognized and respected as the consul of his most Christian Majesty.----------------------

I have the honor to be

Sir,

Your humble Servant,

Signed/ William C. C. Claiborne.

Le Chevalier de Toussard

French Consul.----------------------

New Orleans March 15th 1815

Sir,---------------

The Proclamation of the President announcing the Treaty of Peace reached us on the thirteenth Instant, and has diffused the greatest Joy.---------- The terms

are certainly as favorable, as in the present state of the
world could have been expected, and I tender you my
sincerest Congratulations on an event which under the
favour of Heaven, cannot fail greatly to contribute to
the prosperity and happiness of our Country._____
Among the blessings which the news of Peace have
brought to the Inhabitants of this city, is a restoration
of their constitutional rights._____ The Martial
Law has been recalled by the same authority which imposed it, and we have today had the pleasure of witness-
ing the return of the honorable Judge Hall to this city.
_____ I enclose for your perusal a letter which
was addressed to me on the eleventh Instant by the
French Consul together with a Copy of my answer._____

I am Sir,

Your humble Servant,

_____Signed William C. C. Claiborne

_____Private_____

New Orleans March 16th 1815

Dear Sir_____
GREAT is the change which the return of Peace has
already made in this Capitol.— Our harbor is again
whitened with canvass; The Levee is crowded with Cot-
ton, Tabaco and other articles for exportation;_____
The merchant seems delighted with the prospect before
him, and the aggriculturists in the high price for his
products, finds new incitements to Industry._____
There will doubtless be Individuals who will take exception to the conditions of the Treaty, but in the present
State of the world, it seems to me we could not have expected to have sheathed the sword upon better terms.__
It is presumable that the army will speedily be

placed on the Peace Establishment, and in which event, will you excuse me for expressing a solicitude that among the officers retained, may be those very deserving officers, Colonel William McRea of the artillerists and Major Wicks of the Seventh Regiment of Infantry, the former has long been in service and I believe always acted worthily._____ He has been in command at New Orleans and the vicinity for eight Years, and I have had frequent occasion to notice his great attention to duties, and sincere attachment to Government._____ Major Wicks is a young man of great promise; with the advantages of an accomplished education, and a deportment in life which commands great Respect and esteem. _____May I also take this occasion to remind you of the great desire, which my friend, Mr. Thomas Johnson of this city stil feels to be sent to some Port in France in character of a Consul._____ I have heretofore taken the liberty to express to you my opinion as to Mr. Johnson's fitness for such employment and the high Character I then formed of him is confirmed by his uniform correct and honorable deportment.

I am Sir,

Your humble Servant

Signed/   William C. C. Claiborne____

THE HONORABLE, James Monroe

_____Secretary at War_____

To Genl. Lambert.

New Orleans 25th March 1815.____

Sir,_____

I have the honor to introduce to your excellency and to recommend to your friendly attention, Colonel Michael Fortier and Mr. Chevalier de la Croix, two distin-

guished citizens of this State._____
These Gentlemen at the solicitation, and in behalf of the owners of the negro Slaves, who are understood to have followed the English Army to Dauphine Island, have repaired to your head quarters for the purpose of receiving and providing the means of sending back to their masters such of the negro slaves aforesaid, as in conformity to the first article of the Treaty of Peace between the United States and Great Britain, Your Excellency shall deem proper to decline *carrying away.*_____
A Copy of the Treaty as officially transmitted to me by the Secretary of State for the United States, is herewith enclosed._____ It happily terminated the War between our two Countries and lays the foundation of an honorable Peace._____ A Peace alike interesting to our two nations and which our respective rulers, may I trust Cherish and perpetuate.—

I have the honor to be
Sir,
Your humble Servant,
Signed/   William C. C. Claiborne.

HIS EXCELLENCY, Major General Lambert or the officer Commanding the English army on Dauphine Island._____

_____Answer._____

Dauphine Island March 30th 1815

Sir_____
In the absence of Major General Lambert, and being left in Command of the Troops here, I have the honor to acknowledge the receipt of your Excellency's letter of 25″ Instant introducing to me, Colonel Michael Fortier, and M″ Le Chevalier de la Croix, two citizens of the

State of Louisiana.----------------------

I should feel happy, in rendering any assistance to those Gentlemen, to enable them to execute the object of their mission, but agreeable to the determination of Major General Lambert before he went away, all those slaves who were not willing, and who objected to return to their former Masters, have been embarked for the Island of Bermuda, to be sent from thence to Trinida, The Major General did every thing in his power, to induce the whole of the slaves you deserted from New Orleans to return. but he did not feel himself authorized to resort to force, to oblige them to do so, as they threw themselves on his protection, which they were entitled to, having served with the British Army and which they did voluntarily and without compulsion.------------------

I have the honor to remain,

Sir,

Your most obedient Servant,

Signed/ John Power---------

Major General Commanding.

HIS EXCELLENCY
    William C. C. Claiborne
    Governor of the State of Louisiana.

To Andrew Jackson.

New Orleans April 5th 1815---------

Sir,

In a Letter which I lately received from Mr. Fromentin of the Senate of the United States /but which I cannot at this moment lay my hand upon/ he informs me that on conversing with the late Secretary at War /Colonel Munroe/ relative to the monies advanced by Louisiana towards completing the Fortifications on the Mississippi, the Secretary had among other things, said that the amount should be repaid to the State, and General Jackson instructed upon the subject. as I desire answering Mr. Fromentin's letter by the next mail, may I be permitted to ask whether any instructions in relation to these monies have yet reached you.------------------

I am Sir,
Your humble Servant
Signed/ William C. C. Claiborne
Major General Jackson,
Commdg the Seventh M. Districk.

To Daniel Patterson.

New Orleans April 5th 1815--------

Sir,--------------
I have reason to believe that a Vessel which sailed lately from this Port under the command of one vincent Gambier /Formerly a Chief of the Barataria Association/ is at this time cruising in the Gulph of Mexico, and has already captured two vesesls bound to New Orleans. no time and no expence should be spared, to put down at once this Pirate, or otherwise we may expect a repetition of those practices at Barataria and its vicinity, which so long existed to the dishonour of Louisiana, and to the great Injury of the commerce and revenue of the United States.--------- If you do me the favour to call at my office on Tomorrow, or if convenient at my house on this afternoon, I will give you the particulars of the information.--------------------

I am Sir
Your humble Servt--------
Signed/ William C. C. Claiborne----
COMMODORE
Daniel Patterson.--------------------

To Jean Blanque.

New Orleans April 6th 1815------

Sir,----------------

On the 29th of December last you will recollect, that I met you and Mr. Marigny, at the quarters of Major General Jackson, when a conversation ensued between the General and yourself, relative to the causes, which led on the day previous, to the orders for closing the doors of the Legislature.------------ In the course of the conversation, do you not remember, that I took the occasion to assure the General of my confidence in the Patriotic disposition of the Legislature, and my conviction that the information to the contrary, which had reached him, was a Calumny?---------- And did you not understand the General to reply in substance, that he also had confidence in the Patriotic disposition of the Legislature that their address to him on the day of his arrival, and their subsequent conduct had assured him of their support, and that the closing the doors, had arisen *wholly in a mistake* which he was happy had been explained?----

I will thank you as early as your convenience may permit to answer these inquiries, and to state fully your present impressions, as to the tenor of the conversation alluded to.------- A Conversation which on the part of the General was conducted in English, but which your knowledge of that Language /independent of the translation which at the time was furnished, enabled you to comprehend.[1]------------------

I am Sir,----------------

Your humble Servant--------

Signed/   William C. C. Claiborne--

Jean Blanque Esqr.
a member of the Legislature.

---

[1] The defence of the legislature may be found in a letter from Fulwor Skipwill to Genl. Jackson dated May 15, 1827, in the West Florida Papers, prompted by an attack on Skipwill by Jackson.

To William Piatt.

New Orleans 10th April 1815____

Sir_____

You will recollect, that I told you some time since, that several Planters of whom M" Lecesure had obtained negro labourers, design to claim no compensation for the same, and that I had requested you to pay the amount for negro hire, alone to the Individual Claimants or to their order. Mr. Lauve is one of those Planters, and he now attend at your office for the purpose of entering on the account his abondment of claim._____ It is very possible that some of the Claims exhibited against the Government for cart hire were never exacted by the Individuals furnishing the same; Among them is the Bearer Mr. Lauve who sent to the Mayor two carts and four horses, which although not yet returned he waves all claim for remuneration._____

I am Sir,
Your Obedient Servant
Signed/   William C. C. Claiborne
Colonel William Piatt,_____
late Quarter Master General._____

To Edmund P. Gaines.

New Orleans April 14th 1815____

Sir,

The Bearer Francis Alvarado a Spaniard by Birth and late a Captain in General Humbert's legion, comes to Complain to you of the miserable State in which he and his Companions now discharged find themselves; ____ without money, without rations, lodgings or the means of procuring them. Alvarado comes to entreat

you to direct that his men be as speedily paid of as the
public funds will admit, in order that they may depart
from this city._____ To Alvarado's entreaties upon
this Point, I beg leave, to add my own, for I entertain
serious apprehensions, that if the men, late of Humbert's
Legion, Composed as I learn of all Colours and description of Character, should no longer remain in this City,
and in a State of Suffering, they may and will depredate
upon the properties of the Citizens._____

I am Sir

Your humble Servant

Signed/   William C. C. Claiborne

Brigadier General
_____Edmund P. Gaines____

New Orleans May 1st 1815

Sir,
     Your letter of the 18″ of March with its enclosures,
did not reach me until the 29th Ultimo.   The mail has of
late been very irregular and letters by it, often meet
with great delay._____ The Blank in the Commission for the principal assessor of the third Collection
district, I have filled up with the name D. R. D. Dessessarts Frenchman by birth, but for many Years, an Inhabitant of Louisiana, and a worthy and useful member
of Society._____ Mr. Dessessarts resides in New Orleans and the Commission bears date on this day the
First of May 1815— as an inducement to Mr. Dessessarts' Acceptance, and immediate entrance on the duties
of his office, I have agreed to allow him, and the assistant assessor, the full extent of the compensation mentioned in your letter._____ I will as soon as I can select suitable persons fill up the blanks on the Commissions for the collectors of the first and the Principal As-

sessor for the fourth District, and inform you of the causes of the person chosen, their residence and the date of the Commissions._____

I am Sir
Signed/   W. C. C. Claiborne.

The Hble. Mr. Smith, Comm of the Revenue.

To James Monroe.

Louisiana Parish of Iberville July 26″

Sir,_____

Its my duty to inform you that efforts are now making within this State to prepare the means of a Military expedition against the Interior Provinces of Mexico. _____ The expedition professes to have for object, the best interests of humanity._____ The generous enlargement of an oppressed people._____ *Belle Isle* near the Mouth of Chaffalaya is appointed the place of Rendezvous, where from four to five hundred men are said to have assembled and to be well supplied with arms, ammunition and Provisions._____ Some late commissioned officers of the United States Army and Navy, recently discharged, Privates are also stated to have joined in the enterprise._____ The expedition proceeds from *Belle Isle* by water to *Matagorda,* a small Port near the Gulph of Mexico, from thence to Labahaia a little village on the River San Antonio about forty miles from the Sea Coast and Eighty from the town of San Antonio the Capitol of the province of Texas._____ It is also said another expedition is to move from Nachitoches, and "Labahaia" is fixed upon as the point of reunion._____ One thousand men /it is reported/ are already engaged and a much greater number calculated upon from Kentucky and Tennessee._____

Among the Persons now at belle Isle is a Spaniard of the name of Labalac,''— he is represented to be a native of the Province of Yucatan, and late a delegate from said Province to the Cortez of Spain._____ I do not know, who is to Command these expeditions;_____ In this quarter, a Mr. Henry Perry a native American /Formerly a conspicuous commander under Toledo in his late unsuccessful attack on Texas/ is considered the more prominent character._____ Having been much of the greater part of the last months in retirement at my Plantation about eighty five miles from New Orleans, and most of the time confined to the house, either from my own or the Indisposition of my Family, it was not until very lately, that I became acquainted with the particulars, which I now communicate._____

The civil authority of Louisiana is not competent to the suppression of these expeditions, and if the Government wish them put down Force must be applied._____ On former occasions the civil authority of the State interposed, but to no effect; nor does a like interposition at this time promise a more favorable result._____ The proposed enterprises againt the Spanish Provinces, meet in Louisiana the more Support from an impression that they are Secretly countenanced by the administration._____ I have endeavored to remove this impression and quoted your former Letters to me on this Subject. But until the Government shall apply the only sure corrective force many of the Persons concerned will continue to think that these projects are not disapproved by the Executive._____

I have the honor &c &c_____
Signed Willm. C. C. Claiborne
THE HONORABLE James Monroe_____
Secretary at War._____

Louisiana,—Iberville July 29" 1815

Sir, _____

Your Letter of the twenty third of June has been duly received. _____ The four Packets of Stamps for the First Collection district, and to which you allude were forwarded to Mr. Ryson the gentleman First named the collector of that district; he declined accepting but acknowledged to me the receipt of the Packets. A Mr. Carson was next appointed, and to him Mr. Ryson was requested to deliver the Stamps; But Mr. Carson declined, and the papers I understood remained in the hands of Mr. Ryson. _____ Mr. Marshall was informed of all this, and desired by me to call for and receipt for the papers, Mr. Ryson died a few months since, but he was a man of business and Integrity; _____ The Stamps therefore I have no doubt, were carefully put away, and will be safely delivered by his representatives to Mr. Marshall. _____

I do not know how to account for the deficiency you notice in the Stamps acknowledged to have been received by P. A. Delachaise the Collector of the Second district, and those forwarded from your office. _____ The Fact is that the Packets of Stamps, as received from Mr. Morgan were delivered by me to Colonel Thompson, then a member of the Legislature of Louisiana, and Brother in Law of Mr. Delachaise, and were I am assured placed by the former into the hands of the latter. _____ The deficiency in the Stamps received by Mr. Ficklein, was at the time communicated from the Treasury Department to Mr. Morgan, and to whom I gave such information on the subject as came within my knowledge. _____ The Several Packets of Stamps delivered by Morgan, were deposited in the office of the Secretary of this State, and conseqeuntly under the care of the Secretary. _____ They were forwarded to the several Collectors by the first Convenient occasion, and allways under the care of some honest citizen. _____ It is possible, some of the Stamps for the fourth district, may have been lost on their passage, or through mistake forwarded to the Collector of the first district, and should this last be the fact, you will learn from the return, which Mr. Marshall may make of the Stamps received from the Representatives of Mr. Ryson, the gentleman first appointed Collector._____

I have the honor, Sir
to be very Respectfully &c
Signed____William C. C. Claiborne.

Mr. Smith, Collector of the Revenue
Washington, City.—

To Thomas Gales.

New Orleans September 10th 1815—
Sir, _____
_____ Your Letter of the 29th Ultimo complaining that your former communication to me had remained unanswered has been duly received._____
Not long since my friend Colonel Shaumberg visited Natchitoches, and was specially charged to inform you the reasons which induced me to decline giving any general Instructions, relative to the agency, and had he met you at Nachitoches the cause of my silence, would have been satisfactorily explained._____ It is known to you, that General Armstrong when Secretary at War, confided to me the trust of selecting an Indian Agent in the place of Doctor Sibley, and to that end enclosed me a blank Commission; That the general also authorized me to give,— "To the agent such additional Instructions as may be necessary for his immediate government, and to establish him at such place as shall promise best accommodations."_____ Previous to the selection of the Agent I determined to advise with General Jackson com-

manding the seventh military district, as to a suitable character because being informed, that the General was authorized to embody and to receive into the service of the United States the Caddoe and other Indians on the Frontiers of Louisiana, it was by me deemed important that the New Agent should possess his entire confidence. _____ General Jackson being then on the Mobile, the nomination was necessarily delayed, but you sir, was ultimately chosen with the entire approbation of that officer.— Subsequent to your appointment and previous to your departure from New Orleans, I received a letter from Munroe the Successor of general Armstrong instructing me to fill the blank in the Commission for Indian Agent with the name of _____ Gauvin; But the Commission was no longer within my controul of which fact I informed Mr. Munroe by letter under date of the _____ day of _____, and enclosed him a duplicate of my letter of the _____ of the same month, which announced your appointment._____ You will observe, Sir, that my only authority to exercise the smallest Controul over your acts was derived from the letter of General Armstrong already alluded to._____ The Communication from his Successor M. Munroe furnished evidence of a wish, not to have confided to me the Selection of the Agent, and this circumstance induced an unwillingness on my part further to interfere in the affairs of the agency, unless Mr. Munroe should invite me to do so._____ This he has had an opportunity of doing in reply to the several letters I addressed him relative to your appointment, but to this moment, the receipt of these letters have not been acknowledged._____

As regards the delay and difficulty in honoring your Bills for expenditures incurred, in embodying the Indians, I can only express my regret._____ I had understood that your Predecessor, Doctr Sibley had instructions from General Jackson on that point, and I knew how anxious, the General was for your arrival at your Post, in order that the warriors of the Caddoes, and other Tribes, who were invited to rendez-vous at Nachitoches might be mustered into the service of the United States. _____ On this subject I never supposed it my province to give you any instructions, always believing that it was exclusively committed to the officer commanding the Seventh Military District, and I am persuaded sir, that on application to that officer, he will promptly and cheerfully Sanction, all such expenditures by you incurred in embodying the Indians, as shall appear to have been directed by a prudent discretion._____

Such information relative to the Indians as may immediately interest Louisiana, or any portion of it, will be thankfully received, & on all points, which shall concern the State or its Citizens, I shall from time to time, take the liberty of writing you._____ As regards the general policy, which the Government of the United States, would wish to pursue towards the Tribes committed to your care, it can I presume, be collected from the official communications to and from your predecessor. _____ But if these are not sufficiently explicit, the Secretary at war, will doubtless on application, give you ample Instructions._____

It is rumoured here, that efforts are making to set on foot, in the vicinity of Nachitoches an other expedition against the Spanish Province Texas, and that the Caddoe and other Indians are likely to prove zealous auxiliaries; _____ Will you be pleased to inform me how far these rumours may be accredited._____ No man wishes more sincerely than I do, that Mexico, and the other Spanish Provinces, should become free of all European influences, and placed under a Government of Laws;_____ But I must confess, I shall learn with regret, that any portion of our Citizens should engage in enterprises which the government of the United /as far as I know and believe/

does not approve, and the laws positively forbid._____

I am sir

With Respect

Your humble Servant_____

_____Signed_____ William C. C. Claiborne

Major Thomas Gales,

Indian agent.

_____NACHITOCHES_____

Circulars to Governors.

New Orleans September 15th 1815—

Sir, _____

I have the honor to enclose you a copy of an act of the Legislature of Louisiana, entitled *"An Act to Regulate the Administration of the Charity Hospital of the City of New Orleans,"* Together with the plan of an edifice, which under the direction of that administration, is now completed._____ YOUR EXCELLENCY will observe by a reference to the Twelfth Section of the act, that the Funds of the Hospital are deemed inadequate to the purpose of giving to it, all the extent required by the Situation of this Metropolis, "To which great numbers of our Fellow Citizens, Inhabitants of the States and Territories bordering on the Mississippi, the Ohio, and other water courses, annually repair;"__ _____ And that it is made the duty of the governor of this State, to propose to the several State Legislatures, "A Subscription for the benefit of Said Hospital, which will thereby be enabled to receive a greater number of sick, and to participate to them the necessary relief."_____

For several years past it has been found that among the Patients admitted into the hospital gratis, the greater proportion were Inhabitants of the Western States and

Territories who descend annually to New Orleans, with their surplus productions._____ The Peace which our country now happily enjoys, cannot fail to promote a more frequent intercourse of the industrious and enterprising Citizens of your State with this Capitol, nor is it improbable but among them, there will be Individuals, who afflicted with the diseases prevalent here during the summer season, may seek an assylum in the benevolent Institution, in whose behalf I now address your Excellency._____ This consideration, no less than that generous disposition to relieve suffering humanity, which the American States have at all times manifested, will I am persuaded induce the Legislature of_____ to extend to the Charity Hospital of New Orleans its support._____ With sentiments of great Respect His Excellency the Governor of the State of Tennessee_____
__ ditto _____ ditto _____ Kentucky _____
__ ditto _____ ditto _____ Ohio_____
__ ditto _____ ditto _____ Pennsylvania___
__ ditto _____ ditto _____ Virginia_____

I have the honor
to be
Your Excellency's
most obedient
and humble servant
Signed   William C. C. Claiborne

To Genl. Labatat.

New Orleans September 22. 1815
Sir,_____
The Command of the Brigade of Militia which includes the city and suburbs of New Orleans, previous, pending and Subsequent to the late Invasion, having de-

volved upon you, I know not any officer who has had so good an opportunity to notice my general conduct, in character as Commander in Chief, and I therefore request you, Sir, as far as your knowledge of facts will permit, and as early as may suit your convenience, to respond the Following Questions._____

FIRST, Did I not some time previous to the late Invasion, advise the Militia by General orders, and otherwise of the dangers which menaced the State, and strongly urge the expediency of introducing order, and discipline, and being at all times prepared to receive the Enemy?

SECOND, When on the twenty third of December, the alarm was given, did not the Frst, Second and Fourth Regiments of Militia, and Choveau's Troop of horse, all under your Command, rendez-vous in obedience to my orders in front of the Principal, between two and three O'clock?

THIRD, Did I not on the same day, repair to the Principal, and assume the command of the Detachment?

FOURTH, To such Privates as had no muskets were not Pikes furnished, and in what manner, were they directed to use them._____

FIFTH, Did I not as soon as ball Cartridges were distributed inform the men, that they were to be immediately marched against the enemy, and in what manner was this information received?_____

SIXTH, How far had the Detachment moved on the road, leading to Villere's Plantation before it was halted, and ordered to move on the Gentilly road, and in what manner was this last order received._____

SEVENTH, During the night of the twenty third of December, was not the Detachment under arms, or on the march the greater part of the night?_____

EIGHTH. Until the First and Second Regiments were withdrawn from the Gentilly road, did I not remain with

the Detachment and participate in all its Toils _____
NINTH. During the period that the Command of the
City of New Orleans was confided to you, did I not often
visit the guards, and repeatedly urge the expediency of
enforcing, the greatest vigilance and attention to duty?
_____
TENTH. Very early on the morning of the Eighth of
January, and immediately after the firing General Jackson's lines commenced, did I not *previous to going to the
lines,* repair to the government house, and what were the
orders I then gave you?_____
ELEVENTH. On my return from the lines, were you
not ordered by me to press every boat in the harbour with
their crews, not omitting the little market boats, for the
purpose of facilitating the passage of the River by the
troop destined to reinforce the Detachment on the Western Bank which had given ground to the enemy?_____
TWELFTH. Did you not by my orders, cause domicil-
iary visits to be made, within the City and Suburbs of
New Orleans, and were not all the Spare arms found, immediately placed at General Jackson's disposition?
THIRTEENTH Previous and Subsequent of the Battle of the Eighth, did I not in general orders express my
highest disapprobation of the desertions which had taken
place in some of the Militia Corps, and were you not expressly commanded to cause the Deserters to be arrested?_____

It only remains for me to apologize for the trouble I
am about to give you, and to assure you of_____
_____My great Respect and Esteem____
        Signed,____William C. C. Claiborne_____
____Brigadier General
        John Baptiste Labatat_____
        ____of the First Brigade._____

New Orleans October 1st 1815.____

To Col. Shaumburg.

Sir,_____

As far as your recollection may serve, and as soon as your convenience shall permit, will you have the goodness to respond to the following questions._____

*FIRST.*_____From the Second day of September Eighteen hundred and fourteen, the period of your appointment as my aid-de-camp to the present day has there not existed between us the most friendly intercourse, and a frequent and unreserved interchange of Sentiments and opinions._____

*SECOND.*_____Have you at any time heard from me a Sentiment expression or wish indicating other feelings, than those of the warmest attachment to my Country's interest, and the greatest solicitude for the safety, welfare and tranquillity of this Section of the Union.____

*THIRD.*_____Is it not within your knowledge that every effort was made by me to array and bring into the Field, the auxiliary militia Force, required from this State under the orders of the Secretary at War of the fourth of July eighteen hundred and fourteen.

*FOURTH.*_____Is it not within your Knowledge that some months previous to the Invasion of Louisiana, in my character as commander in chief, I apprised the Militia of the dangers which menaced the State and strongly urged the necessity of union, vigilance, and the strictest obedience to orders._____

*FIFTH.*_____Have you not heard me acknowledge the chagrin which the opposition to general Flournoy's requisition, by the city militia, and the countenance which the Legislature of this State afforded such opposition, had occasioned me, accompanied with an apprehension, lest

a similar opposition might arise to the requisition of the
Fourth of July eighteen hundred & Fourteen._____

*SIXTH.*_____When it was found that the last requisition was cheerfully and promptly met, that several volunteer Corps had offered their services, and that the old
men throughout the State, were /in conformity to my request forming military associations/ did I not express to
you an opinion that the people were becoming sensible of
the dangers to which they were exposed, and that they
would in the hour of Peril prove faithful to themselves
and to their Country._____

*SEVENTH.*_____Was you not in the month of October
Eight hundred and fourteen the bearer of Letters from
me to Major general Jackson, then at Mobile._____ did
I not previous to your departure communicate freely to
you the condition in which Louisiana was placed as related to defence, and were you not particularly instructed
to make General Jackson fully sensible of the Same?____
Did I not also furnish you with a memorandum in writing, which conveyed my impressions as to the defensive
measures which ought immediately to be taken, with a request, that you would explain the same to the General?
and finally did I not authorize you to assure the general
of my disposition to co-operate with him, hand and heart?

----

*EIGHTH.*_____Is it not within your Knowledge that immediately on your return from Mobile, I caused Posts to
be established on the Lafourche, and on the waters of
Barataria?_____

*NINTH.*_____Did I not also employ Spies, or Scouts,
and receive information daily from Chef Menteur and
Terre aux boeufs, did I not also in general orders advise
the militia generally, in what manner they were to act in
case the enemy should effect a landing in any part of
this State?_____ and did I not establish within the
City of New Orleans, Signals of Alarm by day and night,

and designate the points of rendez-vous for the different Corps?_____

TENTH._____When a part of the Louisiana contingent took Post at the english Turn, is it not within your Knowledge, that I advised an Intrenchment in their front, extending from the river to the Cypress Swamp.___

ELEVENTH._____Previous to General Jackson's arrival in Orleans, is it not within your Knowledge, that I spoke respectfully of him as a man and officer?_____And on his arrival, is it known to you, that I evinced every disposition to give him a friendly and respectful reception._____

TWELFTH._____When I yielded the command of the Militia of Louisiana to General Jackson, did I not acquaint you with the motives which influenced me?_____ and what were those motives?_____

THIRTEENTH._____Previous to the general's arrival in New Orleans, was not the Patriotic disposition of the Militia of the City, and indeed throughout the State often spoken of, by me, & noticed by you?_____

FOURTEENTH._____When on the Seventeenth of December Eighteen hundred and Fourteen, the General announced in general orders, his volunteer aids-de-camp, and Judge-Advocate, did I not say to you that the general had taken into his confidence men, whose primary object would be to create a Schism between him & me?_____ And was it not observable, that from that moment, the intercourse between us became every day the less friendly, until it finally ceased?_____

FIFTEENTH._____On the twenty third of December, when the alarm was given did I not hasten to place myself at the head of the city militia?_____On taking up our lines of march towards the enemy, did you not notice the enthusiasm with which the militia were animated, and when we were halted, and ordered to proceed on the gentilly road, did I not observe to you, that this was part of a System decided on, to keep me in the back ground?_____

SIXTEENTH._____Did I not remain on the gentilly, or chef menteur road, until by sending reinforcements to general Jackson, the detachment was so reduced, as not to present a suitable command for a Colonel?_____

SEVENTEENTH._____Whilst commanding in person, on the Chef menteur road, did I not maintain the strictest police, and cause the greatest vigilance to be observed, and a *Defile* which I occupied, to be strongly fortified?__

EIGHTEENTH._____When I returned to the City, is it not within your Knowledge that in addition to the care and vigilance which I continued to extend to Chef Menteur, I took frequent occasion to visit the guards in New Orleans, and inforced in the city the greatest vigilance?

NINETEENTH._____Early on the morning of the eighth of January, did I not /yourself in company) arrive at the lines of general Jackson, soon after the enemy's Infantry had retreated, but at moment when he directed against our lines a heavy cannonade._____

TWENTIETH._____Did I not leave the lines and return to the city for the express purpose of reinforcing the Detachment under general Morgan on the West Bank of the Mississippi which had given ground to the enemy?_____

TWENTY-FIRST._____Did I not soon after reaching the City, hand you for perusal a note addressed me by general Jackson, and which determined me to cross to the West Side of the river and to assume command;— That note is at this time in your possession, will you state its contents?_____

TWENTY-SECOND. Did you not *immediately* after my receiving the note above alluded to, cross the river, with express orders from me to assist in rallying the retreating Troops, and in placing them in a situation to be led back to the ground they had lost?_____

TWENTY-THIRD. In what situation did you find gen-

eral morgan's Command?— and who at the moment of
your arrival was the commanding officer?_____ did
not the greatest confusion reign?_____ and was there apparently any uniformity of opinion, except as to the in-
expediency of attempting at that moment a second ren-
contre with the enemy?_____

TWENTH-FOURTH. Did I not reach general Morgan's Camp as soon as the reinforcing Troops could all
be brought up?_____ And is it not within your Knowledge, that I was discouraged from hazarding an immediate attack, from the then disorganized Condition of Morgan's detachment the opinions of the Superior officers,
the state of the weather, and the further circumstance,
that the reinforcing Troops /most of whom had fought
in the morning at general Jackson's lines/ were at the
moment worn down with fatigue?_____

TWENTY-FIFTH. When on the sixteenth day of January I again crossed the river /agreeable to general Jackson's request/ and assumed the command, is it not within
your Knowledge that general Morgan hesitated to obey
me? and did you not understand, that general Morgan,
shewed a letter from general Jackson instructing him to
consider his command as a separate one, and independent
of my controul?_____

TWENTH SIXTH. Was not general Morgan, the day
after my assuming the command, detached by order of
general Jackson with six hundred picked men?_____

TWENTY SEVENTH. Morgan being so detached,
were the troops on the lines on the opposite shore, greater
in number, than a Major could with propriety be in-
trusted with? and were not these Troops badly armed,
thinly Cloathed, unhealthy, discontented and dispirited?
_____

TWENTY EIGHTH. It is not within your Knowledge
that to supply all the men on the opposite Shore, with

arms of some kind, I caused two hundred Pikes to be made and brought to the Lines._____ and_____

TWENTY NINTH. Was it not after general Morgan was detached with the best men, and after the Commanding general by Letter, had directed Brigadier general Morgan not to consider himself under my orders, that I resolved to leave the command of the small party of troops with Brigadier general Hopkins and return to the city.— and did it not appear to you, that the commanding general designed to render any command under him disagreeable to me._____

It only remains for me to ask pardon for the trouble I impose upon you and to assure you of,_____

_____my Esteem and Respect

Signed   William C. C. Claiborne.

Colonel Bartholemew Shaumburg.

_____ Answer. _____

New Orleans October 30th 1815____

Sir,_____ I comply with your request of the First of this month, with great pleasure._____ The following answers to your queries are as nearly as I recollect and to the best of my belief correct._____

FIRST. I have reason to believe that from the moment I became your aid-de-camp on the second day of September, eighteen hundred and Fourteen, I enjoyed your entire confidence in matters of war, men and measures.____

SECOND. None other but the sentiments of a man who loves his country and had particularly at heart the Safety and welfare of the State over which he presided._____

THIRD. From my own Knowledge of your personal exertions, you have left nothing undone, that ought to have been done to bring the *quota* of a thousand militia of the State into the Field, and the greatest part of this quota was actually in the Field, and served out their term._____

FOURTH. I recollect well because I copied many of the

letters and orders in which the danger which menaced the State was fully impressed on the minds of the militia, I think it had the desired effect; and I believe also inconsequence thereof all the old men in the city formed themselves in militia companies and Corps, and to the vigilance of those Veterans, I think our city has been preserved from many evils._____

FIFTH. I have often heard you express much regret that the city militia particularly on a former requisition, made by Brigadier general Flournoy should have behaved badly in refusing to turn out, and I think too, I heard you complain of the State Legislature for countenancing this opposition._____ and I remember well that you expressed much Joy on this occasion, when you was informed that the greatest part of the quota of militia under the requisition of the fourth of July were assembled at the respective rendez-vous?

SIXTH. You certainly did make use of those expressions and opinions,_____ "That the People would be finally faithful to themselves and their Country."_____

SEVENTH. I was the bearer of your dispatches in the fore part of October, eighteen hundred and Fourteen to Major general Jackson who was then at Mobile._____ You did communicate with me freely before my departure on the situation in which Louisiana was placed as related to its defence, and what further defence was in your opinion necessary;_____ In addition to this communication, you gave me a written memorandum to Strengthen my memory._____ I had the honor to deliver your letters to the major general, he was at that time much engaged /Fort Boyer having been attacked by a British Squadron./ But he granted me a half an hour conversation, during which time, I said what I had to say to him._____ And he appeared to be well pleased with those communications, and promised to write to you fully in answer to those objects;_____ I left with him the written memorandum above alluded to, nor did I fail to assure the Major General from you, that you would co-operate with him, *hand & heart;* you did also authorize me to press upon the general's mind, the necessity and utility of his early repairing to this city._____

EIGHTH. It is perfectly within my recollection that immediately after my return from Mobile, you ordered me to reconnoitre the shores of the waters of Barrataria and the Mississippi near Plaquemine /Fort St Philips/ to choose sites for Fortification; and that, you caused works to be established on the Shores of Barataria and Lafourche, and that those works were garrisoned by the militia of this State._____

NINTH. I remember well that you did employ Spies and scouts to watch chef Menteur and Terre aux Boeufs, Two Places most likely for the enemy to land;_____ This was continued till the arrival of a Troop of Dragoons and a mounted company of riflemen both from the Parish of Feliciana, when the duty devolved upon them, and from whom you receive reports daily._____

TENTH. You did instruct the commanding officers of the Louisiana Militia by general orders how to act in case the enemy should effect a landing in any part of the State; Signals for alarm in the city were also established by you and alarm Posts assigned for the different city Corps._____

ELEVENTH. Previous to the arrival of General Jackson, in the city, you directed me to go to the english Turn, and their advice with Mr. Lafou the engineer, on the erection of a temporary defence, for the Barrack at that place which was occupied by part of the Louisiana Militia under the command of Colonel Declouet._____ I proceeded to the place, and it was thought proper by the engineer and myself to open a ditch about four feet wide, and to throw up a parrapet high enough to cover musketry._____ The ditch was about a hundred and fifty yards in front of the barrack, and to be extended from the river to the Swamp; these works were raised by the Louisiana Militia._____

TWELFTH. It is on record, with what respect you spoke of Major general Jackson, before and after his arrival in this city to your militia, and it is known to me, that the day after his arrival, you ordered the uniform companies to parade in review before his quarters, and that you introduced all the principal militia officers, and other gentlemen to the major general._____

THIRTEENTH. The militia of the State were badly supplied with almost every war like implement, such as arms, Flints and Cartridges, and wholly without Knapsacks, and Camp equipage;_____ The resources of the State did not enable you to procure these necessary supplies, and much less to provide the means of transportation, and to pay, equip and victual the militia, all which must have been done at the expence of the State, had you retained the command, agreeably to the principle laid down by the general government, in the case of the governor of Massachusetts, and of which you were apprised. _____Under these circumstances, you relinquished the command of the militia to general Jackson, and consented to receive his orders, not however without evidencing much feeling and regret on committing to an other the direction of the whole force of the State, and that too at a moment when its safety was menaced, these were your motives, as communicated to me at the time.__ _____I then thought your course correct and I still think it so._____

FOURTEENTH. Anterior to general Jackson's arrival in this city, the Patriotic disposition in the people of this State generally and particularly in the city, and its vicinities increased as the danger became more visible, and I heard you often express satisfaction, when you was told by letters from the militia throughout the State, /that the people were united, and would turn out._____

FIFTEENTH. You did say to me, when the appointments of the volunteer aids-de-camp and the Judge advocate appeared in the general order of the Seventeenth of December eighteen hundred and fourteen, that those men would do you much harm, if the general suffered himself to be imposed on._____ From that moment the intercourse between you and the general became less frequent, I know also that the general often found fault with you; but whether it proceeded from the intrigues of those gentlemen, I am not able to determine._____ I am however aware that they were every one your enemy._____

SIXTEENTH. On the twenty third of December eighteen hundred and fourteen, when we had *suffered ourselves to be surprised* by the landing of the Enemy, within seven miles of the city, the First, Second and Fourth Regiments of militia from the city and the Faux-Bourgs were assembled, and formed as quick as the Forty Fourth Regiment of Regular Troops; that you was at their head, and on your march towards Villeré's where the enemy was understood to have landed, when you received an order from general Jackson to turn, and march towards the gentilly road; The order apparently damped the enthusiasm of our men, as all of them were anxious to meet the enemy, and occasioned for a moment a murmur among them._____and it was on this occasion that you said to me, dont you see, that this is the beginning of a system decided on to keep me in the back ground! But I could not altogether agree with you, in that belief, because it was in my opinion highly necessary that that pass should be strongly guarded, the landing of the enemy below Town, might have been intended for a false attack._____

SEVENTEENTH. You remained at the Post assigned to you, until your command by sending reinforcements from it to general Jackson's line, had been reduced to a Subaltern's command._____

EIGHTEENTH. While you commanded on the chef menteur road, I believe no better vigilance, police and order, was observed in any other camp, and you did fortify the position on which you encamped, which was a *defile,* and in my opinion well chosen to oppose an enemy.
_____

NINETEENTH. Besides the care and attention you bestowed towards chef menteur, you exerted all the means, in your power to maintain that good order and vigilance, which was observed by the Veteran Corps in the city._____

TWENTIETH. On the report of the first gun fired in general Jackson's camp on the morning of the eighth of January, I mounted my horse and rode as fast as he could carry me to Fort St Charles where I found you already mounted, and you immediately required me to ride with you to the point of attack on general Jackson's lines, and we arrived soon after the firing of small arms had ceased, but under a heavy canonade from both sides of Shells, Balls and Rockets._____

TWENTY FIRST. While we were in conversation with some of our militia officers of the uniform batalion, and now and then evaded an enemy's shell, an eighteen pound Shott, or a rocket, and viewing the astonishing slaughter our artillery had done, I heard the sound of a trumpet on the right bank of the river opposite our lines;_____/It happened to be very foggy and could not see more than half way of the river./ I enquired of others and they likewise heard the trumpet; I then was sure that the enemy had crossed, and were attacking the lines on the right Bank; at the moment, I saw adjutant general Buttler coming on foot from the right;_____I met him and asked whether the right bank was attacked, he replied yes, and I am going now to try to send a reinforcement from the line;_____ But said he, had you not better

go to town, and muster all the men you can find, and cross
them to the other side;_____ I told him, there were
none, but the old men who were guarding the city; well
said he there is a general Villeré, he has two hundred and
fifty men, order him over._____ I asked the adjutant
general whether this was intended as an order to general
Villeré he said yes;_____ deliver it to him as an order.__
_____during this conversation my impression is that
you came up, and that the adjutant general communicated
to you the necessity of reinforcing the other side without delay;_____ We left the line together, and ran to
the place where we had left our Servant with the horses,
but could not find him; We then took two horses belonging to Doctor Flood at the hospital, and rode to Town
with all Speed._____ When we came to the place where
general Villeré was posted I left you to deliver the orders
and did deliver the orders; But the general remonstrated,
and said that he was posted there by the express orders
of general Jackson, that his detachment had only a hundred arms; that he had Five hundred negroes to take
care of, and all the english Prisoners that were made on
the morning of the eighth._____I told the general, I
saw the necessity for him to remain where he was, but I
wished it to be understood by him, that I had delivered
the adjutant general's orders, upon which I left him,
and found you employed with general Labatut, in getting
boats ready to cross any troop, which might be sent from
general Jackson's lines, to reinforce the right bank._____
Two hours afterward a detachment from general Jackson's lines, arrived in Town but these troops were rather
slow in crossing the river;_____ They had had but
little rest, the night before they had fought at Jackson's
line; they had marched about *four miles* from camp to
Town in a heavy Shower of rain, their arms and ammunition were wet._____ Some without arms and in fact
they were in no way fit for a new combat for that day.___

TWENTY SECOND THIRD FOURTH and TWENTY FIFTH You did hand me a note for perusal from general Jackson to you the content of which is this._____
_____HEAD QUARTERS 7th Military Distri
Sir_____
"I have sent you all the reinforcements I can spare, "or that I have arms for; The enemy on the other side, "are not more than Five hundred Strong, *they must be* "*destroyed.*"_____
_____Signed   ANDREW JACKSON.____
Major general Cordg
"HIS EXCELLENCY,_____
____William C. C. Claiborne.
Governor of the State of Louisiana.

After perusing this note you told me that you should cross the river immediately with the reinforcements and take the command; In the mean time, you ordered me to proceed immediately to Morgan's lines, to consult with him, and see what could be done;_____ I did so but I found general Morgan's command greatly scattered, disheartened and discontented._____ I spoke to several of the men, and reprobated their conduct, and they said, "give us officers and we will fight better."_____ I went to general Morgan shewed him general Jackson's note to you, and asked him if he would be able to get men enough together to execute the general's orders; he said he thought not, and indeed by the looks of things I thought so too.— The reinforcement from general Jackson's lines had not then reached general Morgan, the road being very bad, and the men fatigued._____ In this State of things a French general Humbert who it would seem was a Volunteer in general Jackson's service, but I know not in what capacity came to Brigadier general Morgan and told him, that he had been sent by general Jackson to

demand four hundred men to destroy the enemy on the
right bank._____ I think general Morgan asked him
if he had a written order; he said no, that it was a verbal
Message; Brigadier general Morgan then asked whether
he was an aid de camp to general Jackson he said no,
general Morgan then told him, if he had the men, he could
not give them to him._____ Monsieur Humbert was then
displeased and went off._____ At this time you arrived
noticed the unpleasant situation of the Troops, and had
Brigadier general Morgan and other officer's opinions on
the subject of attacking the enemy._____ Under these
circumstances together determined to make a true Statement to general Jackson, which you did personally._____
But the fact is the enemy did not wait to be attacked for
he retreated soon after forcing our men from the en-
trenchment._____
TWENTY SIXTH. On the Sixteenth of January you
crossed the river, with an intention to take the command
on the right bank /as you informed me by request of
Major general Jackson/ and immediately issued an order
announcing that you had taken the command at the request of general Jackson, and which being promulgated
to the Troops afforded as was understood at the time
much satisfaction._____ Soon afterwards I had some
business with Brigadier general Morgan, and he told me,
he was not quite sure, he should give up the command;
_____ and I understood on the evening of the day
from Colonel Laneuville our adjutant general, that Brigadier general Morgan had shewn him a letter from Major
general Jackson directing him to consider himself stil
in Command and independent from your Controul.
TWENTY SEVENTH. Yes, general Morgan was detached on Command._____
TWENTY EIGHTH. General Morgan being detached,
with six hundred picked men the remaining Force, was in-

deed but small, besides they were disspirited, discontented, badly armed and thinly Cloathed.

TWENTY NINTH. It is within my Knowledge that you ordered two hundred Pikes to Morgan's lines for the use of men who were without arms.—

*THIRTIETH.*___It was on the day following on which general Morgan was detached that you determined to give up the command of the handfull of troops on the right bank of the River;_____ The commanding general's orders which appeared, *so much to your prejudice* and was so apparent to every officer around you, that they could help advising you to adopt the measure._____ I myself was one of your staff who gave that advice._____

Such are the only answers which keeping in view, truth and Justice, I can return to your several questions. _____I know not how far efforts which have or may be made to injure your standing in life shall receive the countenance of the American government, and people. But this I do know, that previous, during and subsequent to the late Invasion your conduct was such as to encrease your claims to the Public Confidence._____

I am Sir,

With great esteem & Respect

Your humble Servant

_____Signed   B. Shaumburg.____

TO HIS EXCELLENCY,
    William C. C. Claiborne
Governor of the State of Louisiana.

To Daniel L. Patterson.

New Orleans November 10th 1815.

Sir,_____
    Will you be good enough to answer the following questions as soon as your convenience permits._____
FIRST. Has there not from the period of your appoint-

ment as my aid de-camp to the present day, existed between us the most friendly and confidential understanding?_____

SECOND. It is not within your Knowledge, that my
efforts have been unceasing to excite among the militia of
Louisiana, a spirit of union and devotion to their country and government?_____

THIRD. During the late war did I not often by general
orders, and otherwise advise the Militia of the dangers to
which the State was exposed, and urge upon every officer
and private the expediency of holding himself in readiness to take the field at a moment's warning?____ _____

FOURTH. Previous to the arrival of general Jackson,
in New Orleans, did not the militia generally manifest
the most Patriotic disposition, and had not the old men
/at my request/ formed themselves into military associations?_____

FIFTH. Pending the late Invasion of Louisiana, did
you discover any want of disposition on my part to share
with my fellow Citizens in all their toils and dangers.____

SIXTH. Did you not witness, the ardour with the city
militia under my immediate command advanced against
the enemy on the twenty third of December?_____

SEVENTH. When on the twenty third of December the
city militia under my command were halted on their
march to Villere's Plantation, and ordered on the gentilly road, did I not accompany the detachment, and remain with it until the twenty seventh of December when
the First and Second Regiment were sent to reinforce
general Jackson?_____

EIGHTH. Did you not on the eighth of January, witness my exertions to reinforce the detachment under
General Morgan on the West Bank of the River, which
had given ground to the enemy?_____

NINTH. Did you not cross the river with me on the
eighth of January, and notice my chagrin on our arrival

at general Morgan's head quarters on finding the troops not in a situation to be led back to the ground they had lost._____

TENTH. Is it not within your Knowledge that in consequence of my invitation bearing date the _____ day of december 1814, to the Inhabitants to furnish negroes to assist in the completion of the works and fortifications, destined for the defence at New Orleans, that several hundred Slaves were immediately placed by the farmers at the disposition of the public agents._____

I am, Sir,

With respect and esteem

Your humble Servant,

Signed—William C. C. Claiborne

COLONEL Michael Fortier, Junior.——

_____ Answer. _____

New Orleans November 11th 1815.

Sir._____

I have the honor to acknowledge the receipt of your letter of this morning, and to reply to your several questions as follow._____

FIRST. Since the beginning of the year *Eighteen hundred and four,* period of my appointment as your aid-decamp to the present day, I have every reason to believe that I possessed, that which I endeavored to deserve, your confidence and esteem._____

SECOND. It is within my Knowledge that you have exerted every means to excite among the militia of Louisiana, a Spirit of union and devotion to their Country and government, and their conduct during the late Invasion proves the success which attended your efforts.—

THIRD. That you often during the late war, advised the militia of the dangers to which the State was exposed, and urged on every individual the expediency of holding himself in readiness to take the field, is not only known to me, but to every Inhabitant of this State.------------

FOURTH. Previous to general Jackson's arrival in New Orleans, I well remember that the old men of the city had formed military associations, and the militia of the State generally manifested the most patriotic disposition.--------------

FIFTH. During the late Invasion of Louisiana so far from your manifesting a want of disposition, you discovered the greatest solicitude to share with your fellow citizens all their toils and dangers.-----------

SIXTH. I did witness the ardour, with which the city militia under your command, moved towards the enemy on the twenty third of December, and well remember that when you said to them they were to be led immediately against the enemy who had effected a landing near Villeré's Plantation, the men replied with cheers and moved off.-------

SEVENTH. When the city militia was halted on their march to Villeré's Plantation and ordered on the gentilly road, you did accompany them, and remained in command on the gentilly road, until the twenty seventh of December, when the *First* and *Second* Regiments & I believe some other detachments composing the greater part of your command were sent to reinforce general Jackson.-------------

EIGHTH. I did on the eighth of January witness your exertions to forward reinforcements to general Morgan.

NINTH. I did cross the river with you on the eighth of January, nor could I avoid noticing your pain, on your observing the disorder which reigned on the opposite Shore, and the impossibility of an immediate advance, against the enemy with a prospect of success.

TENTH. It is within my Knowledge, that in consequence of your invitation, bearing date I believe *fourteenth of December eighteen hundred and fourteen,* many negroes were sent immediately to New Orleans, and placed at the disposition of the public agents._____
I have the honor to be
Sir
Very Respectfully
Your most obedient Servant,

HIS EXCELLENCY   Signed—J. M. Fortier,
   William C. C. Claiborne   aid-de-camp.
   Governor of the State of Louisiana.

To Daniel L. Patterson.

Parish of Iberville, October 25th 1815.

Sir._____

The enclosed Letter from Major Lockett of Attakapas /which only reached me on yesterday/ will advise you of an act of violence committed by Perry and his associates._____ The letter also designates the Island to which these violators of the Law have repaired and hazard a Conjecture /perhaps well founded/ as to their future designs._____ How far it may be in your power, with the force under your command to disperse them, you can best decide;_____ But if they are not speedily put down, I much fear we shall hear of still greater outrages._____ I shall descend to New Orleans by the next steam boat, and will co-operate with you in all measures having for object the support of the Laws._____

I am Sir_____
Your humble servant,
Signed__William C. C. Claiborne.

COMMODORE,_____
____Daniel L. Patterson.

To Maj. Lockett.

Parish of Iberville, October 25th 1815.

Sir,------------

Being absent from New Orleans, your communication of the tenth Instant, did not reach me until yesterday; the conduct of Perry and Brunson as detailed in the Disposition, you refer to is daring act of violence, and it was your duty to notice the same.--------- The attorney general for the district /Mr Wilson/ has I hope been advised of your proceedings, and it will remain for him, to take such other measures against the offenders as the laws prescribe.----------- The *expedition* which Perry professes to have in view, falls within that description of illegal enterprises to which the President in a late Proclamation alludes, and you sir, and every other faithful officer, and citizen, should use every effort to prevent this expedition from being carried into effect.----------

I am Sir,

Major------   With due Respect,

Winfrey Lockett.------

Signed   William C. C. Claiborne

Baton Rouge October 30th 1815

Sir.------------

Will you do me the favour to answer, as far as your memory serves the following questions.----------

FIRST. About the *last* or *First* of november *eighteen hundred and fourteen,* very soon after the drafted militia of Louisiana had taken post at the english Turn, did I not direct a breast work, with a wide and deep ditch to be thrown up, in their front extending from the river to the Cypress Swamp.--------------

SECOND. Is it not within your recollection, that in a conversation I had with the officers at the time, I stated the facility with which New Orleans might be protected, against any approaches by way of the Levee, the precaution being previously taken to place the defending force behind a Strong work extending from the river to the Swamp?_____

THIRD. Did not the militia at first manifest an unwillingness to labour on the works I had advised, and did I not in consequence repair a second time to the Turn, and in conversation with the officers Strongly urge the necessity of completing the works advised without delay, and saying at the time if my example would induce the men to labour the more cheerfully, I would readily take the first spade._____

I am Sir._____
Your humble Servant,
Signed__William C. C. Claiborne

Major Charles Tessier_____
of the drafted Militia_____

_____ Answer.   .   .   .   _____

Baton Rouge October 30th 1815____

Sir,_____

In reply to your questions addressed to me, in your note of this morning, 1 answer._____

FIRST. That very soon after the drafted Regiment of Louisiana militia took post, at the english Turn, you did direct a breast work /with a wide and deep ditch/ to be thrown up in their front extending from the river to the Cypress Swamp._____

SECOND. Previous to the landing of the enemy in December last, I have heard you give an opinion, that new Orleans might be easily defended against an attack by land and by way of the Levee, the precaution being previously taken to place our forces behind a strong field work which should extend from the river to the Swamp.___

THIRD. It is within my recollection, that the men at the english Turn, did at first seem unwilling to labour on the works, you had directed, and I also recollect, that in a conversation you had with the officers at the Turn you enforced the necessity of the works in question, and that you stated your willingness to be yourself attached to the fatigue party if the example was thought necessary. The works proposed were laid out by Mr. Lafou and it is my belief that the opinion and influence of your excellency induced the men to labour on them with cheerfulness and industry._____

I have the honor to remain

Sir,

With great Respect

Your most humble Servant,

____Signed__Charles Tessier

His Excellency_____
    William C. C. Claiborne_____
    Governor of the State of Louisiana.

To Daniel L. Patterson.

New Orleans November 28th 1815

Sir._____ \

Designing by the next mail to communicate to a friend of mine some general information relative to the military operations on the west bank of the Mississippi, previous to and during the eighth of January last, and feeling solicitous to render such information correct as possible, I have to request of you the favour to answer as soon as your convenience permits the following questions._____

FIRST. How many pieces of cannon, had you mounted at the batteries, which you commanded in person, and of what callibre._____

SECOND. How many effective men, do you think general Morgan had at his lines on the evening of the Seventh of January, and how were they armed._____

THIRD. Were you not apprised, early in the evening of the Seventh of January that the enemy was passing boats by way of a canal which he had cut into the river, and anticipating an attack, did you not suggest by letter to general Jackson the expediency of reinforcing Morgan's lines?_____

Fourth. At what hour in the night of the Seventh of January, was Morgan reinforced by what number of Troops, and how were they armed._____

FIFTH. In what force do you think the enemy crossed the river on the morning of the eighth of January?_____

SIXTH. At what period of the night of the Seventh of January, did the enemy get his boats into the Mississippi._____

SEVENTH. have you reason to believe, that the sudden fall of the Mississippi during the night of the Seventh of January materially affected the plans of the enemy, and delayed his movements._____

EIGHTH. How many cannon fell into the hands of the enemy on the west bank of the Mississippi; and of them how many did he carry away?_____

It remains for me to apologize for the trouble I give you, and to assure of_____

My esteem and Respect._____

Signed—William C. C. Claiborne

Captain
Daniel L. Patterson._____

To Genl. Thomas.

Baton Rouge October 30th 1815____

Sir,

_____Will you have the goodness to return an answer to the following questions as soon as your convenience may permit._____

FIRST. Did I not from time to time during the late War, advise the division under your command, of the dangers to which Louisiana was exposed, and order the whole militia of the State to be holden in readiness for service?_____

SECOND. It is not within your Knowledge that I made every effort promptly and effectually to meet such requisitions for an auxiliary militia force as were made of me, under the authority of the President._____

THIRD. Previous to your receiving information of the actual landing of the enemy below New Orleans in December last, were you not ordered by me to embody the militia, and to be prepared to defend any point within the limits of your Command, which should be menaced?

FOURTH. Were you not specially instructed by me, in case the enemy should land within your district to remove beyond the reach the Stocks of Cattle, hogs and provissions of every kind;_____ To impede his movements by falling of trees, and filling up the water courses in his route, to attack his foraging parties, and harrass his advance and distress him in every manner?_____

FIFTH. Were not my orders on all occasions promptly and cheerfully obeyed by the division under your Command._____

SIXTH. Were not my orders for the march of detachments from your division to New Orleans pending the siege of that city, obeyed not only readily but with an enthusiasm evincive of the most pure and ardent patriotism?_____

SEVENTH. So far from any reluctance being manifested in descending to New Orleans, did you not on some occasions find it difficult to restrain men, whom you wished to occupy some other exposed post from marching direct to this city.

EIGHTH. Previous to the actual Invasion of Louisiana, were you not impressed with an opinion that the people of the State were generally determined on the most spirited resistance in case of such an event, and previous to Major general Jackson's arrival at New Orleans or his exercising any Controul over the Louisiana militia, did you not observe in your division evidences of the greatest devotion to our Country & Government._____

It remains for me to apologize for the trouble I impose upon you and to assure you of,_____

My Esteem and Respect._____

Signed—William C. C. Claiborne____

Major General_____

Philemon Thomas._____

Answer.

Baton Rouge 30th November 1815.

Sir,_____

I acknowledge the receipt of your letter dated the thirtieth of October eighteen hundred and fifteen, putting a number of questions to me, I shall answer them one by one._____

TO YOUR FIRST QUESTION. I answer you did and I have your orders to prove the same; I took immediate steps to have my division in readiness to march when called on._____

TO YOUR SECOND QUESTION. I answer that I receive your orders for raising the quota of my division of six months men called by the United States and it was immediately carried into effect and the men brought into the field, agreeably to those orders, and I heard no murmuring on the occasion except some officers contending to go on._____

TO YOUR THIRD QUESTION. I answer that on the twentieth of december at night I received your orders as stated, and they were promptly executed; I brought seven Regiments into the field as quick as possible, the other four Regiments, I held in a State of readiness to march at a moment's warning; all this before it was known where the enemy would land._____

TO YOUR FOURTH QUESTION. I answer you did, and I am ready to produce the orders, and I took immediate steps to have the same carried into execution Should the enemy land within my division._____

TO YOUR FIFTH QUESTION. I answer they were, by the division I have the honor to command, and I saw no kind of reluctance with respect to obedience of orders but a real willingness to meet their enemy._____

TO YOUR SIXTH QUESTION. I answer they were, as nothing but true patriotism would ever have moved militia in the rapid manner in which they marched to the scene of action; for the men and officers appeared to me to be glad of having an apparent chance of fighting the enemy._____

TO YOUR SEVENTH QUESTION. That from my knowledge of the division which I have the honor to command, the men composing the same, are with few exceptions, as firm American in principles, as those of any division in the United States. I have now had a full proof of the fact, for I had to make use of the most positive orders to keep a few men at some points, that I thought necessary to keep up, so great was their desire to be at the real scene of action._____

TO YOUR LAST QUESTION. I answer that I have always found my division obedient to orders, and as before stated with some few exceptions, I never had a doubt of being able to call the whole strength into the field, when ordered by the Chief Magistrate of the State, or any officer authorized by the United States, as to Major general Jackson, but few of my division knew any thing of him, but they had heard that he was a brave man and I heard none say they were unwilling to fight under his command, but I am equally sure on such occasion, it was no matter who would command, my division would have come forward to defend the country, and I do believe, that the men had no other stimulation, but the love of the country, and the protection of their Liberty, and their property._____ I am truly sorry that any misunderstanding should have taken place when all, with the hands of a kind providence have terminated so well._____

I have answered all the questions, that you have called on me to answer, and have all your orders ready to produce if necessary, which will prove your statement to be facts._____

May God grant you and family prosperous days._____Signed—Philemon Thomas.

Major general of the Second Division.

HIS EXCELLENCY
    William C. C. Claiborne.
Governor of the State of Louisiana.

To Genl. Morgan.

New Orleans December 1st 1815.—

Sir,_____

Being engaged in communicating to a friend a detailed account of the military operations in this State during the past Winter, and feeling desirous that the same should be strictly correct, I must ask the favour of you to answer the following questions, as early as may suit your convenience._____

FIRST. When did you assume command of the Troops stationed at the english Turn?_____

SECOND. What was the force under your command at the english Turn on the twenty third of December eighteen hundred and fourteen?_____

THIRD. At what hour of the day on the twenty third of December eighteen hundred and fourteen did you receive information that the enemy had effected his landing near to Villeré's Plantation, and how was the information conveyed?_____

FOURTH. How long did you remain at the english Turn after the auction on the night of the twenty third at Villeré's?_____

FIFTH. Did you cross the river in conformity to orders, or on your own responsibility?_____ If the former where were your orders dated?_____

SIXTH. On what day did you take up a position on the west Bank of the Mississippi nearly opposite to general Jackson's lines?

SEVENTH. What was the effective force under your command on the evening of the seventh of January Eighteen hundred and fifteen.__

EIGHTH. Where your lines of defence completed on the evening of the Seventh of January Eighteen hundred and fifteen._____

NINTH. Did you ask a reinforcement from the Commanding general on the evening of the Seventh of January and by what numbers were you reinforced?_____

TENTH. How many cannon had you on your lines, and of what Calibre?_____ were any of those cannons received during the night of the Seventh of January, and had you a plentiful supply of ammunition?

ELEVENTH. Were the men under your Command during the attack on the eighth of January well armed?_____ and

TWELVE. Were the batteries commanded by Commodore Patterson so situated as to co-operate in the defence of your lines, against an assault by land._____

I am Sir,

With great Respect

Your humble Servant,

Signed__William C. C. Claiborne.

BRIGADIER GENERAL_____

David B. Morgan._____

To. Col. Croghan.

New Orleans December 20th 1815

Sir,_____

Several militia Corps of this City, with grateful recollections of the triumphs of their Country, design to parade on the twenty third of the present month, the anniversary of the first defeat of the late Invaders of Louisiana._____ Among these Corps is the battalion of Orleans volunteers, for whose use I request of you the *loan for* and during Saturday the twenty third Instant of two pieces of field Artillery with their necessary appendages._____ This brave and Patriotic battalion having borne an honorable portion the conflict they design to communicate, you will I am persuaded take a pleasure in meeting my request, if the convenience of the service presents no obstacle._____

I am Sir,

very respectfully

Your humble Servant,

Signed__William C. C. Claiborne

Lieutenant Colonel Graghan,

Commanding the United States troops.

At New Orleans.

To his Excellency William C. C. Claiborne

Governor of the State of Louisiana.

_____Sir_____

_____ The House of Representatives participate in the pleasure expressed by your excellency on the happy change of affairs and reciprocate with sincerity their Congratulations on the restoration to our country of the great blessing of peace._____

_____ The meritorious conduct of the citizens of Louisiana in the late arduous conflict in which the nation was involved, we are happy has been justly appreciated, and honorably rewarded by the Congress of the United States._____

_____ Great indeed is the cause for patriotic exaltation in the glorious defence of this country, and the rescue of this Capitol from the manifold dangers with which it was menaced "to heaven to the hero who led our forces, and to the brave men composing them, and we owe and feel the greatest gratitude, and where there is so much to admire, we are not disposed, to dwell upon some deeds, which we cannot approve._____

_____ The House of Representatives embrace with pleasure this opportunity to assure your Excellency, that they have every reason to be satisfied with the correctness of your motives and the propriety of your conduct in Submitting at the late momentous period to the call of Major general Jackson, and placing under his command the militia of this State._____

_____ In the liberal advances made by your excellency from the funds of this State for the promotion of the military and navy; service on this Station you have Conformed to the will of the Legislature._____

In the mean time we are happy to find from your Excel-

lency's Statement, that the funds appropriated to the common defence during our last session, proved more than adequate to the demands of the respective Commanders of the United States Army and navy._____
_____ The different subjects of the Legislation both general and local, to which you have adverted Shall receive the prompt and immediate attention of this house; and we are convinced of the necessity of the municipal changes and provisions, which you have so forcibly and happily recommended._____
_____ It remains for the house of Representatives to assure your Excellency, that they will cooperate with alacrity in all measures which promise to promote the welfare of the State._____
_____signed_____Magloire Guichard._____
Speaker of the House of Representatives.
_____signed_____August Daverac de Castrac.
Clerk of the House of Representatives.

To Andrew Jackson.

New Orleans April   1816.__
Sir,_____
Shortly previous to the late Invasion of Louisiana fifteen hundred stand of new muskets the property of this State, which were at the time deposited in the United States Arsenal, were by my request to Captain Humphreys placed into the hands of the Louisiana Contingent and other corps of Militia ordered into the service of the United States._____ Of these arms six hundred and forty three were returned to me by the officer commanding the Louisiana Contingent, and the residue has or I presume will be delivered to the United States Commissary of ordnance in this city._____ The last of-

ficer having invited the return of all public arms I have endeavored to enforce his call by two militia orders in the last of which with a view of avoiding all pretese for avoiding it, I particularly ordered,_____ The immediate return to Major Woolstoncraft of the United States ordnance department of all muskets and other arms now in possession of Individuals, or Corps, which were received at the United States Arsenal in this city whether the said arms were delivered as "the property of this State or of the United States."— Under this circumstances, I have thought that the State could justly claim of the United States, the deficiency in the arms, /*Eight hundred and fifty seven*/ furnished as aforesaid, and therefore take the liberty to ask of your an order on the proper officer for the delivery to the Governor of Louisiana or to his order *eight hundred and fifty seven* Stand of Muskets._____

I am Sir,
Very Respectfully
Your hunble Servant
_____Signed   William C. C. Claiborne—

Major general Jackson_____
Commanding the Second Military_____
_____DIVISION_____

To John Jamison.

New Orleans May 18th 1816

Sir,_____

_____ Your letter bearing date at Natchez the 4th Instant reached me by the last mail._____ In my Judgment it is no less essential to the interest of the United States and of the Indians than to the convenience of the Inhabitants of the Parish and Town of

Natchitoches that the factory and agency be removed.

----------------- The policy of the government has been to keep the Indians at their homes, to guard against those impositions to which they were exposed by an indiscriminate trade and intercourse with the whites, to introduce among them, husbandry and the art of Civilization, finally by supplying all their wants to impress them with grateful and friendly Sentiments.----------- With these views, agencies and trading houses were established, and to promote them, the removal of the factory and agency from Natchitoches the center of a compact and rich Settlement of Louisiana to some frontier position is deemed advisable.-----------------

----------------- It however is thought a measure of Prudent precaution, to place the establishment, under the precaution of a military Post, and to this end, I shall recommend to the Secretary at War, the immediate establishment of a garrison on the Sabine, at or near the Spot where the Nocogdoches road crosses the Same, and which I consider as the most convenient Scite for the factory and the residence of the Agent.------------ In the mean time you will remain at Natchidoches, and here if the buildings appertaining to the Factory do not furnish comfortable accommodations and I learn they do not I advise that you rent suitable Apartments.--------- It is not in my power to say, what are the emoluments to which you may be entitled, but I give it as my opinion that the government ought, and will make you a reasonable allowance for quarters.-----------------

----------------- The Honorable the Secretary at War requests me to give you such additional Instructions, as I may deem necessary for your immediate government. ------------- It is very probable that you may have received from the Secretary some general *Instructions,* and I therefore must in the First place ask for a Copy of them, in order to prevent mine from being in any manner opposed._____ In the mean time, I recommend the Following Points to be attended to._____

FIRST. That the act of Congress regulating trade and intercourse with Indian Tribes be strictly enforced._____

SECOND. That no traders be permitted to reside among the Indians, but such as have been licensed according to law._____

THIRD. That you press upon the minds of the Indians the benefit resulting to them by exclusively trading with the Factory.—

FOURTH. That so soon as the Indians visiting the Factory shall have their trade, you hasten their return home._____

FIFTH. That you discourage and take all the means in your power to prevent the Indians from exchanging their peltry with the whites for ardent spirits._____

SIXTH. That you bring the provisions of the law, to bear against such citizens as shall sell ardent spirits to the Indians.—

SEVENTH. That you endeavor to excite among the Several Tribes a disposition to live in peace with all nations._____

EIGHTH. That you protect and treat with kindness not only our own Indians but Individuals of such other Tribes without the limits of the United States as may visit your agency._____

NINTH. That you endeavor to ascertain the policy observed by the Spanish Authorities towards the Indians residing on the Waters of Red River, and how far the same may be friendly or otherwise towards the United States._____ and _____

FINALLY. That you keep the governor of Louisiana informed of such occurrences within the limits of your

agency as may in any manner affect the interest of this
State or the views of the government.---------------
I am Sir,-------------
Very Respectfully--------
Your humble Servant.------
-------- Signed—William C. C. Claiborne
John Jamison, Esquire------------
Indian Agent,-----------
Nachitoches.------------

To William H. Crawford.

New Orleans May 18th 1816.—
Sir,------------

----------------- Your letter of the twentieth of January last came, enclosed to me the other day, under cover
of one from Colonel Jamison, dated at Natchez the fourth
of this month.---------- The Colonel was then on his
way to Natchitoches, to assume the duties of his agency.
and I have addressed to him at that place a letter of instruction, of which the enclosed is a Copy.----------
---------------- You will observe that the removal of
the *factory* and *Agency* from Nachitoches to a position
on the Sabine, is deemed by me highly estimable;--------
But in as much as it is necessary to place them under the
protection of a military Post, I take the liberty to recommend that orders be given for the establishment of a
small garrison on the Sabine, at or near the Nacogdoches
road crosses the same, and that the factory and agency
be removed to that place as soon as the suitable buildings
can be erected.---------- The Inhabitants of the Parish
and Town of Natchitoches have long complained of the
Inconvenience to which they were subjected by the frequent visits of Indians and I really think that the Inter-

est of all concerned requires that the cause of Complaint be removed which can only be done by locating the Factory and Agency at some more frontier position._____

I have the honor to be

Sir

With great respect _____

Your obedient Servant,

Signed—William C. C. Claiborne

THE HONORABLE,_____

    William H. Crawford_____

        Secretary at War_____

WASHINGTON CITY._____

To Daniel L. Patterson.

New Orleans, May 18th 1816

Sir,_____

Elias amirault Duplessis a native of Louisiana and Inhabitant of this city, in a trading voyage to cap Henry in the Island of Hayti, has I am informed been imprisoned by the authorities there, under. charges of being an emigrant from that Island, and a French Spy._____ The Father and the Brother of Mr. Duplessis Solicitous to forward by some safe and Speedy conveyance to cap Henry documents to prove his nativity, place of Residence and the innocent object of his voyage, I am induced to ask, how far you may feel at liberty, to order the commander of some vessels attached to your command and cruising in the gulph to call at cap Henry, and to deliver to the authorities there the aforesaid documents._____ If the convenience of the service would admit of your giving such an order, you will contribute to the release from confinement perhaps to the preservation of the life of a fellow citizen whose course of conduct has I am persuaded been uniformly correct and honorable._____

I am Sir

Very Respectfully

Your humble Servant

Signed____William C. C. Claiborne._____

COMMODORE_____

Daniel L. Patterson_____

New Orleans_____

To the Governor of Pennsylvania.

New Orleans 7th June 1816._____

Sir, _____

I have the honor to acknowledge the receipt of your Excellency's letter under date of the 28th of March last, enclosing an authenticated Copy of an Act of the Legislature of Pennsylvania, Entitled *"AN ACT FOR THE RELIEF OF THE HOSPITAL OF NEW ORLEANS AND the PENNSYLVANIA HOSPITAL.* _____

This act shall be submitted to the general Assembly of Louisiana at an early day of their ensuing session, nor do I doubt, but they will readily accede to the terms on which the State of Pennsylvania consents to grant to the hospital of New Orleans, an annuity of Five hundred Dollars for Ten Years._____ In the mean time, I have acquitted myself of a pleasing duty in laying a copy of the act aforesaid before the administrators of the hospital, and in obedience to their request, I now transmit to your Excellency, an extract from the Journal of their proceedings._____ It will shew the grateful Sentiments which the very generous donation of Pennsylvania has inspired and the high sense entertained of the truly human benevolent and honorable motives which influence Coun-

cils of that great and respectable State._____
_____ I tender to your Excellency the assurances of_____

My Sincere Esteem and Respect._____

Signed—William C. C. Claiborne

HIS EXCELLENCY_____ „ _____
The governor of the State of Pennsylvania.

To William H. Crawford.

Sir,_____   New Orleans July 13th 1816._____

I have the honor to acknowledge the receipt of a letter
from Mr. P. Haytum the additional accountant of the
war department under date of the twenty fifth may 1816,
announcing that the claim of the State of Louisiana for
the disbursements for Fortifications have been adjusted
and settled and the sum of $16480,,17/100 admitted and
which amount was subject to the disposition of the authority of the State of Louisiana._____ In consequence of the high rate of exchange, and indeed the im-
practicability of passing bills in Washington, at this moment, I have to request that you would transmit me the
amount aforesaid in Treasury Bills or in an order on the
Banks of this city payable to the order of Felix Armand
Esqr. Treasurer of the State of Louisiana, who will for-\
ward duplicate receipts therefor._____ In the mean
time you will hold this letter as a voucher for the payment of the sum of $16,480,,17/100 admitted to be due to
the State of Louisiana as aforesaid._____

I have the honor to be
Very Respectfully
Your humble Servant—
Signed—William C. C. Claiborne

THE HONORABLE_____
_____William H. Crawford, Secretary at War
WASHINGTON CITY._____

PARALLEL PRINTED AND MANUSCRIPT SOURCES RELATING TO HISTORICAL FACTS CONTAINED IN THE CLAIBORNE LETTER BOOKS.

LOUISIANA 1803–1816

Account of Louisiana laid before Congress Nov. 1803. Washington [1803]

Adams, Henry. History of the United States 9v. New York, 1896
    v. 1: p. 338–40, 423–46
    v. 2: p. 8, 42–50, 74–134, 160–90, 252, 399–403
    v. 3: p. 26–42, 219–378, 441–71
    v. 5: p. 162, 239, 323–6
    v. 6: p. 220–44
    v. 7: p. 172–206, 232–61
    v. 8: p. 311–85
    v. 9: p. 4, 6, 8, 149, 152

—— —— Life of Gallatin. p. 318–22. Philadelphia, 1879

—— —— Life of Randolph. p. 74–8, 84–93. Boston, 1893

Adams, John Q. The duplicate letters, the fisheries and the Mississippi. Washington, 1822

Analysis of the third article of the treaty of cession. [Washington, 1803?]

Annuaire louisianais . . . 1808–9

Arthur, Stanley C. The Story of the Battle of New Orleans. New Orleans, 1915

American State Papers. Foreign Relations v. 2, p. 295–355 [treaty &c] 475, 510, 512, 516, 517, 540, 556, 558, 559, 563, 569–72, 573 [Also v. 3].

—— —— Public Lands. v. 1, p. 193, 106 [lead mines upper La.] 250, 258, 586, 587–90

Babcock, Kendric C. Rise of American Nationality, 1811–19. New York, [American Nation ser.] v. 13: p. 15–19, 21–25, 50–83. 1906

Baudry des Lozières. Second voyage a la Louisiane. Paris, 1803

Blanchard, Rufus. Documentary history of the cession of La. Chicago, 1903

Brackenridge, Henry M. History of the late war between the United States and Great Britain. 1817

—— —— Views of Louisiana [mainly upper La.] pt. 3 Louisiana (State). Pittsburg, 1814

Brannan, John ed. Official letters of the military and naval officers of the United States, 1812–15. Washington, 1823

Brazer, Samuel jr. Address May 12, 1804 on the cession of Louisiana. Worcester, 1804

Bristed, John. Resources of the United States. p. 18, 395. New York, 1818

Brown, Chas. Brocden. Address to government on the cession of Louisiana. Philadelphia, 1803

Brown, Jeremiah. Short letter to a member of Congress concerning the territory of Orleans. Washington, 1806

Burr, Aaron. Reports of trials. 2v. Philadelphia, 1808. Trial for treason. Richmond, 1807

Burr Papers. Library and Rolls Dept. of State, Washington

Butler, Nicholas Murray. The effect of the war of 1812 upon the consolidation of the Union. Baltimore, 1887

Castellanos, H. C. New Orleans as it was. p. 248, 294–344. New Orleans, 1895

Cession of Louisiana [Old South leaflets no. 128]. Boston, n. d.

Channing, Edward. The Jeffersonian system. p. 60–85, 155–168. New York, 1906

Claiborne Papers. Library and Rolls Dept. of State, Washington

Clark, Daniel. Proof of the corruption of Gen. James Wilkinson. Philadelphia, 1809

Colvin, John B. Republican policy. Frederick, Md., 1802

Cox, Isaac J. Exploration of the Louisiana frontier, 1803–6 [in Am. Hist. Assoc. rept. 1904, p. 149–74.] Washington, 1904

Cullum, George W. Campaigns of the war of 1812. p. 305–41. New York, 1879

Darby, William. Geographical description of Louisiana. Philadelphia, 1816

DeBow, J. D. B. Industrial resources . . . of the Southern & Western States, . . . 3v. New Orleans, 1853

         v. 1: p. 425–30

         v. 2: p. 136–9

Debouchel, Victor. Histoire de la Louisiane. p. 91–139 [résumé of
    Code noir]. New Orleans, 1841
Deiler, John H. Germans on the coast of Louisiana. p. 129 [letter of
    Laussat]. Philadelphia, 1909
Duvallon, Berquin- *ed.* Travels in the two Floridas and Louisiana in
    1802 [trans. by John Davis]. French edition Paris 1803.
    New York, 1806
Esquisse de la situation politique et civile de la Louisiane [1803–4].
    New Orleans, 1804
Faithful picture of the political situation in New Orleans at the be-
    ginning of 1807. Boston, 1808
Favrot, Henry L. The State Seal [in La. Hist. Soc. v. 2, pt. 4, p. 18].
    New Orleans, 1902
Fay, Edwin W. History of Education in Louisiana. p. 19–40. Wash-
    ington, 1898
Ficklen, John R. History and civil government of Louisiana, p. 81–109.
    Chicago, 1901
—— —— Northwestern boundary of Louisiana [in La. Hist. Soc. v. 2,
    pt. 2, p. 26]. New Orleans, 1899
—— —— Was Texas included in the Louisiana purchase? [in Southern
    History Assoc. pub. v. 5, p. 351–87]. Washington, 1901
Fortier, Alcée. History of Louisiana. 4v. New York, 1904
    v. 2, chaps. 8–11
    v. 3, chaps. 1–7
Foster, John W. A Century of American Diplomacy. p. 187–204.
    New York, 1900
Gayarré, Charles. History of Louisiana. The Spanish Domination.
    p. 386–628. [New Orleans etd. 1903, complete in 4v. with
    bibliography]. New York, 1854
—— —— The cession of Louisiana to the U. S. Letter to Hon. J.
    Perkins. [Washington?] 1861
Gallatin, Albert. Writings. v. 1, p. 153, 162–6, 212–14. [on boundary]
    p. 110, 145, 242–3, 247, Philadelphia, 1879
Geer, Curtis M. The Louisiana purchase, &c. [in Hist. of N. America,
    v. 8, p. 167–221, 239–53 app. 273–83], Philadelphia, 1904
Gilman, Daniel C. Monroe. p. 74–93. Boston, 1892.
Gleig, George R. Narrative of campaigns of the British army at Wash-
    ington, Baltimore and New Orleans, 1814–15. p. 252–350.
    London, 1821
Goodloe, Daniel R. The purchase of Louisiana and how it was brought
    about [in Southern History Assoc. publications, v. 4,
    p. 149–71]. Washington, 1900

Goodspeed, W. A. *ed.* The Province and the States Louisiana and the states formed therefrom, v. 2, p. 104–425, v. 3, p. 17–66. Madison, 1904

Green, Thomas M. The Spanish Conspiracy. Cincinnati, 1891

Guénin, Eugene. La Louisiane [cession] Chap. 12. Paris, 1904

Hart, A. B. Formation of the Union, 1750–1829. p. 185–9 [La.] 189–91 [Burr] 203–9, 213–14, 220 [war 1812] 233 [La, boundary]. New York, 1892

────── Foundations of American Foreign Policy. p. 145–7, 186–207. New York, 1901

Hermann, Binger. Louisiana Purchase. Washington, 1900

Hobby, C. M. The Louisiana Purchase [in Iowa Historical Lectures]. Iowa City, 1893

Holmes, Gov. David. Letter Book, Miss. Dept. of Archives and History.

Houck, Louis. History of Missouri. 3v. Chicago, 1908
v. 2, p. 348 *seq.*

────── *ed.* Spanish Régime in Missouri. v. 2, p. 285 *seq.* [translations of docs. in Seville archives, 1800–05.] Chicago, 1909

Howard, Azel B. Louisiana purchase, its history &c. St. Louis, 1901

Hunt, C. H. Life of Edward Livingston. New York, 1864

Hunt, Gaillard. Madison. p. 285–98, 319–59 [war 1812]. New York, 1902

Ingersoll, Charles J. Historical sketch of the second war between the U. S. and Great Britain. 2v. Philadelphia, 1845–9

────── History of the second war. Ser. 2. 2v. Philadelphia, 1852

Jackson, Andrew. Papers Mss. Div. Library of Congress

James, William. Military occurrences of the war of 1812 [only valuable for official documents]. London, 1818

Jay, John. Life [by William Jay]. v. 1. p. 444–8. New York, 1833

────── Correspondence, etc., ed. by H. P. Johnston. New York, 1890–93

Jefferson Papers. Library of Congress. Mss. Div.

Jefferson, Thomas. Limits and Bounds of Louisiana. New York, 1804

────── Proceedings of the U. S. government . . . against Edward Livingston. New York, 1812

────── Writings ed. by Paul L. Ford. v. 8: p. 144, 192, 205, 209, 241, 244–5, 247, 249, 251, 265, 278. New York, 1892–9

Johnson, Emory *et al.* History of Commerce. v. 1, p. 209–16. Washington, 1915

Johnston, Alexander. Louisiana purchase, war of 1812: articles in Lalor's Cyclopedia of political science. Chicago, 1881–4

King, Grace. New Orleans, p. 157-87 [Lafitte, p. 191-211; Battle of N. O., p. 213-56]. New York, 1895

King, Rufus. Life and correspondence. 6v. ed. by Chas. R. King. v. 4, p. 122-4, 262-3, 323-5, 329-32, 363, 513-4, 554-5, 559-75, 591-7. New York, 1894-1900

Langford, Nathaniel P. Louisiana purchase and Spanish intrigues. [St. Paul, 1900?]

Latour, A. Lacarrière Major. Historical memoir of the war in W. Florida and Louisiana 1814-15, p. 461-9, 470-83. Philadelphia, 1816

Letters to Williams, Mead and Holmes, Governors of Mississippi Territory. Miss. Dept. of Archives and History. See Official Guide to Mississippi Archives. 1914

Lewis, Virgil A. Story of the Louisiana purchase. St. Louis, 1903

Livingston, Edward. Papers of (owned by Hon. Carleton Hunt a distinguished lawyer of New Orleans)

Lossing, Benson J. Field Book of the War of 1812. p. 1018-53. New York, 1896

Louaillier, Louis, sr. Appeal against charge of high treason, explaining transactions at New Orleans. New Orleans, 1827

Louisiana. A Topographical & statistical account &c. Hagertown, 1803

Louisiana—Boundaries. Official correspondence between de Onis and J. Q. Adams. London, 1818

—— —— Documents relating to Spanish grants. Washington, 1835

—— —— Constitution or form of government of the State of Louisiana. English & French. [n. p. 1812]

—— —— General Assembly. Representation and Petition [to Congress] Jan. 4, 1805   Washington, 1805

—— —— Judiciary. Act to organize Supreme Court, &c. New Orleans, 1813

—— —— Annotations on Louisiana codes . . . 1809-1843. P. J. A. Deslix. New Orleans, 1847

—— —— Condensed reports Supreme Court from 1809 . . . J. B. Harrison. New Orleans

—— —— Decisions Superior Court of the Territory of Orleans, 1809-16. New Orleans, 1811 . . .

—— —— Digest of decisions from 1809-12, New Orleans, 1840

—— —— Digest of decisions from 1809-1843. Boston, 1853

—— —— Laws, etc. Acts of the Legislative Council territory of Orleans 1-2 session, 1804-5. New Orleans, 1805

—— —— Acts of the Louisiana legislature 1806-11. New Orleans, 1807-11

—— —— Acts of the 2d Legislature. New Orleans, 1809

—— —— Acts of Congress relative to land claims. [1807?]

—— —— Compilation:—treaty of cession, laws of Congress for territory of Orleans, etc. [in French also] New Orleans, 1806

Louisiana Laws, etc. Debate in the House on memorial to Congress *in re* Wilkinson. New Orleans, 1807

—— —— Digest of acts of the Legislature of the late territory of Orleans and State of La. . . governor's ordinances, etc. F. X. Martin. New Orleans, 1816

—— —— Digest of civil laws in the territory of Orleans "Old code" [French & English]. New Orleans, 1808

—— —— Digest of acts of the Legislature 1804–27. New Orleans, 1828

—— —— Digest of laws from 1804–41. Grenier. New Orleans, 1841

—— —— Exposition of criminal laws, territory of Orleans. Lewis Kerr. New Orleans, 1806

—— —— Index to acts of the legislature of the territory of Orleans 1st sess. 1st legislature to 2d sess. 3d legislature. New Orleans, 1812

—— —— Journal House of Representatives. 1st sess. 2d legislature. New Orleans, 1814

—— —— Journal Senate 1812 . . . [in French also]. New Orleans, 1812

—— —— Laws of Las Siete Partidas still in force. Trans. by L. M. L'Islet. New Orleans, 1820

—— —— Laws of the State Session acts 1812–1908. New Orleans, 1812–1908

—— —— Lois du territoire d'Orleans 1804–8. New Orleans, 1808

—— —— Lois de la Louisiane. 1808–9. New Orleans, 1809

—— —— Ordinance establishing the Bank of Louisiana. New Orleans, 1804

—— —— Report of committee investigating cause of military orders against the Legislature [session 1814–15]. [New Orleans]

—— —— Statement of facts occurring during the invasion of the British [session 1814–15]. [New Orleans]

Louisiana Maps 1803–16. Library of Congress. Map Div.

Louisiana Newspapers 1803–1816. New Orleans

Newspapers in City Archives.

City Hall, New Orleans, La.

Louisiana Gazette:

July 31, 1804, to Oct. 17th, 1806

Oct. 28th, 1806, to Oct. 21st, 1808

Oct. 25th, 1808, to Mar. 30th, 1810

April 3rd, 1810, to April 3rd, 1811
April 4th, 1811, to April 1st, 1812
June 9th, 1811, to Oct. 27th, 1814
March 28th, 1811, to Dec. 5, 1815
Jany. 2nd, 1811, to Dec. 30th, 1816
Louisiana Courier:
    July 4th, ———, to Dec. 5th, 1810
    July 29th, ———, to November 29th, 1811
    Jany. 6th,———, to December 31, 1818
    Jany. 5th, ———, to December 30th, 1816
L'Ami Des Lois:
    June 1st, 1813, to Nov. 29th, 1814
    Jany., April, Sept. and Dec., 1816.

Louisiana—Treaty. Debates in House of Representatives. Philadelphia, 1804

Louisiana and Florida. Documents relative to 1799, 1800. Spanish regime. Washington, 1833

Louisiana Historical Society publications. v. 4, p. 141–4 contains list of documents relative to La. in Madrid Archives. New Orleans, 1908

Louisiana purchase. Article in Columbian Centinel. Boston, July 2, 1803

——— ——— Article by "Fabricius". Boston, July 27, 1803

Lyman, Theodore. The Diplomacy of the United States, v. 1, p. 367–405. Boston, 1828

M....... Mémoires sur la Louisiane et la Nouvelle Orleans . . . les avantages que le commerce doit tirer de l'art. 7 du traité. Paris, 1804

Madison Papers. Library of Congress. Mss. Div.

McAfee, Robt. B. History of the late war . . . [Creek war and battle N. O.] p. 454–534. Lexington, Ky., 1916

McCaleb, Walter F. The Aaron Burr Conspiracy. New York, 1903

——— ——— The Aaron Burr Conspiracy and New Orleans [in Am. Hist. Assoc. Rept., 1903 v. 1: p. 131–43]. Washington, 1904

Magruder, Allen B. Reflections on the late cession of La. Lexington, Ky., 1803

Marbois, Barbé. F. de History of Louisiana, particularly of the cession of the colony to the U. S. Philadelphia, 1830

Marigny, Bernard. Thoughts on the foreign policy of the United States [French & English] p. 23–32. New Orleans, 1854

Martin, François X. History of Louisiana. New Orleans, 1829

Mead, Cowles. Letter Book Miss. Dept. of Archives and History

New Orleans. Code de police, etc. New Orleans, 1808–14

Ogg, Frederick A. The Opening of the Mississippi, p. 486–656. New York, 1904

[Onis Luis de] supposed author, signed "Verus" no t. p. general subject West Florida. 1810

Orr, George. Possession of Louisiana by the French as it affects . . . Great Britain, America, Spain and Portugal. London, 1803

Parton, James. Life and times of Aaron Burr, 2v, New York, 1864

Perez, Luis M. French refugees to New Orleans in 1809 [in Southern History Assoc. publications 1905, v. 9, p. 293–310]. Washington, 1905

Perrin du Lac, F. M. Travels through the two Louisianas in 1801–02–03 [French edition Paris, 1805]. London, 1807

Phelps, Albert. Louisiana, p. 178–283. New York, 1905

Pike, Zebulon B. Expedition to the headwaters of the Mississippi through La. territory and in New Spain, 1805–6–7, edited by Elliott Coues. New York, 1895

Powell, E. Alexander. Gentlemen Rovers. p. 91–124 [Lafitte]. New York, 1913

Prendergast, Garrett E. Physical and topographical sketch of Miss. territory, lower Louisiana &c. Philadelphia, 1803

Quincy, Josiah. Speeches, 1805–13 [Admission of Louisiana, 1811]. Boston, 1874

Robertson, Chas. F. Bishop. The influence of the Louisiana purchase on the American system. New York, 1885

—— —— Attempts made to separate the West from the American Union. St. Louis, 1885

Robertson, James Alex. Documents in Spanish archives relating to the U. S. with transcripts in American libraries, p. 290–323. Washington, 1910

—— —— Louisiana under the rule of Spain, France and the United States, 1785–1807. Cleveland, 1911

v. 1, p. 29–232 [Alliot's Reflections on La. 1803–4] p. 359–76

all of v. 2 that fall within this period [translated documents entirely]

Robin, Claude C. Voyage dans l'intérieu de la Louisiane . . . l'état des Anglais-Americains, etc. 3v. v. 2, p. 62–206, 384 seq. v. 3, p. 137–62, 245–64. Paris, 1807

Roosevelt, Theodore. Winning of the West. v. 4, p. 258–342. New York, 1900

——— ——— Naval war of 1812. pt. II, p. 198–243. New York, 1904

Russell, J. jr. [compilation of letters]. History of the War [1812]. p. 276–90, 333–41. Hartford, 1815

Safford, William H. The Blennerhassett Papers. Burr Conspiracy, p. 63–583. Cincinnati, 1861

St. Louis Mercantile Library. Notes on ms. records, Spanish, French and American. The library has the Supreme Court records from 1813, and Claiborne's journal 1805–7. Reference list No. 1. St. Louis, 1898

Scroggs, William O. Archives of Louisiana [in Am. Hist. Assoc. rept. 1912, p. 275–93]. Washington, 1914

——— ——— Rural life in the Mississippi Valley about 1803, Vol. VIII. Proceedings of the Mississippi Valley Historical Association. Cedar Rapids, 1916

Seybert, Adam. Statistical Annals of the United States. p. 22, 32–7, 344–6. Philadelphia, 1818

Shepherd, W. R. Wilkinson and the Spanish Conspiracy [in American Hist. Review, v. 9, p. 490, 748]

Sloane, William M. The world aspects of the Louisiana purchase. Washington, 1904

Smith, Walter R. Brief history of Louisiana territory. p. 62–92. St. Louis, 1904

Smith, Zachary F. The Battle of New Orleans. Louisville, 1904

Stevens, John A. Life of Gallatin, p. 201–3, 212–24, 238–45, 260–74, 295, 312–37. Boston, 1892

Stoddard, Amos. Sketches, historical and descriptive of Louisiana. Philadelphia, 1812

Sullivan, William. Familiar letters . . . [anti-Jefferson] Letters 43, 46, 47, 48. War of 1812 letters 59–65. Boston, 1834

Sylvestris. Reflections of the cession of Louisiana to the United States. Washington, 1803

Transcripts of Spanish Archives. Miss. Dept. of Archives and History

Transcripts of French Archives. Miss. Dept. of Archives and History

Turner, Frederick J. Diplomatic Contest for the Mississippi Valley [Atlantic Monthly, 1904, p. 676–91]

United States. Annals of Congress. 8th Cong. 1st sess. p. 432–515 [House] p. 35–73 [Senate]. Washington 1803

——— ——— Debate on Orleans territory govt. [House] p. 1054–79. Senate not reported. Washington 1803–4

——— ——— Convention between the French Republic and the U. S. Washington, 1801

—— —— 7th Congress 2d. session, The Mississippi question. Debate Feb., 1803 on right of deposit at New Orleans. Philadelphia, 1803

—— —— Land Office. Historical sketch of Louisiana and the La. purchase, p. 8–11. [maps] by Frank Boyd, chief clerk. Washington, 1912

—— —— Papers and correspondence bearing on the purchase of Louisiana. Washington, 1903

—— —— Treaties 1801–9. President's message on treaty of cession. [Washington, 1803]

—— —— Treaty of cession. [Washington, 1803]

Vaughan, Benjamin. Remarks on dangerous mistake made as to eastern boundary of La. Boston, 1814

Villiers du Terrage, Marc Baron de. Dernières années de la Louisiane française [Laussat] p. 366–451. Paris, 1804

Voyage fait dans 1816–17 etc., . . . de N. York à la Nouvelle Orleans [Montlezun baron de] v. 1, 251–361. Paris, 1818

Walker, Alexander. Jackson and New Orleans. New York, 1856

Warden, D. B. Statistical, political and historical account of the United States. [La. purchase v. 3, p. 490–568] Edinburgh, 1819

Webster, Sidney. Two treaties of Paris and the Supreme Court, p. 1–32. New York, 1901

West Florida Papers. Library of Congress. Mss. Div.

White, J. M. Collection of the laws of England, France and Spain relating to land. . . . 2v. Philadelphia, 1839

Wilkinson, James. Memoirs. v. 2. Washington, 1810

Williams, Gov. Robert. Letter Book Miss. Dept. of Archives and History

Workman, James. Letter to the respectable citizens of the county of Orleans. New Orleans, 1807

Wright, Marcus J. Account of the transfer of the territory of Louisiana [in Southern History Assoc. publications v 2, p. 17–28]. Letters of Madison, Jefferson, Dickson and Sevier. Washington, 1898

Zacharie, James S. New Orleans—its old streets and places [in La. Hist. Soc., v. 2, pt. 3, p. 45]. New Orleans, 1900

INVENTORY.

DOCUMENTS AND PAPERS CONCERNING TRANSACTIONS DURING CIVIL COMMOTIONS IN WEST FLORIDA.
MSS. DIV. LIBRARY OF CONGRESS.[1]

1. Fulwar Skipwith to the President of the United States relative to the protection of Florida by the U. S.. Dec: 5, 1810.
2. Audibert to Fulwar Skipwith, concerning loyalty of the French to the cause, Sept. 4. 1810.
3. John Mills and C. M. Audibert to Fulwar Skipwith, relative to pecuniary matters and contains list of Spanish vessels, &c. Dec. 4, 1810.
4. C. M. Audibert to F. Skipwith (private) Dec: 6, 1810.
5. John Mills and C. M. Audibert to Fulwar. Skipwith, relative to privateers, Dec: 7, 1810.
6. Same, Dec: 14, 1810, relative to purchase of two schooners.
7. Same, relative to letters of marque and arming of two schooners, Dec: 10, 1810.
8. Petition of the Inhabitants of W. Florida, State of Louisiana, for adoption of permanent and uniform principles for adjustment of land claims.
9 Petition of the Inhabitants of East Baton-Rouge for the abolishment of Parish Juries.
10 Fulwar Skipwith to the President of the U. S. relative to actions of Gov: Claiborne, &ct, Dec. 9, 1810.
11 Same to C. C. Claiborne in relation to his taking possession of West Florida as a part of the Territory of Orleans, Dec: 10, 1810.
12. Fulwar Skipwith to Jno: Graham, Chf. Clk: Dept. of State, Washington, relative to the Government taking possession of Florida, Dec: 23, 1810.
13. Fulwar Skipwith to—January 14, 1811, Relative to affairs in Florida, the revolution and F. S.'s connection with same; also lands owned by F. S.

---

[1] This very interesting collection of papers is of the highest value to the student of American-Spanish relations in the Southwest, and of the Revolution of West Florida. This material is valuable as a supplemental source to the Claiborne Letter Books, and the Letter Books of Governors Robert Williams, Cowles Mead and David Holmes of Mississippi Territory. Its value is augmented by the fact that it has never been used.

14. Reuben Kemper to Convention of West Florida, Nov: 19, 1810, Condition of affairs and states that the flag will be raised on east side of Mobile River.

15. Same to Same, Nov: 23, 1810, Condition of affairs and what is going on in the Pensacola Districts.

16. Same to Same, Dec: 16, 1810, Condition of affairs.

17. Jno: Nicholson to Same, Dec: 17, 1810, Condition of affairs.

18. Reuben Kemper to Same, Dec: 20, 1810, Condition of affairs.

19. Same to Same, Oct. 28, 1810, Condition of affairs.

18. Joseph Pulaski Kennedy, Nov: 3, 1810, Condition of affairs.

20. Reuben Kemper to Don Perer, Commandant, Civil and Military of Mobile, Nov: 3, 1810.

21. Same to Convention of West Florida, Nov: 5, 1810. Condition of affairs.

22. Same to Same, Nov: 6, 1810, Condition of affairs.

23. Same to Same, Nov: 10, 1810, Condition of affairs.

24. P. Grymes to F. Skipwith, October 6, 1810. Relative to printing Declaration of Independence, etc.

25. Constitution of the State of Florida, Convention of Oct. 24, 1810.

26. Order for the transfer of Public Stores from Baton Rouge to Pensacola, Oct 29, 1810.

27. Letters to Capt. Ballonger, Oct 29 & 30, 1810.

28. Order of the Committee of P. S. to get in readiness 2 brass field pieces, Nov 2, 1810.

29. Orders to General Thomas, Nov. 12, 1810.

30. Citizens of Pensacola District to Reuben Kemper and his reply to same, Nov: 12-15, 1810.

31. John Innerarity to Mr. Sanderson, Nov. 23, 1810, Condition of affairs at Pensacola.

32. Abner L. Duncan to the President Committee of Public Safety, Nov 23 & 20, 1810.

33. And. Steele to Gov: Skipwith, Nov. 26, 1810.

34. Collins's affidavit and complaint against Sterling Dupree et al. for violence and robbery on Mrs Wilson.

35. Capt. Smith's Report of Arms, etc, Nov. 30, 1810.

36. Proceedings of a Board of Militia Officers, Dec. 1, 1810.

37. Appointment of Sam'l Baldwin Navy Agent for Springfield, Dec: 3, 1810.

38. Quarter Master's Return of Military Stores, Dec: 1, 1810.

39. Extract from the Journal of the Senate, Dec. 4, 1810.

40. Orders for Capt. Collins, Dec: 4, 1810.

41. Writ of Election in Florida.

42. Orders to the Navy Officers. Commanding Vessels.

43. Copy of F. Skipwith's letter to Gov: Claieborne recommending Genl McCausland.

44. French Minister of Foreign Relations' Letter to F. Skipwith. Legislature of Florida's Address to F. S.

45. Printed Speech of Gov: Skipwith to Senate & House of Representatives of the State of West Florida, Nov 29. 1810.

46 To the Inhabitants of the State of Florida (Printer) Fulwar Skipwith, Dec. 23, 1810.

47. Fulwar Skipwith to the Inhabitants of the State of Florida, declining to serve in the Legislature of the Territory of Orleans, when elected from the County of Feliciana. April 1, 1811

48. Speech of Fulwar Skipwith, April 1, 1811.

49. Oration delivered at St. Francisville, West Florida, July 4, 1811, by James Turner. (Printed.)

50. Fulwar Skipwith to the Free and Independent Electors of the Parish of East-Baton-Rouge, August 30, 1812. (Printed.)

51. An Act Apportioning the representative of that part of Florida annexed to the State of Louisiana, and for other purposes. Approved, August 25, 1812. (Printed.)

RELATIVE TO GENERAL ANDREW JACKSON.

52. Militia General Orders, Head-Quarters, New-Orleans, September 8, 1814. (Printed)

53. General Andrew Jackson to the Mayor of New Orleans, Jany 27, 1815. Printed in French & English.

54. Case of Louaillier

55. General Andrew Jackson to the Post-Master General, March 22, 1824, alleged misconduct of F. Skipwith during the late war.

56. F. Skipwith to Wm. Y. Lewis, April 23, 1827, requesting his aid in disproving the charges of Gen'l Jackson.

57. F. Skipwith to Editors of the Richmond Enquirer, May 13, 1827, Requesting them to print material in connection with charges of General Jackson.

58. F. Skipwith to General Jackson, May 15, 1827, Relative to charges brought by General Jackson against him.

59. General Jackson and the Louisiana Legislature—

60. District Court of the U. S. The United States vs Major Genl Andrew Jackson. Transcript. ————————

61. T. B. Robertson's Address to the People of Louisiana, June 10, 1820, Relative to land claims &c. (Printed.)

INDEX

Andrews, —, V, 204.
Andrews, W. L., correspondence with Claiborne, VI, 247.
Andrion, Capt. Louis, IV, 382.
Andry, Col. Manuel, II, 3, III, 106, 118–19, V, 95–96, 104, 346, VI, 229; characterized, IV, 375; recommended, IV, 378-79; letters of Claiborne to, III, 92–93, 118, V, 97, 99, VI, 18.
"Ann" an American vessel, III, 271–72.
"Ann," an English schooner, II, 99.
"Anna", American sloop, IV, 131.
Annetto, an Indian, IV, 146.
Antilles. See West Indies.
Antonie, Father, Seditious priest, IV, 25–26, 28.
Antonio, a pilot, VI, 128.
Arbean, Jean Marie, trial of, IV, 391-95, 397-99.
Arbitration, settlement by, I, 369–370, II, 79–80, 105, 127–128.
Arbuckle, Lieut. —, I, 231.
Archives. See Louisiana: records.
"Arctic", vessel, IV, 381, 410, 413–15.
"Argo", French brig, I, 387.
Arkansas-Post, II, 96, 101.
Arkansas River, store on,
Arman, John, II, 128.
Armas, Christoval de, VI, 191.
Armesto, Don André de, secretary of Spanish government, II, 21, 151, 163, 188, 227, 281, III, 250, 260.
Armesto, Madame Don Audre, II, 47.
Armstrong, John, secretary of war, VI, 327, 362–63; letter to Claiborne, VI, 242–43; letters of Claiborne to, VI, 233–35, 243–44, 252–53, 277–78.
Armstrong, John, pardoned, IV, 146.
Armand, Felix, V, 237, 377; treasurer, VI, 406.
Arnauld, T. E., VI, 187, 197.
Arroya Honda, IV, 161, V, 334, VI, 34–36, 38–39, 104, 160, 271, 277.
Asage Indians. See Osage Indians.
Asburn, Audley L., letter of Claiborne to, V, 44–46.
Ascension Parish, IV, 224, VI, 177, 197.
Assumption Parish, IV, 221, 386.
Atchafalaya (Chaffalaya) River, VI, 359.
Attakapas Country, I, 336, 338, 347, 349, 362–63, II, 155, 158–59, III, 81, 239, 307, 378–79, IV, 15–16, 221,

256–57, 259–60, 271, V, 9, 242, VI, 9, 100, 172, 176, 242; religious dispute in, II, 169–71, 274–75; commandant, II, 275, 283, 298–99, 305–6; sheriff, II, 30, VI, 106; militia, II, 209, III, 235–37, IV, 28, VI, 272, 289, 317; officers, IV, 385, VI, 75; exposed to attack, III, 388, 399, VI, 181; troops from, II, 384, VI, 297, 315, 318; land claims in, II, 282–83; visited, III, 370, 373–76, 399, IV, 108–9, 187–90, 400, 403, 410, 419, V, 2, 13, 361, VI, 60, 65, 73, 222, 224; representatives, V, 262, 277.
Attakapas Indians, IV, 224.
Aubert, P. —, IV, 315.
Au Boeuf Bayou, III, 350, 368.
Aubry, —, French officer, II, 152.
Aucion, Pierre, justice of peace, IV, 386.
Auctioneer, office of, I, 311, II, 117, IV, 147.
Auditor, a Spanish officer, II, 357-58, 370.
Augustine, a mulatto, V, 87.
Ausark River. See Ozark River.
Austria, alliances, V, 246.
Avoyelles Parish, II, 87, IV, 146, 221–22, V, 308, VI, 162; judge, VI, 172, 178; complaints from, II, 200.
Babet, a negro, III, 133.
Babin, Bonaventure, II, 127.
Baccus, Maj. —, V, 339.
Backer, Evan, justice of peace, IV, 146.
Bahia (Tex.), VI, 359.
Bailey, Thomas, II, 66–70, 81; affidavit, IV, 395 96.
Bailey, Pierre, ship owner, I, 393.
Bainbridge, Capt. William, V, 174–75, 177, 211–12, 299, 302–3; letters of Claiborne to, V, 280, 287, 294; commended, V, 299.
Daker, Col. Joshua, boat attacked I, 91–92; Corner, I, 188; deposition, IV, 339; justice of peace, V, 277; letter of Claiborne to VI, 75–76.
Baldwin, —, prisoner, V, 275.
Baldwin, Capt. —, V, 98.
Baldwin, Abraham, Commissioner for Georgia, I, 173.
Balize, I, 366, IV, 318, 337, 352, 357, 359; fort at, II, 359–65, IV, 84, 101, 157, 169, V, 18, 24–25, 29–31, 202, 264, VI, 15, 22, 26, 112, 116, 123, 125, 129, 306–7; lighthouse at 11, 42; repairs, IV, 346–47, VI,

Guerin, Marie Catherine, Cuban emigrant, IV, 412.

Guice, James, justice of peace, I, 188.

Guichard, Magloire, speaker, V, 131, VI, 399.

Guillotte, P. A., auctioneer, IV, 387.

Guinea, slaves from, IV, 387.

Guiterras, José Bernardo, VI, 71-72, 79.

Gurley, Henry A., V, 354-55, 375, 76, VI, 14, 47; letters of Claiborne to, V, 381, 386.

Habeas corpus, in Louisiana, II, 282; Orleans Territory, IV, 50, 64, 68-69, 118-19, 121, 123; during War of 1812, VI, 344.

Halifax, IV, 192, VI, 28.

Hall, Dominic A., judge, III, 63, 66, 71, 73, 76, 177, IV, 56, 78, 391, V, 184, 263, VI, 53, 193; judge of Supreme Court, VI, 212; arrest of, VI, 344, 348; return, VI, 351; letters of Claiborne to, III, 73-75, IV, 70-71, 78-79; letters to Claiborne, III, 55-56, 60, 73-76, 78; decision in Batture case, VI, 258, 260.

Hames, —, IV, 99.

Hamilton, Jett, militia officer, IV, 144.

Hamilton, Paul secretary of the navy, V, 24; letters of Claiborne to, V, 175, 181-83, 192-93, 201-02, 210-11, 212, 231-33, 245-48, 253-54, 271-72, 274-75, 283-85, 285-86, 289-91, 326-28, 331-33, 356-57, 358-59, 360, 369, 395-98, VI, 4-5, 12-13, 19, 20-22, 27-29, 37-39, 45-46, 57-59, 125-27, 129, 199-200.

Hamilton, Samuel, letters of Claiborne to, IV, 264-65, 356.

Hamos Indians. See Oumas Indians.

Hampton, John P., judge of Feliciana, VI, 60, 204; letter of Claiborne to, VI, 59.

Hampton, Gen. Wade, military commander, IV, 122, V, 70-71, 100, 111, 135, 137, 144, 148, 155-57, 180, 187, 206, VI, 11, 23, 36-37, 39, 50, 57, 80; goes to Washington, V, 246, VI, 100, 105; letters of Claiborne to, V, 91-94, 106-7, 115-17, 147-48, 153-54, 200-1, 215-16, VI, 22-23, 34-36.

Hampton (Va.), in the War of 1812, VI, 258.

"Happy Star," merchant ship, I, 383.

Harding Lyman, I, 34, 177, 377; letter of Claiborne to, I, 53.

Hardy, Capt. Pierre, IV, 384, 413-14.

Hargrave, Maj. William H., justice of peace, I, 279; imprisoned, V, 85-86, 160, 165-68, 172, 177-78, 191, 225, 249, 267; characterized, V, 178, 370-71; intercession for, VI, 112-13, 239-40.

Hargrave, Mrs. William H., petition of, V, 177-78, 191; letter for, V, 249, VI, 267; letter from, VI, 240; at Havana, V, 344.

Harman, James, justice of peace, I, 65, 141.

Harpe, Wiley, a robber, I, 91, 93-94.

Harper, D., VI, 185.

Harper's Ferry (Va.), V, 267; arsenal at, VI, 219.

Harris, E. L., I, 38.

Harris, Eldredge, I, 2.

Hart, —, New Orleans merchant, V, 9.

Harty, William, pardoned, IV, 146.

Haughney, William, III, 47-48.

Havana (Cuba), I, 257, 289, 315, 351, 387, II, 193, 285, 322, III, 31, 120, 122-23, 191, 212, 217, 234, 362, 368, IV, 26, 120-21, 149, 202, 214, 259, 269, 289, 352, 354, 357, 365, 381, 387, 399, V, 1-2, 5-6, 60, 89, 91, 142, 144, 165, 167, 167-72, 174-77, 191, 193, 212, 268, 276, 301, 343, 370, VI, 20-21, 28, 45, 62, 90, 110, 112, 211, 224, 227, 235; consul at, VI, 111, 117, 125.

Havens, James, IV, 246, V, 87.

Hawkins, Benjamin, Indian agent, I, 86-87, VI, 223; letter to Claiborne, I, 21-22; letter of McKee to, I, 22-23; letter of Claiborne to, I, 23-24, V, 315.

Hay, Daniel, private soldier, II, 132.

Hayti, VI, 404.

Haytum, P., accountant, VI, 406.

Hayward, Dr. —, III, 396.

Health, regulations for, I, 164, II, 169, 172, 194, 204, 242-43, 364, III, 137, 144, V, 337; vaccination, II, 208-9; board for, II, 202, 204, 241, 261, 377; conditions of, II, 306-7, 311-12, 328, 337, 346, 350, III, 86, 176, 193, 200, IV, 134, 392-93, 404-6, 410, V, 343. See also Smallpox and Yellow Fever.

Helisson, Francois, Cuban emigrant, IV, 412.

Heins, H. A., II, 82, III, 296.

McDonough, John, II, 30, 172, IV, 245.

McFarland, —, VI, 166.

McGachan, Peter, smallpox patient, I, 198.

McGee, David, letter of Claiborne to, VI, 319.

McGrew, John, justice of peace, I, 65, 189.

McKee, Col. John, Indian agent, I, 72, 109, 152, 158, 194; commissioner at Fort Stoddart, V, 199, 247, 316, VI, 93; letters of, I, 22-23, 192; letters of Claiborne to, I, 59-60, 78-79, 94, 120-22, 130.

McNeal, Capt. —, III, 132.

McNeil, Joseph, V, 231.

McUutt, Isaac, justice of peace, IV, 386.

McQuean, Capt. —, VI, 268.

McRea (McCrae), Col. William, V, 91, 263, VI, 289; defenses of, VI, 306-7; commended, VI, 352; letters of Claiborne to, V, 306-7, 320, 350-51, V, 118-19, 362-63, VI, 16-17, 49-50, 309-10, 315.

Macon, Nathaniel, speaker, II, 21; letters of Claiborne to, I, 102, VI, 51.

Madison, James, commissioner, I, 173; secretary of state, I, 5; president of the United States, IV, 289, 324, 334; reëlected, VI, 206; opposition to, V, 327; message to Congress, V, 396, VI, 12; petition to, IV, 417; proclamation concerning West Florida, V, 40, 42-43, 46-50, 54, 59-60, 71-72, 78-80, 90, 112, 115, 121, 154, 156, 280, 305; letters to Claiborne, I, 89, 115, 135-36, 173-76, 255, 273-74, 282-83, II, 56-57, 93-94, 122-24, 140-41, 177-78, 278-80, VI, 191-92; letters of Claiborne to, I, 6-14, 27-32, 34-35, 38-42, 46-47, 53-54, 69-70, 89-90, 107-8, 114, 116, 139-40, 161-62, 176-77, 210-22, 232-33, 250-51, 253, 262-64, 267, 275, 277, 279-80, 283-87, 294-95, 297-307, 312-16, 322-33, 339-41, 344-49, 352-56, 358-60, 362-63, 371-73, 375-78, 387-88, II, 13-16, 21-26, 40-48, 60-62, 76-77, 81, 83-85, 88-91, 95-97, 109, 118, 124-26, 134, 137-38, 143-44, 146-48, 151-52, 165-66, 170-74, 178-82, 186, 190-92, 196-99, 209-12, 216-17, 227-29, 230-31, 233-38, 239-40, 244-46, 248-50, 266-68, 269-72,

274, 280-82, 284-86, 290-93, 298-301, 306-307, 312, 313, 315, 327-28, 336-37, 337-39, 340, 341, 344-49, 352-60, 366-70, 373-79, 381-93, III, 7-8, 9-11, 13-16, 23-29, 34-36, 38-40, 51-52, 53, 57-59, 60, 68, 76-83, 96, 105, 114-16, 120, 127-28, 131-32, 136-38, 141, 142-43, 145-46, 146-47, 148-49, 150-52, 154, 156-57, 158, 165, 169-70, 176, 178-79, 180-83, 186-87, 190-92, 198-99, 201-2, 211-13, 215, 223-24, 225-27, 229-30, 230-31, 234-35, 241-43, 246-48, 251-54, 254-56, 260-61, 264, 266-72, 281-82, 283, 284-85, 289-91, 293-94, 297-300, 305-6, 309-11, 313, 319, 323-24, 345-47, 367, 391-92, IV, 27, 35, 36-38, 40-44, 46, 47-48, 50-52, 68, 71, 95-97, 108-09, 114-15, 121-22, 123-25, 129-31, 134-36, 142-43, 147-49, 155-57, 160-62, 167-70, 173-75, 175-87, 199-02, 209-13, 234, 244-46, 250-51, 258-59, 267-68, 278, 282-85, 288, 299, 303-05, 311-12, 316-17, 320, 332-34, 335, V, 173, VI, 65, 138, 235-39, 334-35.

Madison, Mrs. James, present for, "Madison", ship, IV, 404.

Madisonville (La.), VI, 266.

Madrid (Spain), III, 368, IV, 206. See also Treaty of Madrid.

Magic Lantern, Burr's proposed journal, IV, 167, 317; characterized, V, 16.

Magruder, Allen B., VI, 11, 42-44, 118; resignation, VI, 56; successor, VI, 206, 210; letters of Claiborne to, V, 392-93, VI, 208-9.

Mahan, Samuel S., I, 245.

Mails. See Postal Service.

Mairot, J. C., IV, 418.

Malherbe, Capt. Le Jeune, IV, 417.

Malingues, La, IV, 418.

Mallet, Pierre, II, 150.

Malliar, Jean Louis, II, 127.

Malone, Thomas, clerk for Washington District, I, 188.

Manchac, IV, 235, 322, IV, 195; fortified, III, 329; patrolled, IV, 102; church at, IV, 221; priest, V, 252.

Mannadell, Henry, justice of peace, I, 140.

Manon, —, negro woman, II, 92.

Many, Capt. James B., II, 96, 100-1; letters of Claiborne to, IV, 358, 367, 378.

Naples, Kingdom of, III, 316.

Nashville (Tenn.), I, 6-8, 211, 222, 371, II, 132, 207, IV, 96, 98, 105, 123, 154, 182, VI, 234; Burr at, IV, 33; letter to post-master, I, 344.

Natchez, capital of Mississippi Territory, I, 3, 277, II, 283, 345, II, 31, 70, 180, 183, 191, 194, 200, 202, 228, 281, IV, 15, 22, 39, 134, 182, 184, 213, 215, 228, 241, 380, 393, 407, V, 46, 80, 188, VI, 135, 153; Indians at, I, 13-14, 70, 73, 121; artillery company, I, 46, 67; officials of, I, 281; harbor, V, 36; mail route to, IV, 245; postmaster, II, 212; visited, III, 373, 377, 387, V, 25, 34, 347, 350; Burr at, IV, 48, 94-95; 100, 115, 151; Jackson, VI, 213; troops from, V, 39, 46, 50; gambling at, IV, 123.

Natchez Trace, mail route via, I, 4, 27, II, 328; resident on, VI, 234.

Natchitoches, American flag raised at, II, 145; a border post, II, 119, 131, 145-46, 320, 328, III, 80-83, 100, 239-40, 284-85, 288, 290, 328, 342, 375, 378, 380-84, 391, 395, 398, IV, 9-10, 12-17, 20, 24-25, 27-28, 31, 55, 152, 154, 167, 188, 190, 194, 199-200, 254, 256, 283, 286, 421, V, 8, 17, 92, 174, 207, 252, 320, 383, VI, 34, 38, 122, 151-52, 159-60, 163, 165, 167, 229, 283, 389; fort at, II, 148, 286-89, 872-74, 380-90, III, 8-9, 27, 30-33, 155-56, 163-64, 186, 198, 241, 260; commandant, II, 197, 215, 289, 313-14, III, 30, 41-43, 80, 197, 242, IV, 18, 149; troops from, IV, 41, 47, 83, VI, 50, 51; lack of officials at, IV, 116; Indians near, II, 292-93, 341-42, 348, III, 70, VI, 328, Indian agent, VI, 274, 331, 362, 401, 403; trading house, II, 2, VI, 401; militia, III, 7, 27, IV, 20, VI, 39; land commissioner, IV, 23; judge, IV, 221-22, 244, 258, 334, V, 242, VI, 172; school at, VI, 87; visit to, III, 343, 378, 387, IV, 1-2, 6-7, 29, 109, VI, 69, 72, 275; officer at, V, 18; disaffection, II, 268-69, III, 81; expedition from, VI, 364.

Natchitoches Parish, I, 385-86, III, 161-64, 284, 332, 388, 399, V, 334, VI, 73, 403; militia of, III, 235-37; representatives, V, 262, VI, 9; courts, III, 218, IV, 90; judges,

III, 232, V, 176, 319-22, 328, VI, 34, 36, 39, 149, 151, 200.

National Intelligence, IV, 393, V, 159.

Navigation Company, VI, 20.

Neely, Maj. William, I, 66.

Negroes. See Free People of Color, and Slaves.

Neil, Samuel, alderman at Natchez, I, 281.

Nelson, James, I, 169, 188; letter of Claiborne to, V, 311, VI, 195.

Nelson, Jr., James, sheriff of Baton Rouge, V, 140, 138; resigns, VI, 195.

Nelson, William, Coroner, I, 188.

Nemours, Depont de, III, 126.

Neufbourg, Philippe de, IV, 418.

"Neustra Del Carmen", IV, schooner, IV, 381.

"Neustra Senora Del Carmen", schooner, IV, 381.

Neutrality of U. S., I, 353, II, 93-95; of Spain, II, 133-134.

New England, in War of 1812, VI, 321.

New Iberia, V, 221, 398, VI, 100.

New Iberia Parish, V, 217, 243.

New Madrid, I, 9-10.

New Orleans (La.), possible capture of, I, 8, 253, 286, 288-89, 298; Spanish forces at, I, 344-45, 355, 372, 375-76, II, 21-22, 40, 55, 58, 61-62, 77, 84-85, 88-89, 147-48; French forces, I, 344-46, 355, 372, 375-76, II, 56-57; General Victor at, I, 226, 230; American right of deposit, I, 207-10, 221, 229, 233-36, 239-40, 245-47, 250-51, 253, 255-56, 261-63, 267, 273-75, 282; American flag raised at, I, 299, 307, 385; population in 1803, I, 315; Claiborne describes, I, 313-14; order in, I, 363, 375, II, 15, 21-22, 47, 61, 63, 77, 84, 88-89, 96, 108-9, 130, 152; disorder and discontent, I, 330-31, 358-59, 372, 376, II, 22, 46-47, 84-85, 88, 91, 367-69, 376; complaints, I, 348-49, II, 1; public anxiety, I, 392, II, 160-61, incendiarism, I, 381-83, II, 15; mob, III, 16; conspiracy, IV, 279-83, 304, 309-10; commerce at, I, 320-22, 329, 331, II, 188, 216; shipping regulations, I, 320-22, 329, 334-35, 338-39; port of, IV, 247-48, 251, 275, 319, 355, VI, 128, 258; harbor master, I, 320-21, 334-35, 338-39; port wardens, III, 104; port sur-

DATE DUE